Age cannot wither, nor custom stale, her infinite variety.

ANTONY AND CLEOPATRA (2.2.243–244)

INFINITE VARIETY

Exploring the Folger Shakespeare Library

Edited by Esther Ferington
The Folger Shakespeare Library
Washington, DC

Distributed by
University of Washington Press
Seattle and London

Photographs by Julie Ainsworth,
unless otherwise noted.

Cover images: On the front cover, a detail from the 1513 Strassburg edition of Ptolemy's *Geography* includes a web of rhumb lines (the routes sailed by ships on fixed compass bearings) as well as latitude numbering based on the Hellenistic coordinate system. The map that includes this section appears on the back cover.

Frontispiece: A pair of masks denoting Tragedy (shown here) and Comedy are central features in the tiled floor of the Exhibition Hall.

Printed in England.

Distributed by University of
Washington Press, Seattle and London
ISBN 0-295-98231-4 (cloth edition)
ISBN 0-295-98232-2 (paper edition)

Library of Congress Cataloging-
in-Publication Data
Infinite variety: exploring the Folger
Shakespeare Library / edited by
Esther Ferington.
p. cm.
ISBN 0-295-98231-4 —
ISBN 0-295-98232-2 (pbk.)
1. Folger Shakespeare Library.
2. Shakespeare, William, 1564-1616—
Library resources. 3. Library
resources—Washington (D.C.)
I. Ferington, Esther.

Z733.F6632 I54 2002
027.753—dc21 2001055652

CONTENTS

FOLGER SHAKESPEARE LIBRARY

In the course of its entire history, the Folger Shakespeare Library has never before produced a comprehensive survey of its collections and activities for the general public. Leaving aside careful and descriptive annual reports, which provide snapshots of the institution's work over a brief period, and the useful booklet *The Widening Circle,* published in 1976 and long out of print, there has been no visual and textual record of the library's programs and resources. *Infinite Variety: Exploring the Folger Shakespeare Library* meets that long-felt need.

The Folger opened its doors for the first time on April 23, 1932, with President Hoover and many dignitaries in attendance. In the intervening seventy years, the Folger has received presidents, prelates, and princes. It has entertained notables from the worlds of government, diplomacy, commerce, and the visual, performing, and literary arts. It has published a vast array of scholarly and popular materials relating to Shakespeare and early modern times—enough to have become, in Yeats's words, "a world's delight." Above all, it has become an incomparable resource for scholarship on, and public appreciation of, European civilization, 1500–1750—the age of Shakespeare, and of his predecessors and successors. In many and generous ways, it provides pathways we can all use to better understand our own civilization.

It is fair to assume that the Folgers' hopes for their library have been amply fulfilled over time, albeit in ways they could hardly have imagined. The Elizabethan Theatre, where the Folgers envisioned lectures and elocution lessons, now hosts full-scale theatrical productions, readings of modern poetry and fiction, and a celebrated series of early music performances. In the Exhibition Hall, which was designed to house a permanent display of Shakespeareana, several major exhibitions of rare books, manuscripts, prints, and drawings take place each year, most of them accompanied by ambitious catalogs. Hundreds of scholars now pursue their research in expanded study facilities planned to accommodate a happy few, while others find their way to the Folger Institute's seminars, conferences, and colloquia. Extending the institution's reach beyond anything envisioned as recently as five years ago, the printed word and the Internet take the Folger's educational

Bas-reliefs depicting scenes from Shakespeare's plays adorn the white marble facade of the Folger Shakespeare Library, a block from the US Capitol in Washington, DC. Research, performances, education, and exhibitions all contribute to the lively mix of Folger programs.

and scholarly programs to millions of readers around the world.

The Folger also serves as the professional home of a staff of nearly a hundred women and men, whose dedication to the work of the library is legendary. That tradition of service now extends back through several generations, and an impressive phalanx of young people is in place to carry it forward. Of this large and varied company, many have devoted time, thought, and energy to this project. Richard Kuhta and Garland Scott oversaw the enterprise from its earliest stages to its conclusion. Rachel Doggett and Georgianna Ziegler brought their learning and curatorial skills to the complex task of vetting the entire text. Erin Blake, Janet Field-Pickering, Janet Griffin, Kathleen Lynch, Barbara Mowat, J. Franklin Mowery, Elizabeth Walsh, and Heather Wolfe all contributed within their respective areas of expertise. Julie Ainsworth and her staff from the photography department combed the archives and contributed dozens of splendid new photographs.

A doorway ornamented on the exterior with Art Deco grillwork opens outward at the west end of the East Capitol Street facade. A matching door on the east end leads to the Elizabethan Theatre.

Other members of the staff lent their diverse talents to the project, including Linda Blaser, Carol Brobeck, Melody Fetske, Jane Kolson, Rachel Kunkle, Karen Lyon, Jane Pisano, Anita Sperling, and Mary Tonkinson. Gerard Passannante, a Folger intern, compiled the chronological appendix, and contributed and researched descriptions of a number of objects from the collection.

The library extends its particular gratitude to Esther Ferington, who edited the book and managed its production at every stage; to Antonio Alcalá of Studio A in Alexandria, Virginia, who designed it; and to Stephen Hyslop, who wrote "The Folger Story." Roxie France-Nuriddin checked all the historical references, while copyeditor Anne Farr and proofreader Celia Beattie brought it to its current state.

Here and there, readers of this book will notice signs of the immense philanthropic energy that has enabled the library to become the mature institution that enlivens these pages. Over the years, thousands of individual donors, together with dozens of foundations and corporations, have made many important gifts and grants to the Folger. Too numerous to mention by name, all have earned honorable mention in the annals of the library. Their names are proudly displayed in our annual reports, upon the walls of our buildings, and in the catalog of our restricted endowment funds. These vital named funds now number more than seventy. Collectively, they help to underwrite our fellowships, acquisitions, conservation, exhibitions, public and educational programs, publications, and more. The generosity and vision of those who have chosen to support the Folger's mission in lasting and strategic ways give us great hope for the future. In a very real sense, this book is both a tribute to, and an embodiment of, their philanthropic spirit.

Werner Gundersheimer, Director
April 2002

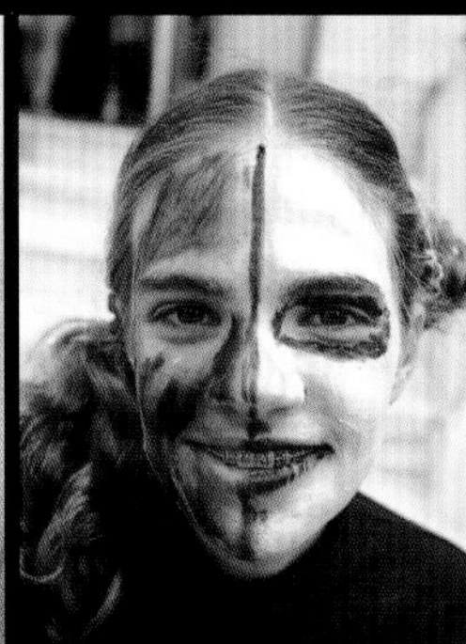

It was a beautiful spring day at the Folger Shakespeare Library. Outside the white marble building, visitors of all ages walked or sprawled on the expanse of emerald green grass. Brad Waller, the fight director for many Folger Theatre productions, demonstrated stage combat with sticks and swords to a circle of onlookers consisting mainly of small boys. A troupe of women Morris dancers performed along East Capitol Street, framed by a cascade of brightly colored balloons. Crowds filled the Folger's Elizabethan Garden, where on this one day they could purchase herbs of their own, many accompanied by apposite Shakespearean quotations in neat calligraphy. Others, meanwhile, crossed Third Street to explore the recently dedicated Haskell Center, where Folger staff and docents coached novices in the Elizabethan games of ninepins and hoops and ribbons. Jugglers, fortune-tellers, and other entertainers strolled through the throng, which included local families, visiting scholars, tourists, and even some Annapolis midshipmen in their gleaming whites.

Inside the library's Elizabethan Theatre, Mistress of the Revels Cam Magee, resplendent in period clothing, gossamer wings, and glitter, coaxed volunteers to take part in "spontaneous Shakespeare." The great Exhibition Hall, filled with a visiting exhibition of modern bookbindings, echoed with the voices and laughter of youngsters who tried out mask making and "hands-on heraldry" and munched on empanadas. Behind the hall, the Old and New Reading Rooms—off-limits to the general public on every other day of the year—had flung open their doors. Today, researchers (known as "readers" at the Folger) were welcome to enjoy the festivities, but not to study there. Instead, the rooms filled at different times with the sounds of a cappella singing, the patter of a juggler-magician, and a rap music–based presentation of Shakespearean scenes by seventh graders from the Capitol Hill Day School.

Outdoors, still more children tried on Elizabethan caps and hats, pondered the Folger's Shakespearean bas-reliefs—and waited eagerly for Queen Elizabeth I, ably impersonated by docent Gerry Kasarda, to cut the official birthday cake. By four o'clock, with a lawn full of contented cake eaters, the 2001 Shakespeare's Birthday Open House at the Folger came to an end,

At left, smiling faces provide a glimpse of the 2001 celebration of Shakespeare's birthday. The Folger has marked the day with speeches or other festivities every year since 1932.

concluding an annual celebration that had begun three weeks before with the Shakespeare's birthday lecture, this year given by James Shapiro of Columbia University on the topic "Jessica's Daughters."

It seems safe to say that Henry and Emily Folger did not have face painting and rap music in mind some seventy years earlier, when they planned the building that would house their collection of rare Shakespearean books and manuscripts. But their frequently expressed hopes for the library were very much in the spirit of the day's celebration. By setting a Shakespearean center in the midst of the nation's capital, and equipping it not just with study space but with an exhibition hall and theatre (used for many years as a lecture hall), the Folgers hoped to share their love of the playwright's works with an ever-widening public. As Emily Folger once wrote, Shakespeare is "one of the wells from which we Americans draw our national thought, our faith and our hope."

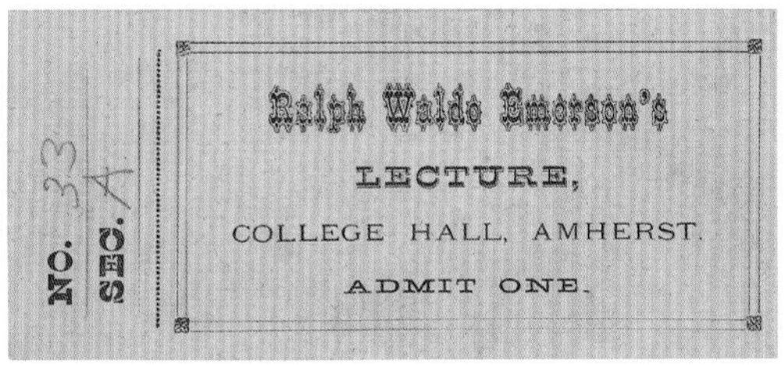

"THE CONSOLER OF OUR MORTAL CONDITION"

If there was any one occasion that led directly to the creation of the Folger Shakespeare Library, it was on another spring day—this one in 1879—when Amherst College senior Henry Clay Folger attended a lecture by the seventy-six-year-old Ralph Waldo Emerson. Emerson was in frail health and spoke quietly (on "superlative or mental temperance"), but he made an indelible impression on the shy, idealistic Folger, who went on to read some of Emerson's other works. Among these was a speech Emerson had given fifteen years earlier, on the 300th anniversary of Shakespeare's birth. "Genius is the consoler of our mortal condition," Emerson had said, "and Shakespeare taught us that the little world of the heart is vaster, deeper, and richer than the spaces of astronomy."

Like most college students, Folger was familiar with Shakespeare's works, but the speech cast them in a new light. The words so profoundly influenced Folger that they led to what became his life's mission—to collect in one place for posterity not only the works of Shakespeare but also the works upon which he drew or that alluded to him, and materials that conveyed the essence of his age. More than fifty years after Folger first encountered it, Emerson's 1864 speech would be read out at the Folger Shakespeare Library's dedication.

In the meantime, however, the young graduate had his way to make in the world. Although he traced his roots back eight generations to Nantucket settler Peter Folger, Henry Folger was not wealthy. He managed to complete his studies at Amherst only with financial help from the families of two classmates, including that of his roommate Charles Pratt. Pratt was the son and namesake of a leading figure in the oil industry, for whom Folger went to work after graduating. After earning a law degree from Columbia University (and a master's degree from Amherst in absentia), Folger spent his entire career as an oil executive, winning the confidence of industry titan John D. Rockefeller Sr. When federal trustbusters later aimed their slings and arrows at Rockefeller's Standard Oil Company, Folger helped pick up the pieces and made a fortune as the president and ultimately the chairman of Standard Oil of New York.

Success in business gave Henry Folger the means but precious little time for amassing a great collection of Shakespeareana. His ability to achieve that goal owed much to the partnership he entered into in 1885 when he married Emily Clara Jordan, a graduate of Vassar College who was a friend of Charles Pratt's sister Lily. Within a few months of the wedding, he gave his bride a reduced-sized facsimile of the 1623 First Folio, the first collected edition of

A born collector, Henry Folger saved the ticket that admitted him to an 1879 lecture by Ralph Waldo Emerson. The talk led indirectly to Folger's lifelong love of Shakespeare. A young Henry Folger is shown in a picture from 1879, the year he graduated from Amherst. Emily Jordan, a Vassar graduate, appears in 1885, the year of their marriage.

Shakespeare's works, commenting, "Here you may see Shakespeare's plays as they were actually given to the world." Emily Folger later called the book, which cost just $1.25, the "cornerstone of the Shakespeare Library."

Emily Folger soon came to share her husband's fascination with the Bard. Some years later, she earned her master's degree from Vassar for a thesis entitled "The True Text of Shakespeare," dealing with variations in early editions of his plays. Among her advisers was Horace Howard Furness, a genial scholar and book collector who entertained the Folgers with readings of Shakespeare at his country home in Wallingford, Pennsylvania. A widower, Furness was cheered by their companionship and once wrote to them, "The sight of husband and wife, both eager in the same pursuit, always touches me deeply." The Folgers' shared devotion to Shakespeare made them a formidable team in the competitive realm of book collecting.

That avocation began in earnest when Henry purchased his first rare book in 1889, bidding in person at Bangs's auction house in New York City on a copy of the 1685 Fourth Folio edition of Shakespeare's plays. He got the volume for $107.50, but needed thirty days' credit in order to pay. Fourteen years later, with his career well advanced, Folger was able to pay £10,000, or nearly $50,000, for the coveted copy of the First Folio presented as a gift on behalf of the printer William Jaggard to his friend Augustine Vincent—a particularly fine copy that Folger thought might be the very first First Folio off the press. He liked to call it "the most precious book in the world."

The Folgers devoted themselves wholeheartedly to their Shakespearean labors. For them, getting away from it all often meant embarking on collecting expeditions to England aboard the merchant freighter SS *Minnehaha* and rereading their favorite author. *The Tempest* reads "best of all in mid-ocean," Henry wrote. "It is fragrant with salt spray picked up from wave crests by driving winds. The enchanted island of Prospero seems to have risen out of the surf." Back home from their travels, Emily kept track of the growing collection through a series of "case books," as she called them, a task that grew more complex as the collection expanded to include tens of thousands of books, manuscripts, paintings, playbills, and objets d'art. She also studied the catalogs from book dealers, marking off items for Henry to consider and often advising him on his purchases. In the evenings after work, Henry would go through the catalogs, decide what to order, and handle the correspondence with dealers, agents, and auction houses.

"Superficially, it may seem curious that an active American business executive should choose deliberately so complex and exacting an avocation," Emily wrote many years later. "But it was a recreation for Henry to step back three centuries at the close of the day and to read old books and examine old prints and reconstruct in his mind the old times from which the new times descend."

In collecting as in business, Henry Folger moved quickly; more than once he obtained a rare find because his agent got there first, armed in advance with Folger's agreement to a particular price. He was also extremely discreet. "I have persistently avoided all publicity," he once wrote, "feeling that book-buying could be done more cheaply and successfully if there was no advertising." While he avoided the limelight, Henry did not mind when Furness nicknamed him Forty Folio Folger—a tribute to his growing roster of First Folios that eventually reached some seventy-nine copies, as well as additional fragments. Other prizes in the collection included more than

"I...have made a collection of material illustrating Shakespeare which I believe will soon be notable."

Henry Folger, 1904

200 quarto editions of Shakespeare's plays and poems, many of which had appeared before the First Folio. Among the quartos was one of particular importance—the sole surviving copy of *Titus Andronicus* from 1594.

Investing in books did not always make sense to Henry Folger's business acquaintances, however. When playing golf with Rockefeller, Folger once found himself challenged about his peculiar hobby of book collecting. As the story goes, Rockefeller said, "Henry, I see from the papers that you just paid $100,000 for a book!" Folger replied obliquely, "Now, John, you know better than anybody else how newspapers exaggerate, especially about things like that. If you buy something for $10,000, it becomes $100,000 in print." Relieved, Rockefeller let it go at that. "Well, I'm glad to hear you say that, Henry," he answered. "We wouldn't want to think that the president of one of our major companies would be the kind of man foolish enough to pay $100,000 for a book!"

Lacking space to enjoy the collection in their own Brooklyn Heights home, the Folgers kept most of their finds in packing cases stored in fire-

A successful oil executive by the time of this 1910 studio portrait, Henry Folger continued to read Shakespeare at home and while traveling. A favorite reading edition was his thirteen-part "handy-volume" Shakespeare, a portion of which appears at left.

proof warehouses. (Still, as Emily later recalled, enough paintings, playbills, and other objects remained with the couple that they carried a hefty additional home insurance policy.) Sometime after about 1910, the Folgers began to think about establishing a library. Emily Folger recalled that Henry considered New York City, Chicago, and even Stratford-upon-Avon as possible locations. "But," she wrote, "as time passed, he came to favor Washington. That city is the common capital of the whole United States; it belongs to all the people." Emily herself had briefly lived in Washington as a child, when her father was solicitor of the treasury in the Lincoln administration.

After some consideration, they chose a piece of land near the Library of Congress on East Capitol Street. The site was then occupied by an array of substantial Victorian town houses known as Grants Row, and the process of quietly buying up lots and waiting for leases to expire consumed nine years. Then, in January 1928, just months after the parcel was finally assembled, the Folgers were stunned to learn that the Library of Congress was planning an expansion onto the very same land.

With characteristic speed, Henry Folger wrote at once to the Librarian of Congress, Herbert Putnam, confiding his plan for a Shakespearean library and expressing great concern that the government's plans might force him to move it to another city. The reaction was all that he could have hoped. In a reply sent by telegram, with a companion letter mailed the same day, Putnam hailed the news as "of extraordinary interest and supreme importance." The Library of Congress pronounced itself happy to adapt its plans to Folger's, and a few months later Congress passed a resolution assuring the Folgers full use of their plot. The same year, Henry Folger retired from Standard Oil to devote himself to the library project.

An unlikely memento of the Folger's construction, this "CC Soda" bottle was discovered inside a wall in 1999 during renovations to the tea room. The fruit drink was bottled by Coca-Cola in Washington, DC, between 1930 and 1932.

The next step was to find an architect. For this the Folgers consulted their acquaintance Alexander Trowbridge, who recommended the well-known Philadelphia architect Paul Philippe Cret; Trowbridge then became the consulting architect. Cret suggested that the New York sculptor John Gregory create the bas-reliefs that the Folgers wanted for the library's facade.

At every step, the Folgers worked closely with the architects; no part of the design was too small for their consideration. One day in May 1930, they visited Gregory's studio as he was refining the panel designs. Henry Folger wrote Cret that they had passed "a very happy hour" at the studio, and suggested a few small changes. "I would have the King Lear head a little older than as now portrayed," he recommended. "He was, as he himself said, an old man—indeed, his words were 'a foolish old man.'"

Although still vigorous at seventy-three, Henry Folger was now an old man himself; sadly, he would not live to see the library completed. A few weeks after writing that letter, he died on June 11, 1930, of heart failure following an operation. Emily Folger was left to continue their work—and to cope with an alarming discovery. Her husband's estate had been so reduced by the stock market crash of 1929 that it would not cover the costs of opening and operating the Folger Shakespeare Library, much less establish a lasting endowment. At this crucial juncture, Emily Folger saved the project by turning over Standard Oil securities worth more than $3 million to the trustees of Amherst College, whom Henry Folger had chosen to oversee the library. "She told us that the Library must open, and that it must be kept open," recalled Stanley King, a trustee and later president of Amherst, who was to

play a particularly active role in the library's affairs. "She would give the Trustees her own fortune and make the gift now."

Emily Folger also continued to take part in the plans for the still-incomplete library. One modification came in March 1931, when she wrote Cret to ask that John Gregory produce a memorial bust of her husband for the Exhibition Hall. She quietly ruled out Cret's countersuggestion of two matching busts. ("I do not need to tell you," he had written, "that Mr. Folger, in our conferences, always spoke of 'the founder' as meaning you, as well as himself.")

On April 23, 1932, at a dedication ceremony attended by President and Mrs. Herbert Hoover and the ambassadors of Great Britain, France, and Germany, Emily Folger presented the key to the newly completed Folger Shakespeare Library to George Arthur Plimpton, head of the Amherst board. A festive gathering with a long reception line followed. "Night fell, and we came away," she later wrote. "Back in my room alone I knew that the dream had come true at last."

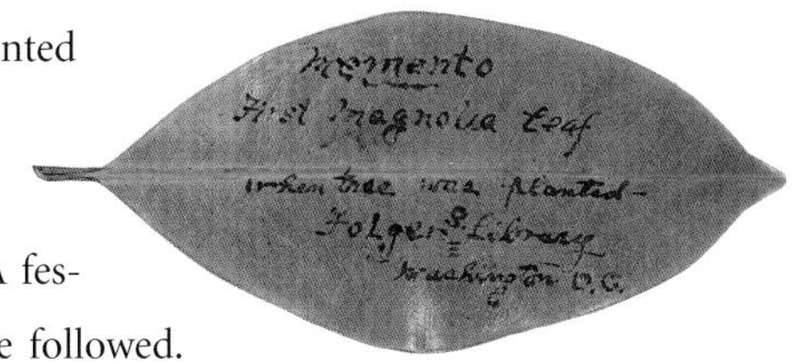

For her own efforts toward realizing that dream, Emily Folger was awarded an honorary doctorate from Amherst College in 1932, a tribute that Henry Folger had received some years before. She remained active in organizing the administration and contents of the library until her death in 1936 at age seventy-eight. Today, the ashes of both Folgers are buried in the Old Reading Room, near where their portraits by the British painter Frank Salisbury hang beneath a memorial bust of Shakespeare.

At left, President Herbert Hoover and George Arthur Plimpton, chairman of the Amherst trustees, stride out of the recently completed Folger Shakespeare Library following the April 23, 1932, dedication. Above, a carefully preserved leaf commemorates the new institution's magnolia trees.

"Upon its establishment near the close of 1931 the Folger had to start from absolute zero," wrote director Joseph Quincy Adams in a report on the Folger's first decade. (With scholarly exactitude, Adams dated the start of the library's work to a point some months before the dedication, when the building was first opened to start receiving the collection from storage.) "Not only did it possess no staff and no plan of operation but its collections had never been classified or even brought together in one place." Nor, he might have added, did it have a single executive. At the beginning, Adams shared leadership responsibilities jointly with the designated director, William A. Slade from the Library of Congress; it was Emily Folger's wish that each should take charge of an aspect of the library's operations. The arrangement came to an end in 1934, when Slade returned to the Library of Congress. Adams was then named acting director, becoming the Folger's first regularly appointed director two years later.

Organizational charts aside, the Folgers' legacy posed two distinct challenges for those guiding the library in that first decade. To begin with, the sheer volume of material the Folgers had collected was staggering; simply moving it into the new building took five months, as the small, newly hired staff unpacked more than 200,000 separate books, manuscripts, prints, sets of playbills, paintings, and other objects from 2,109 packing cases. Assessing and cataloging that material would take many years.

But for all its depth, the collection was limited in scope to Shakespeareana, however broadly defined. And so, early on, Adams and some of the

Emily Folger posed for several photographs in the library she and her late husband created. Here, she stands beside her desk in the Founders' Room, originally intended as a private space for both Folgers.

trustees saw a second challenge: that of expanding the Folger's holdings to encompass the entire English Renaissance. While the staff worked to turn the collection into a usable library, Adams kept an eye out for acquisitions on a grand scale. In January 1938, he proposed to the board the purchase of more than 8,000 volumes printed in England or in the English language before 1641, which had been collected by the late Sir Robert Leicester Harmsworth, a British newspaper publisher. These works, just one part of Harmsworth's large personal library, would be the perfect complement to the Folger's existing holdings, Adams argued; among them were no books by Shakespeare but many other important works the Folger lacked, in areas such as science, politics, and exploration. Following the family's wishes, the early English portion of the Harmsworth collection was being sold intact rather than piecemeal —and in a market severely affected by the Great Depression. Still, Adams estimated that the acquisition might cost $250,000, a sum roughly equivalent to the annual income from the endowment. Only by dipping into the principal, as the trustees were legally entitled to do, could the institution find the necessary cash.

Adams's presentation was "so masterly," as Stanley King later wrote, that the board promptly authorized a bid. King himself then handled the talks, ultimately offering £35,000 for the collection, or about $175,000. As Henry Folger once wrote of one of his own book-collecting adventures, it was "a happy, winning figure." At one stroke, the Folger's collection of early English titles doubled.

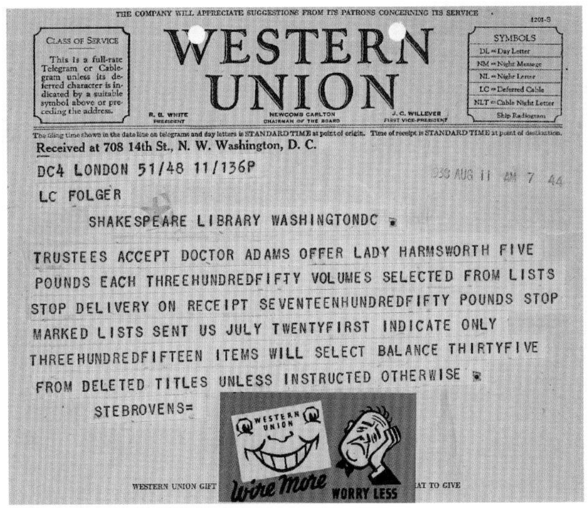
THE COMPANY WILL APPRECIATE SUGGESTIONS FROM ITS PATRONS CONCERNING ITS SERVICE

1201-S

CLASS OF SERVICE

This is a full-rate Telegram or Cablegram unless its deferred character is indicated by a suitable symbol above or preceding the address.

WESTERN UNION

R. B. WHITE, PRESIDENT · NEWCOMB CARLTON, CHAIRMAN OF THE BOARD · J. C. WILLEVER, FIRST VICE-PRESIDENT

SYMBOLS
DL = Day Letter
NM = Night Message
NL = Night Letter
LC = Deferred Cable
NLT = Cable Night Letter
Ship Radiogram

The filing time shown in the date line on telegrams and day letters is STANDARD TIME at point of origin. Time of receipt is STANDARD TIME at point of destination.

Received at 708 14th St., N. W. Washington, D. C.

DC4 LONDON 51/48 11/136P

1938 AUG 11 AM 7 44

LC FOLGER

SHAKESPEARE LIBRARY WASHINGTONDC

TRUSTEES ACCEPT DOCTOR ADAMS OFFER LADY HARMSWORTH FIVE POUNDS EACH THREEHUNDREDFIFTY VOLUMES SELECTED FROM LISTS STOP DELIVERY ON RECEIPT SEVENTEENHUNDREDFIFTY POUNDS STOP MARKED LISTS SENT US JULY TWENTYFIRST INDICATE ONLY THREEHUNDREDFIFTEEN ITEMS WILL SELECT BALANCE THIRTYFIVE FROM DELETED TITLES UNLESS INSTRUCTED OTHERWISE

STEBROVENS=

A 1938 telegram recalls the Folger's second, and smaller, acquisition from the library of the late Sir Robert Leicester Harmsworth, following a purchase of several thousand volumes some months before.

An unexpected sequel came the following July, when Adams traveled to England and visited Lady Harmsworth at her Sussex home. She invited him to have a look around, Adams later wrote, and while rummaging "in a dark unlighted closet in a rambling Elizabethan barn adjoining the Manor House," he came across a few hundred books printed before 1640 that Harmsworth had apparently purchased during his last illness but never cataloged. Many were still in the packaging in which the collector had received them. Lady Harmsworth promptly agreed to sell the Folger the newly discovered volumes as well. Today, the Folger holds almost half of the volumes listed in the *Short-Title Catalogue,* or STC, of early English books, and a portrait of Harmsworth hangs in the vault dedicated to those volumes.

Other acquisitions followed, but soon more pressing concerns were on the way. By the time that Adams's ten-year report was printed in 1942, the United States was at war—and the Folger's greatest treasures were in hiding. Just one week after the Japanese attack on Pearl Harbor, Adams and King had informed the trustees that they planned to ship 30,000 objects from the collection in a sealed railroad car to wartime storage on the Amherst campus. By January 15, 1942, the transfer was complete. There the materials stayed until November 1944, when fears of attack receded and they returned home. Only then was their wartime location revealed.

In the fall of 1946, Adams died at home of a heart attack. For some eighteen months, his second-in-command, James G. McManaway, served as

EVEN WITH ITS GREATEST TREASURES SAFE AT AMHERST, *the Folger still faced the realities of life during World War II in Washington, which included a severe manpower shortage. After a citywide search, only two very senior licensed building engineers—one seventy-two and the other eighty—could be found to run the heating system. Three scholars left the Folger's small staff for service overseas. Yet Joseph Quincy Adams, despite his own failing health, was determined to keep the library open for the duration; somehow, requests from researchers and novelists alike were met, and facsimile reprints of rare Folger holdings continued to be produced.*

Meanwhile, the Elizabethan halls of the Folger became something of an intellectual rest-and-relief center for "war-harassed men and women," as assistant director James G. McManaway wrote in 1944. McManaway described a new kind of visitor to the Reading Room—"the erstwhile professor of English, now a captain in the artillery just back from the South Pacific, who drops in to purge his thoughts of death and destruction by reading Ben Jonson." Nor was it only ex-English professors who found respite there. Crowds of weary clerical workers filled the Exhibition Hall, which the Folger kept open on Saturdays and Sundays throughout the war.

acting director while the trustees searched for a successor. In the process, they concluded that the new director's mission—once they had chosen him—would be to transform the Folger into a modern research center. While a great deal had been accomplished since the first move-in day in 1931, much remained to be done. The Folger's catalog was still incomplete and difficult to use. The Reading Room contained few reference works; readers and staff were expected to cross the street to the Library of Congress for more general materials, a frustrating and impractical arrangement. A postdoctoral fellowship program brought in two Folger Fellows each year, but other scholars complained that it was too hard to gain access to the collection. Those who did enter the Reading Room sweltered there in the hot Washington summers; the Folger's limited cooling system could provide air-conditioning only for the stacks where books were stored. And the sight of guards with pistols—who took target practice on a shooting range in the basement—was not especially inviting.

In 1948, the trustees appointed as the next director Louis B. Wright from the Huntington Library. At the same time, they sent him a letter that described the needed changes in some detail, a document he later called a "blueprint" for the Folger's future. One of Wright's first moves, as he later wrote, "was to take pistols from the guards and remove a barrier blocking entrance to the reading room. The appearance of the place began to look less like a fortress and more like an institution of learning." In years to come, the library would install a thorough, comprehensible catalog, a wide assortment of reference works organized for scholarly use, and central air-conditioning. The Folger's first renovation and expansion program added new underground storage and office space.

There was also, of course, considerable continuity with what had come before. From the beginning, the Folger had prided itself on attracting

100,000 or more visitors a year to the Exhibition Hall, and Adams himself had taken a role in preparing educational prints, facsimiles, and photographs to be sold at modest prices to the tourist crowds. Under Wright, the library added an engaging sequence of illustrated Folger Booklets on Tudor and Stuart Civilization, designed for students and nonspecialists. Among the intriguing titles were *Music in Elizabethan England,* by Dorothy Mason; *The Art of War and Renaissance England,* by John R. Hale; and *English Dress in the Age of Shakespeare,* by Virginia LaMar.

LaMar, who had come to the Folger in 1946, was Wright's executive secretary, and so distinguished herself that a prize was later established at the Folger in her memory. She never went to college, Wright noted, "yet she was one of the best-educated persons on the Folger staff." Unlike gifted secretaries elsewhere whose work went largely unheralded, she was soon given larger responsibilities and received credit as coeditor with Wright of the Folger's General Reader's Shakespeare series—inexpensive paperback editions of Shakespeare's works that won favor for their lucid introductions, accessible notes, and illustrations from the Folger collection. (At century's end, that popular format was retained in the New Folger Library Shakespeare, a completely new treatment of the plays edited by Barbara Mowat, director of academic programs, and Paul Werstine, professor of English at King's College and the Graduate School of the University of Western Ontario.)

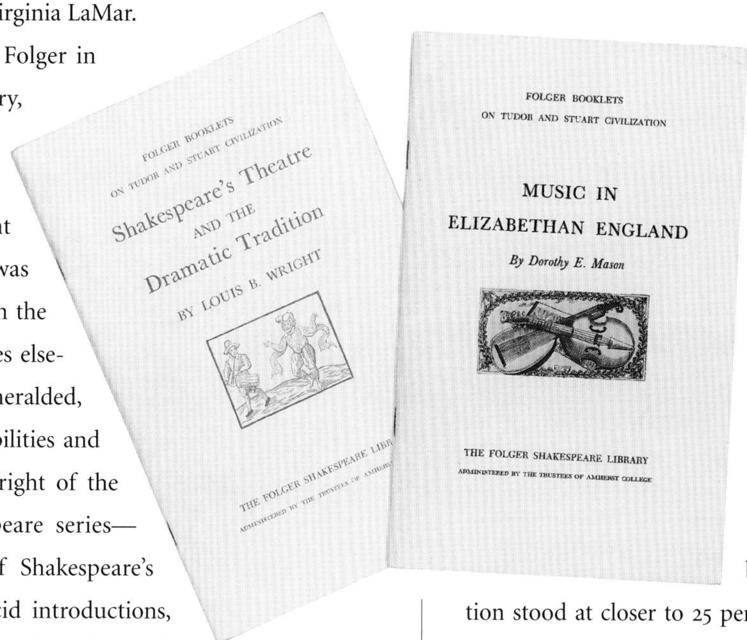

Another publication that brought the Folger praise was a newly inaugurated newsletter, *Report from the Folger Library.* Wright's dry wit made the occasional publication a favorite even among recipients who never set foot in the library, and often enough, the whimsy had a point. In one issue in 1951, Wright noted that Mary McGrory, then book review editor of the *Washington Star,* had recently stopped by the Folger for afternoon tea—a daily gathering of staff and readers that is nearly as old as the Folger itself. McGrory, Wright added, was surprised that "not one visiting scholar in the group had Shakespeare for his subject. 'What, nobody working on Shakespeare?' she exclaimed in some distress. We assured her that we had done our best. We had beaten the Shakespearean bushes for her and could not drive a single Shakespearean out of hiding."

Wright went on to explain that only about 15 percent of the library's visiting researchers in the past year had "displayed any professional interest in Shakespeare." (Shakespearean researchers remain in the minority, although by the early twenty-first century the proportion stood at closer to 25 percent.) For the staff at the Folger, this was no cause for alarm; instead, it showed that the library's scope now went far beyond exclusively Shakespearean matters. Here, too, Wright had expanded on Adams's work. By the time Wright retired, after twenty years, in 1968, the Folger had secured an additional 22,000 European books and some 19,000 English ones, complementing the primarily English-language acquisitions of the Adams years.

WHEN CHARLTON HINMAN ARRIVED AT THE FOLGER *as a research fellow in 1941, scholars had made little progress in collating, or comparing, the First Folios assembled there. The copies of this first collection of Shakespeare's plays differ slightly from one another because the pages were proofread and corrected during printing; once tabulated, the inconsistencies were expected to be of great interest. But finding them was very time-consuming. Hinman had barely started before he left to spend four years in naval intelligence during World War II.*

As Hinman later recalled, the war gave him the answer, when he learned of a machine built to compare before-and-after pictures of bomb targets. On his return, he spent the years from 1946 to 1952, with a two-year absence in Korea, developing a similar device called the Hinman collator. (Folger librarian Giles Dawson kept the work going while Hinman was gone.) To use the collator, an operator set two First Folios in place, then looked through an eyepiece to see them first superimposed, then each alone. As the view blinked back and forth, even a broken comma wriggled noticeably. Hinman found he could collate as many as 180 folio pages in under five hours. In the next decade, he analyzed more than fifty Folger folios, a pair at a time.

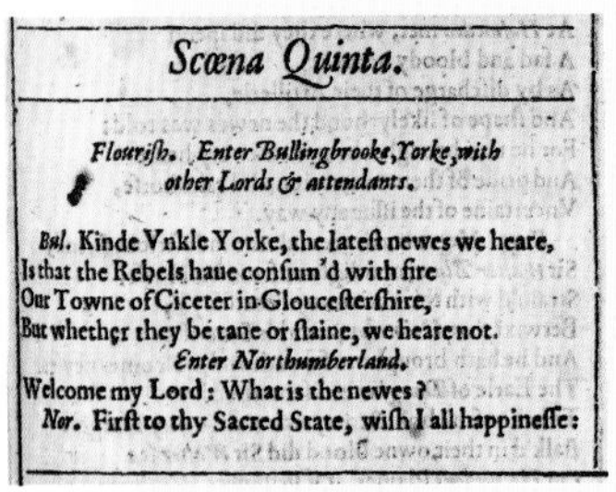
Scœna Quinta.

Flourish. Enter Bullingbrooke, Yorke, with other Lords & attendants.

Bul. Kinde Vnkle Yorke, the lateſt newes we heare,
Is that the Rebels haue conſum'd with fire
Our Towne of Ciceter in Glouceſterſhire,
But whether they be tane or ſlaine, we heare not.

Enter Northumberland.

Welcome my Lord: What is the newes?
Nor. Firſt to thy Sacred State, wiſh I all happineſſe:

The results, published in 1963 in The Printing and Proof-reading of the First Folio of Shakespeare, *were unexpected. Hinman found few substantive differences among the First Folios. Instead, he used thousands of small changes in the type itself to piece together just how the books had been printed, including the sequence in which pages were set and the characteristics of those who set them. The extent of that achievement, wrote the editor of* Shakespeare Quarterly *on Hinman's death in 1977, "is difficult to describe with any adjective other than 'monumental.'"*

TURNING OUTWARD

Fittingly for a place devoted to study of the Renaissance, the Folger underwent a rebirth of its own in the late 1960s and the 1970s, a time when many institutions reassessed their goals in the interest of greater openness and social responsibility. Once again, the Amherst board of trustees helped move the Folger forward by appointing a director with fresh ideas—O. B. Hardison Jr., a professor of English literature from the University of North Carolina. "We are a repository of materials dealing with the life and issues of the English Renaissance," Hardison told one interviewer. "Now we want to present these materials so that they are meaningful to the non-scholar as well."

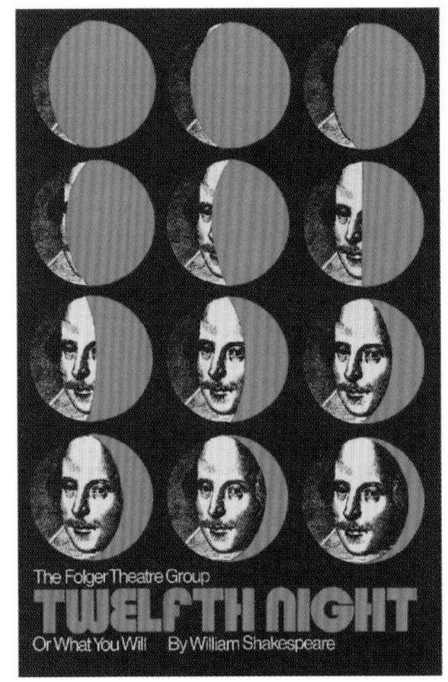

The first step in this process was to transform the Folger's Elizabethan Theatre, previously used mainly for lectures and tours, into a functioning playhouse, a change that included fireproofing its waxed-oak walls. While that makeover was under way in 1970, the newly formed Folger Theatre Group mounted its first production at nearby Saint Mark's Church—the rock musical *Dionysus Wants You!*, adapted from Euripides' *The Bacchae,* in which the god of wine and ecstasy drives his followers to madness. Conceived by Folger artistic director Richmond Crinkley, the production drew the attention of the well-known director Joseph Papp, who picked up the show and took it to New York. Later that season, a production of *Twelfth Night* featuring cast members in bell-bottoms and hot pants was reviewed approvingly by the *New York Times.*

For all the notice the Theatre Group attracted, another innovation did just as much in the long run to connect the Folger with the public. Despite

"I believe that the Folger and institutions like it preserve something even more precious than their collections of rare books and manuscripts: they preserve an idea, and an ideal, of humanity in a world that seems increasingly hostile to things merely human."

O. B. Hardison Jr., 1974

its history of offering exhibitions, booklets, and prints, the Folger furnished little direct guidance to the visitor. In 1970, the Folger began recruiting its first volunteer docents, and by the next year it was able to announce a new tradition of free walk-in tours for the public. Attracting energetic women with lively minds at a time when women's roles were changing, the docent program became a seedbed for educational outreach programs, including school visits with slide shows. In 1980, the docents created a new Folger tradition by sponsoring the first Shakespeare performance festival for elementary-school students. A parallel festival for secondary-school students began the next year.

Nor were the docents and the Theatre Group the only news items in 1970. Modern poetry readings—a continuing tradition at the Folger—began that year, as did the Folger Institute, a joint venture between the Folger

The well-known American poet Reed Whittemore addresses a rapt audience in the Exhibition Hall in September 1975. Poetry and fiction readings remain a vital part of Folger programs.

Dear K.C. Avery,

I thought you were very good playing the Queen. The speech you made was very interesting. I loved your costume. I think the fact that you were there was exciting.

Sincerely yours,
Laura Porkerson
'Tom Snout'
Herndon Elementary

and a growing list of universities to promote the study of Renaissance and eighteenth-century topics through symposia and seminars. In 1972, the year of the Folger's fortieth anniversary, the journal *Shakespeare Quarterly* was transferred to the library from the independent Shakespeare Association of America. And the changes kept coming, with the creation of a Midday Muse series of lunchtime poetry readings and performances, the addition of a film archive to the Folger's collection, and the launching of a new imprint, Folger Books. In 1977, music was added to the mix with the founding of the Folger Consort, a resident ensemble dedicated to the performance of medieval and Renaissance music.

With growing programs, of course, came growing financial needs. Although the Folger had received assistance from a small number of donors since its inception, efforts at development had been largely ad hoc. That changed in 1971 with the founding of the Friends of the Folger. "The Library would obviously benefit from increased contact and wider understanding of its activities," Hardison told the first meeting of the group. "We hoped that its friends would derive genuine personal satisfaction and enrichment from a closer, more intimate association." Early in 1973 came another step forward, as the relatively new National Endowment for the Humanities (NEH) announced some much-needed aid in dramatic fashion. On the opening night of *The Winter's Tale,* the NEH chairman, Ronald S. Berman, took the stage before the play began to announce a grant of $98,609 for central library functions. Berman added that he encouraged the Folger to apply again, foreshadowing what would become an enduring partnership.

Dressed as Elizabeth I, Folger docent K. C. Avery waves regally in front of a Folger bas-relief. Avery played the part for seventeen years before passing the scepter to another docent, bringing history to life for tens of thousands of schoolchildren, including the writer of a 1983 letter.

The same year, the Folger acquired its first development chairman, James Elder, who soon organized so many special events that Hardison called him "my master of revels." A typical instance was a 1975 benefit with the theme "Shakespeare in Italy." As chronicled by society writer Diana McClellan, the evening featured Anna Moffo singing arias, the wife of the British ambassador "spectacular in ermine-trimmed wimple," and O. B. Hardison dressed in "a red moiré doublet and white tights." Some people "got a little tiddly," McClellan confided. "Nothing like last year, mind you, when it was Shakespeare in Scotland and the haggis was swilled down with Scotch whisky."

Fittingly, the Folger in 1979 capped a decade devoted to making connections with a wider audience by mounting a large-scale traveling exhibition, *Shakespeare: The Globe and the World (right).* At the same time, the library closed its Reading Room for renovation, the second phase of a project that started with the construction of new, and much improved, underground vaults. Construction of a second reading room would follow. The $8.5 million modernization project was nearing completion in 1982, when President Ronald Reagan marked the Folger's fiftieth anniversary by accepting the keys to the library from Mrs. Caspar Weinberger, chairman of the trustees' Folger Library Committee, and a plaque from O. B. Hardison. Departing from his prepared text with a characteristic anecdote, the president joked, "I could date myself completely and tell you that once in college I played in *Taming of the Shrew* in modern costume, and my wardrobe was plus-four knickers." Turning serious, he compared the modern Folger to a candle that "throws its beams across our land, adding to the perspective, understanding, and character of our people," a sentiment that Henry and Emily Folger would surely have appreciated.

In late 1983, O. B. Hardison stepped down to teach at Georgetown University; upon his departure, Philip Knachel served as acting director,

THE FOLGER ON TOUR

NO PRODUCTION IN THE FOLGER'S HISTORY *reached a wider audience than* Shakespeare: The Globe and the World, *a traveling exhibition of the institution's treasures that opened in San Francisco in October 1979. Launched while the Folger's Reading Room was closed for renovation, the show attracted hundreds of thousands from coast to coast. Those entering first encountered exhibits on country life and Stratford-upon-Avon, then moved on to London and a model of the Globe Theatre; around the Globe, six "minitheatres" displayed costumes, paintings, and film clips of half a dozen of Shakespeare's plays.*

It was a once-in-lifetime event, and host cities made the most of it. In Kansas City, nearly every schoolchild from St. Louis to Denver saw the exhibition, and universities joined with the Nelson Gallery of Art to hold a three-month "Mid-American Shakespearean Chautauqua." In Dallas and Atlanta, NEH-funded "actors in residence" spent weeks at local campuses. On the final weekend in Pittsburgh, Princess Grace of Monaco twice performed scenes from Shakespeare. And in New York, where a lecture by playwright Tom Stoppard kicked off the run, the Times *hailed the exhibition as "instructive and continuously amusing," singling out S. Schoenbaum's companion book as "a palpable hit."*

The show even got an encore when it was extended for a special three-month run in Los Angeles. With that, however, the extravaganza came to an end. In February 1982, the books, manuscripts, and other rarities returned safely home to Washington, DC, where the Folger's Reading Room was once again open for scholarly use.

a role he had also filled briefly after Wright's retirement. Some months later the Amherst board named Werner Gundersheimer of the University of Pennsylvania as the Folger's fourth regularly appointed director. This time, their choice broke new ground in two respects: Gundersheimer was a historian, not a literature professor, and his background was in the Continental Renaissance, not Elizabethan England. As Gundersheimer commented to the *New York Times*, his selection seemed to "represent a sense on the part of the trustees that the Folger's mission has broadened." The Folger's evolution from a repository of Shakespeareana to a library encompassing first the English Renaissance and then the early modern age had moved another step forward.

STRIKING A NEW BALANCE

A few months after Gundersheimer's arrival, one of the delightful serendipities of rare book collecting occurred in October 1984, when Folger conservator Frank Mowery discovered an unusual manuscript fragment as he was rebinding two sixteenth-century texts. Old manuscript pages were often pressed into service by binders of that era, but an examination by curator of manuscripts Laetitia Yeandle and cataloger Anthony Franks revealed that this one was something very special. Internal evidence showed it was part of a manuscript from the British Isles predating AD 800, the oldest such manuscript fragment known to exist. Well outside the Folger's period of interest, the fragment was put up for auction at Sotheby's the next spring, earning some $100,000 for the Folger, which used the money to establish a special acquisitions endowment fund.

For the Folger's new director, however, the manuscript sale was a rare piece of good financial news. The dramatic changes of the 1970s and early 1980s had broadened the scope of the Folger's concerns and, with the renovations, left it in fine physical condition. But some of the initiatives were becoming a burden on the Folger's endowment, already hurt by the 1970s recessionary inflation. In early 1985, Gundersheimer faced the unenviable task of dissolving the Folger Theatre Group, which had been experiencing significant losses for the past decade despite its local popularity. That November, the group reincorporated as The Shakespeare Theatre at the Folger, an independent entity. With support from the library, the company remained at the Folger six more years before moving to larger quarters downtown. Meanwhile, the Folger began a long process of regaining its financial balance and revitalizing the crucial jobs of cataloging and acquisition, both seriously underfunded, as well as the library's fellowship program, which had lapsed altogether.

Donated in 1987 by Dorothy Rouse-Bottom, this Nicholas Hilliard miniature from the 1590s depicts Lettice Knollys, countess of Leicester.

In addition to renewed fund-raising and major capital campaigns, the years that followed saw a surge of energy in several other programs. The Folger Institute sponsored a continuing series of intensive NEH-funded summer seminars. The PEN/Faulkner Award for Fiction, which had arrived at the Folger in 1983, and new Folger Poetry Board Readings marked a growing involvement with contemporary writers. And the Elizabethan Theatre buzzed with a mix of concerts, plays, and lectures under education and public programs director Janet Griffin, leading in the mid-1990s to a new theatre initiative, the Folger Theatre. Among its early successes was a 1997 production of *Romeo and Juliet* directed by Joe Banno, which won three Helen Hayes Awards.

The last decades of the twentieth century also saw considerable growth in the Folger's educational outreach, an effort that had begun years ago with the docent program, then emerged as a fledgling institutional focus in the early 1980s with the arrival of the first professional staff and grant funding. Peggy O'Brien, the Folger's first head of education, argued that the best way for students to learn Shakespeare was "*by doing* Shakespeare," enacting scenes from the plays and bringing the language to life. This approach offers special benefits for youngsters with poor reading skills, whose ear for language is often better than their eye. "Shakespeare is for all students," O'Brien insisted, "of all ability levels and reading levels, of every ethnic origin, in every kind of school."

To share that notion, the Folger organized the Teaching Shakespeare Institutes, a continuing series of NEH-funded summer institutes for teachers that got them up and performing in front of their peers—and gaining new insight into the texts. *Shakespeare Set Free,* a three-volume set of classroom-proven exercises, spread these ideas still further, as did the later Teaching Shakespeare Web site. In the late 1990s, the Folger education program added a successful program for children in the third through the sixth grades in the Washington, DC, public schools called Shakespeare Steps Out. "Younger children still have a sense of wonder about language," explained Janet Field-Pickering, who succeeded O'Brien as head of education. "They view these plays as musical, rhythmical, and magical." In the year 2000, the expanded education and public programs staff moved into the Haskell Center, a newly renovated office space across the street from the main building.

Among other changes back at the original building, the Folger at last updated its Exhibition Hall, a dimly lit space that had been occupied since 1932 by the same antiquated glass cases. In 1986, a thorough cleaning and renovation left the hall much better lit, with window shades that screened out the sun's ultraviolet rays and safer, more adaptable display spaces. In 1990, Gundersheimer named Rachel Doggett the first curator of books and exhibitions, with responsibility for developing the exhibition program as both a scholarly endeavor and an interpretative program for the public. Exhibitions, access for the disabled, and still more public programs were further aided in 1993 by a grant of $2.5 million from the Lila Wallace–Reader's Digest Fund, the largest single philanthropic award in the Folger's history up to that time.

In 1999, an ambitious multimedia exhibition, *Seven Ages of Man,* funded in part by that grant, took its place beside the Exhibition Hall in the new Shakespeare Gallery. More than 250 digital images of treasures from the Folger's collection were arranged according to the "ages of man" described by Jaques in *As You Like It.* The display also included music by the Folger Consort, passages from Shakespeare, a pop-up glossary adapted from the New Folger Library Shakespeare editions, and a recording of Jaques's speech by the well-known Shakespearean actor Sir Derek Jacobi.

That computerized exhibition was perhaps the most visible part of a sea change that overtook the Folger, as it did other institutions, in the last years of the twentieth century: the digital revolution. After some modest steps forward in the 1980s—the acquisition of a minicomputer with four terminals, a Reading Room connection to the Research Library Information Network (RLIN) database—in the next decade the Folger environment changed forever. In 1990 there was a single fax machine in the building. By 1996 there were computers on every desktop, with voice mail and e-mail at arm's reach. The New Reading Room was soon as well known among researchers for its laptop-computer

"The Folger itself has become a diamond of many sparkling facets. Our task is to keep it safe, to preserve and enhance its beauty and its value to the wide world of scholarship, and indeed to all who benefit from the bright light it tries to cast in the cultural life of this capital and the nation."

Werner Gundersheimer, 1991

connections as for its graceful wall displays. And in a multiyear effort directed by the Folger's librarian, Richard Kuhta, the library's vast card catalog became available online under the felicitous name Hamnet.

The Folger's long-standing interest in facsimiles and photographs of its fragile materials, which make it possible both to share the objects and to protect them from wear, also took on a digital dimension. By the turn of the millennium, some of the library's greatest treasures could be viewed in digital formats by schoolchildren a world away, a situation that could scarcely have been imagined even twenty years before. In ways both new and old, from digital facsimiles to innovative stage productions, from the quiet intensity of its reading rooms to the excited voices of youngsters acting Shakespeare, the twenty-first century Folger continues to realize its founders' dream, delighting in the pleasures of the past made present as it shares a remarkable collection with the world.

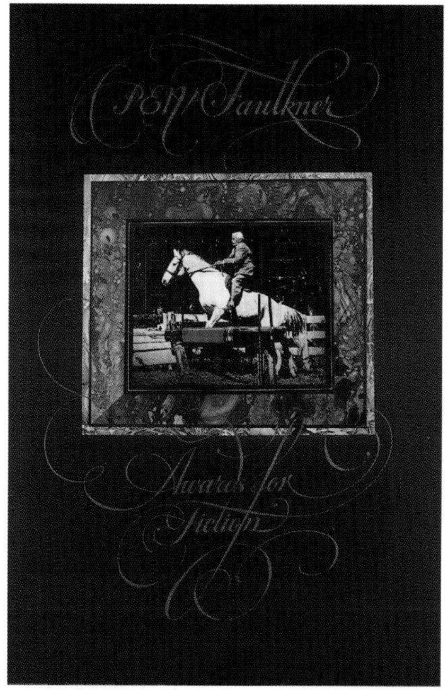

An image of William Faulkner on horseback enlivens this 1993 poster celebrating the PEN/Faulkner Foundation, which makes its home at the Folger. Among other programs, PEN/Faulkner sponsors a major literary award as well as readings by such figures as the writer Eudora Welty (below), who appeared at the Folger four times.

Facing page: Swinging into action on the Elizabethan Theatre stage, students from Washington's Shaed Elementary School enjoy a 1998 stage-combat workshop led by Brad Waller as part of the Folger's Shakespeare Steps Out educational outreach program.

SOLDIER
LOVER
JVSTICE
SCHOOLE BOY
PANTALOUNE
INFANT
OLD MAN

Situated a block from the US Capitol in Washington, DC, the main Folger Shakespeare Library building is an Elizabethan monument in neoclassical clothing. On the outside, the library is clad in the city's familiar white marble with an Art Deco flair. But carved literary quotations and bas-reliefs on Shakespearean themes hint at the very different world that lies within. There, oak-paneled walls and thirty-foot ceilings evoke one of the great English houses of Shakespeare's day—an effect heightened by a large fireplace in the main reading room. (The fireplace, of course, is never used.) Tucked into the east end of the building, an intimate period theatre recalls the sixteenth-century innyards where traveling troupes performed.

From the bas-reliefs to the theatre, these details are based on Henry and Emily Folger's own ideas for their library, as interpreted by the Philadelphia architect Paul Philippe Cret and his Washington colleague Alexander Trowbridge, the consulting architect. Henry Folger did not live to see the building completed, but an elderly Emily Folger was there to welcome President and Mrs. Herbert Hoover and other dignitaries to the dedication in 1932. In the years since then, the library has undergone several renovations and expansions, including the addition of modern, climate-controlled vaults for its especially rare holdings. Yet the building's unique, somewhat idiosyncratic, atmosphere endures unchanged.

In the year 2000, the original building was joined by a second structure just across Third Street, the Wyatt R. and Susan N. Haskell Center for Education and Public Programs. A wholesale renovation of a mid-nineteenth-century office building that was once a funeral parlor, the new center houses the Folger's education and public programs staff in a setting that includes distance-learning equipment, a well-lit rehearsal room, and much-needed office space.

Serving as something of a hyphen between the two buildings is the Elizabethan Garden on the east side of the main library, facing the Haskell Center. This special area, which opened in 1989, incorporates a selection of herbs from Shakespeare's day. Scenes from the garden and both buildings, shown here and on the pages that follow, offer a modern look at the unusual setting that the Folgers first imagined for their collection more than seventy years ago.

In the Old Reading Room, a glowing stained-glass window depicts the "seven ages of man" from Jaques's speech in As You Like It. *The Philadelphia design studio of Nicola d'Ascenzo modeled the stone tracery of the window after the example in Stratford's Holy Trinity Church.*

Built like the great hall of an Elizabethan house, the 131-foot Old Reading Room incorporates sixteenth-century French and Flemish tapestries, carved paneling, a high trussed roof, and a large fireplace, with the Seven Ages of Man window at the west end. A portion of one Flemish tapestry appears below. On the hall screen at the east end, portraits of the Folgers in their academic robes hang near a bust of Shakespeare based on his memorial in Holy Trinity Church, Stratford-upon-Avon; the ashes of both Folgers are interred behind a memorial plaque.

Constructed in the early 1980s as a modern complement to the original reading room, the Bond Memorial Reading Room is topped by glass panes that admit indirect daylight, making it an excellent display space for paintings from the Folger's large Shakespeare collection. The wooden pillars leading from the Old Reading Room into the new one and the stone-trimmed high arches reflect the Renaissance spirit of Paul Cret's original design. Outdoors, the exterior of the new section matches the white marble of his plan as well.

The site of two to three exhibitions every year, drawn primarily from the Folger collection, the Folger's Exhibition Hall evokes the gallery of a sixteenth-century house with its soaring plaster strapwork ceiling. The shield and great eagle of the United States grace the west end of the hall, nearest the Capitol; the coat of arms of Elizabeth I, Shakespeare's queen, represents Great Britain in the east. Each heraldic device is accompanied by a quotation from a theatrical giant—respectively, the American drama critic William Winter and the British thespian David Garrick.

ALL THE WORLDS A STAGE
AND ALL THE MEN AND
WOMEN MERELY PLAYERS

Perhaps the most unusual feature of the Folgers' plan for the library is the small replica of an Elizabethan theatre, shown at left. As Henry Folger himself wisely noted, "Any effort to reproduce permanently any one of the theatres known by name will involve too much risk of criticism, based on what is now known about such theatre, or may later be discovered." Instead, Cret's design uses carved oak columns and three-tiered wooden balconies to suggest the courtyard of an early English inn, where traveling players performed on a raised platform at one end as spectators gathered in the yard below and on the balconies above. Above, a canopy represents the open sky.

"There's rosemary, that's for remembrance. Pray you, love, remember," says Ophelia in her mad scene in Hamlet. *Inspired in part by such herbal references in Shakespeare's plays, the Elizabethan Garden next to the library building also incorporates plants that were simply popular in his time, including lavender, creeping thyme, and English ivy. The armillary sphere at its center, a memorial to former director O. B. Hardison Jr., serves as both a garden ornament and a sundial.*

A MIDSOMMER NIGHTS DREAME

THE TRAGEDIE OF ROMEO AND IVLIET

THE MERCHANT OF VENICE

THE TRAGEDIE OF MACBETH

THE TRAGEDIE OF IVLIVS CÆSAR

THE TRAGEDIE OF KING LEAR

THE LIFE AND DEATH OF RICHARD THE THIRD

THE TRAGEDIE OF HAMLET

THE FIRST PART OF HENRY THE FOVRTH

Spanning the library's north facade, nine bas-reliefs by the New York sculptor John Gregory depict scenes from Shakespeare. By convention, the artwork would ordinarily have been positioned much higher, near the top of the building; the Folgers asked for it to be near street level to give the public a better view. The original Puck sculpture, shown below, was created for the Folger in the 1930s by Brenda Putnam, an award-winning sculptor who was also the daughter of Herbert Putnam, the director of the Library of Congress. By the late 1990s, damage to the outdoor piece was extensive. The statue underwent restoration in 2001.

A modern doorway topped with the original painted street address leads into the Haskell Center, designed to house the Folger's performance and education programs. The architect, Andrew Stevenson, faced several challenges in fashioning this modern work space out of an antiquated office building, not the least of which was a basement less than six feet deep. As part of the project, the existing building was underpinned while a new bottom floor was excavated, creating a functional lower level that became one of four usable floors.

E R
TVTTO VEDO &
MOLTO MANCHA
SEMPER EADEM
SANCHO RIPO
SO & RIPOSATO
AFFANO 1579

Henry and Emily Folger originally meant to call their library the Folger Shakespeare Memorial, and that is the legal name by which it appears in Henry Folger's will. But as planning continued for the building that was to house their vast collection, they changed their minds. It was not a somber "memorial" they wanted, in the sense of a shrine or a monument to a man long dead. Instead, they sought to create a forward-looking institution, which they named the Folger Shakespeare Library, where the books, manuscripts, artwork, and other rare materials they had acquired would serve, in Henry Folger's often-quoted phrase, as a fine "kit of tools for scholars."

In the years since, the collection that Folger thus so modestly described has grown far beyond Shakespeare to encompass the whole of the early modern age in the West. And the list of those who regularly draw on its many strengths has grown as well. Whether directly, or indirectly through Folger programs and publications, the collection serves students, teachers, authors, poets, musicians, actors, audiences, and exhibition visitors, all in addition to a vital core of visiting scholars.

In the pages that follow, several dozen objects from the Folger's collection—many of them photographed for this book by staff photographer Julie Ainsworth—provide a diverse sampling of the institution's holdings. For convenience, they are loosely divided into three sections. The first includes some of the institution's great non-Shakespearean rarities; the second consists of works—some no less rare—that are especially notable for illuminating the early modern age; and the third offers a brief tour of the Folger's unrivaled collection of Shakespeareana, including modern-day materials in theatre history. Where appropriate, the accompanying text suggests some of the more intriguing ways that these materials have played a part in the lives of those who come to the Folger.

The books, manuscripts, and other items pictured here suggest a great diversity of subjects—among them, to cite just a few, politics, religion, zoology, fashion, music, art, and literature. In recent years, scholars at many institutions, including the Folger, have begun to focus on still another topic: the books and other rare objects themselves. Researchers have turned their attention to the relationship between books and readers, with a detailed look at how specific texts and images have been circulated, and sometimes changed, over time.

Although seemingly straightforward, such topics can ultimately prove complex. As the Folger's own rare book catalogers can attest, even the identity of a book was understood differently centuries ago. Copies of the same edition may vary because of stop-press corrections or additions. They may also appear in very different bindings, because it was common to purchase new books unbound and then to arrange for binding. Then as now, books also changed from edition to edition. In contemplating a work such as Isaac Newton's Principia Mathematica, of which a rare first edition is held at the Folger (page 134), or John Foxe's Book of Martyrs, which doubled in size from one edition to the next (page 100), a number of questions arise for researchers, editors, and readers. Is there one best or most complete edition, or can more be learned from textual differences? How did readers understand such variations at the time? How can (or should) a modern editor or reader search for and select the "truest" version, if such a thing exists—the one closest to the author's own intentions?

Inquiries of this kind have become newly urgent in a time when electronic media are adding still more ways to exchange and adapt information. In the case of Shakespeare's own texts, of course, very similar questions long ago drew the Folgers to their lifework of collecting. Recast in a modern light, such questions are part of an ever-expanding web of research and activities that ensures the assortment of rare materials at the Folger is no silent "memorial," but truly a living collection.

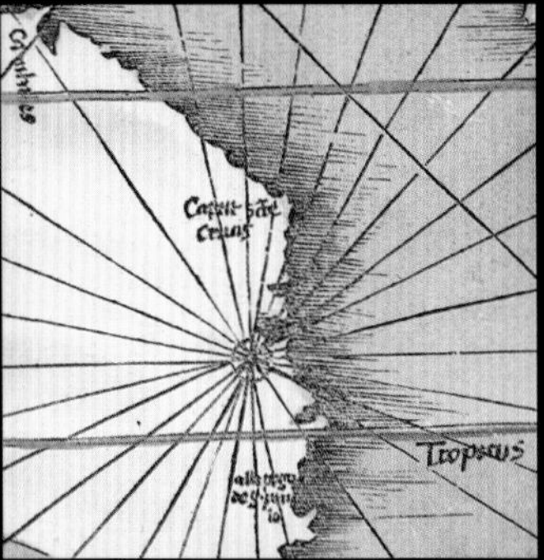
Tropicus

Only one copy is known to exist of the earliest extant manuscript of an English morality play, The Castle of Perseverance. *The same may be said of Elizabeth I's own pulpit copy of the Bishops' Bible and of the individual creations of the seventeenth-century calligrapher Esther Inglis, which appear on the following pages. Other materials included here are notable for their personal association with one of the members of the Tudor or Stuart royal families; still others commemorate great early English writers—Chaucer, Donne, Spenser. Some are books rich with annotations that reveal much about their owners and the world they lived in. All are among the collection's great rarities, either acquired by the Folgers themselves or by purchase or gift over the years, in some cases as recently as the 1990s.*

The rarity of a book, manuscript, or objet d'art like those shown here is a two-sided coin. It marks the object itself as something to be especially cared for and preserved, while adding value and strength to the collection. But making such scarce materials available without wearing them out poses special challenges. In striking the balance between access and excessive wear, nearly all the materials shown here have been exhibited to the public at the Folger or in touring exhibitions, and many have been studied in Folger Institute conferences and seminars as well as by individual researchers. A few have been the subject of painstaking, years-long conservation projects. Some have been published in printed or digital facsimiles, which can sometimes serve in the place of the original for a particular research question. Once captured photographically or digitally, such images can also take on multiple roles, illustrating Folger publications, banners, and teaching packets.

Such a survey of typical uses and curatorial solutions does not, however, fully capture the value of a direct encounter with any of these original objects, or encompass all the reasons for preserving and building a collection of such materials. Original books and manuscripts certainly provide the physical evidence on which bibliographical and textual scholarship are based; they are irreplaceable. But there are other factors at work that speak to scholars and schoolchildren alike, including the immediacy of a physical object and its emotional power to transport the viewer. There is drama in these documents and other holdings that only they themselves can express.

Thomas de
kempis
vide ab

Although few of them were collected for that reason, the rare books at the Folger offer some fine examples of bookbinding—an art that was also a necessity in the early days of printing, when books were often sold without covers. In 1992, more than 160 examples of the binder's art, including the 5 shown here and on the following pages, were displayed in the Folger's Fine and Historic Bookbindings *exhibition, the first major US bindings exhibition mounted solely from one institution's collection; it was also the first large-scale American show of bindings since 1958. The exhibits, which spanned more than four centuries, incorporated materials ranging from leather to jewels and embroidery. Some bore the stamps of kings, queens, and noblemen. Among the earliest was the 1494 Thomas à Kempis text at left, bound in blind-tooled pigskin and equipped with an iron chain; printed books of that era were so valuable that they were often chained in place to foil thieves.*

Other notable leather bindings included the one from 1529 shown overleaf at left, a superb example of a panel-stamped binding, in which heated metal plates, or "panels," often bearing elaborate designs, are stamped into dampened leather. Here the front panel includes portraits of Saints Claud, Barbara, Catherine of Alexandria, and John the Evangelist. The elaborate gold-tooled calfskin binding beside it was created by a master binder whose name is lost to history; he is referred to as the "MacDurnan Gospels binder" for his achievement in rebinding the ninth-century Gospels of Maelbright MacDurnan, abbot of Armagh. Far more is known of the career of the brothers Gregorio and Giovanni Andreoli, two highly successful Roman brothers whose clients included a number of popes and Queen Christina of Sweden. Gregorio, who created the elegant Islamic-influenced design at left on page 49 for Pope Alexander VII's nephew in 1659, became the official Vatican Binder in 1665.

The small red velvet volume on page 49, decorated with raised silver thread and hundreds of seed pearls, holds a 1608 manuscript in the hand of Esther Inglis, whose fine calligraphy appears elsewhere in this book (page 86). Researchers consider it quite likely that Inglis herself created the intricate and delicate binding for presentation to Henry, Prince of Wales, the son of James I, to whom the work is dedicated.

Thomas à Kempis, *Opera,* and Saint Albertus Magnus, *Compendium theologice veritatis* / 1494 and 1489

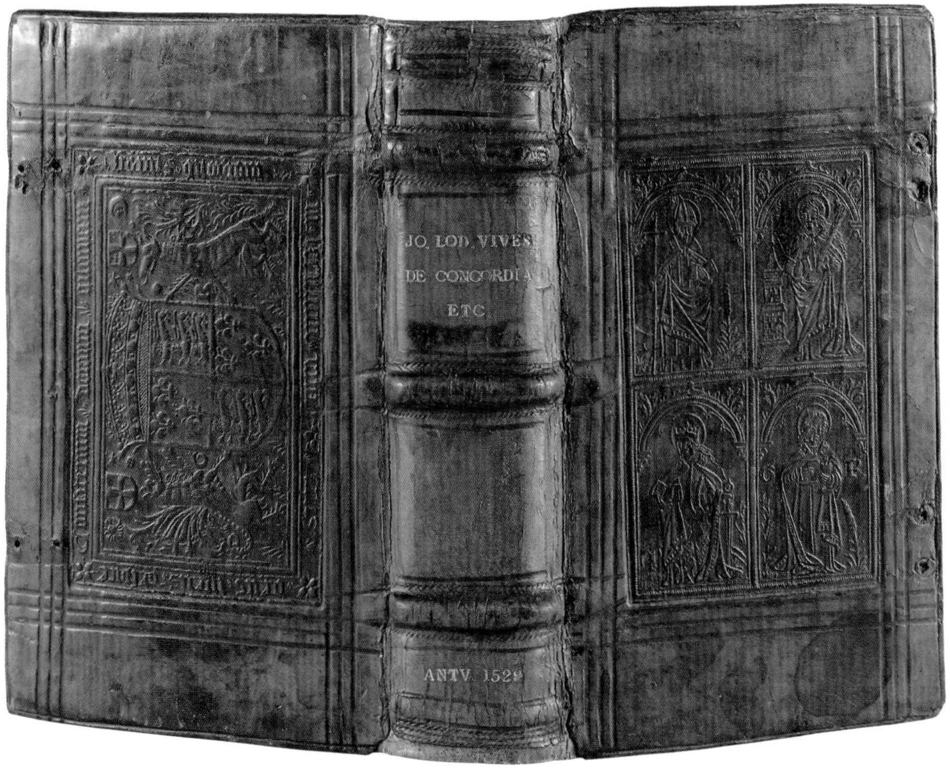

Juan Luis Vives, *De concordia & discordia in humano genere* / 1529

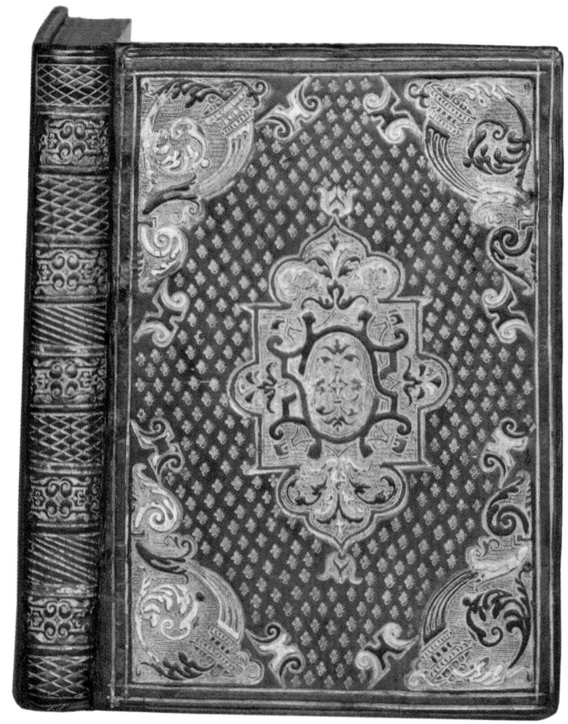

A defence of priestes mariages / 1567 (?)

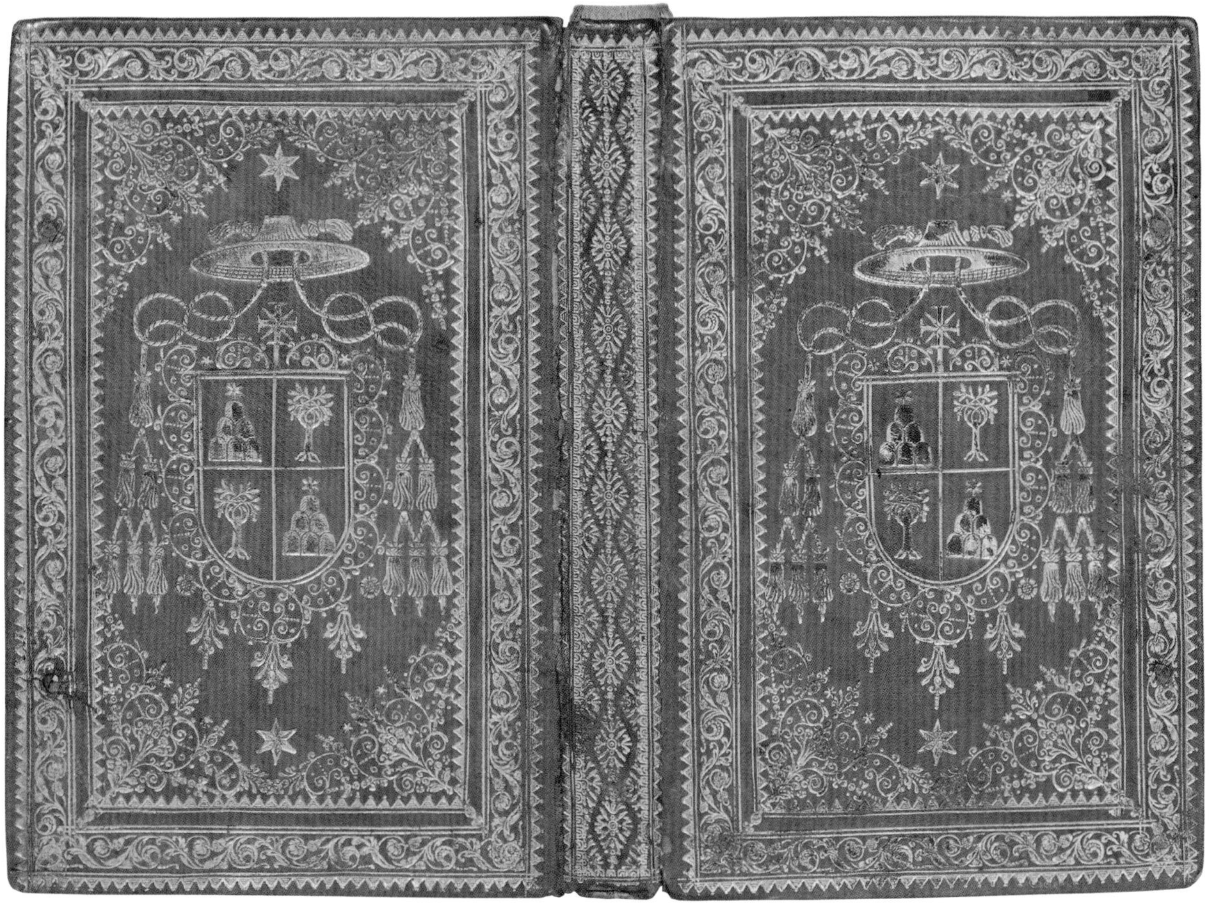

Angelo Petricca, *De nobilitate eiusque origine* / 1659

Esther Inglis, *Argumenta psalmorum Davidis* / 1608

It's been called one of the "Seven Wonders of the Folger," and understandably so. The set of manuscripts known as the Macro Plays (named for an eighteenth-century owner, the Reverend Cox Macro) remains the most important source of knowledge of the early English morality plays—allegorical dramas, with characters like Mankind and the Seven Deadly Sins, which preceded the more realistic theatre of the Renaissance. Two of these plays are known only through this unique source: The Castle of Perseverance, which dates from between 1400 and 1425, making it the oldest-known English morality play to survive, and Mankind, written about 1465. A third play, Wisdom, from between 1450 and 1500, does exist elsewhere, but in an incomplete form.

For students of theatrical history, the most striking feature of any of the Macro Plays is the Castle of Perseverance staging diagram shown here. For decades, this single drawing has been a principal source for theories of how late medieval drama was performed. Set outdoors, it appears to show a circular ditch or moat, perhaps intended to keep spectators out of the main acting area. In the center is the "castle"—a platform on which some of the actors stood. The bed of the character Mankind is located directly below, with the direction, "And there shall the soul lie under the bed until he shall rise and play."

Less lyrical, but more startling, are the directions for the actor playing Belial (the Devil), a figure who may have stood on one of the five scaffolds shown outside the ditch. Reflecting the medieval association of the Devil with firecrackers, these notes instruct, "He that shall play Belial look that he have gun powder burning in pipes in his hands and in his ears and in his ars when he goeth into battle."

Acquired at auction in 1936, the Macro Plays proved to be such magnets for researchers that by 1970 the manuscripts were showing distinct signs of wear. Two years later, the Folger created a facsimile edition to serve in the manuscripts' place for many research purposes.

The Castle of Perseverance / ca. 1400–25

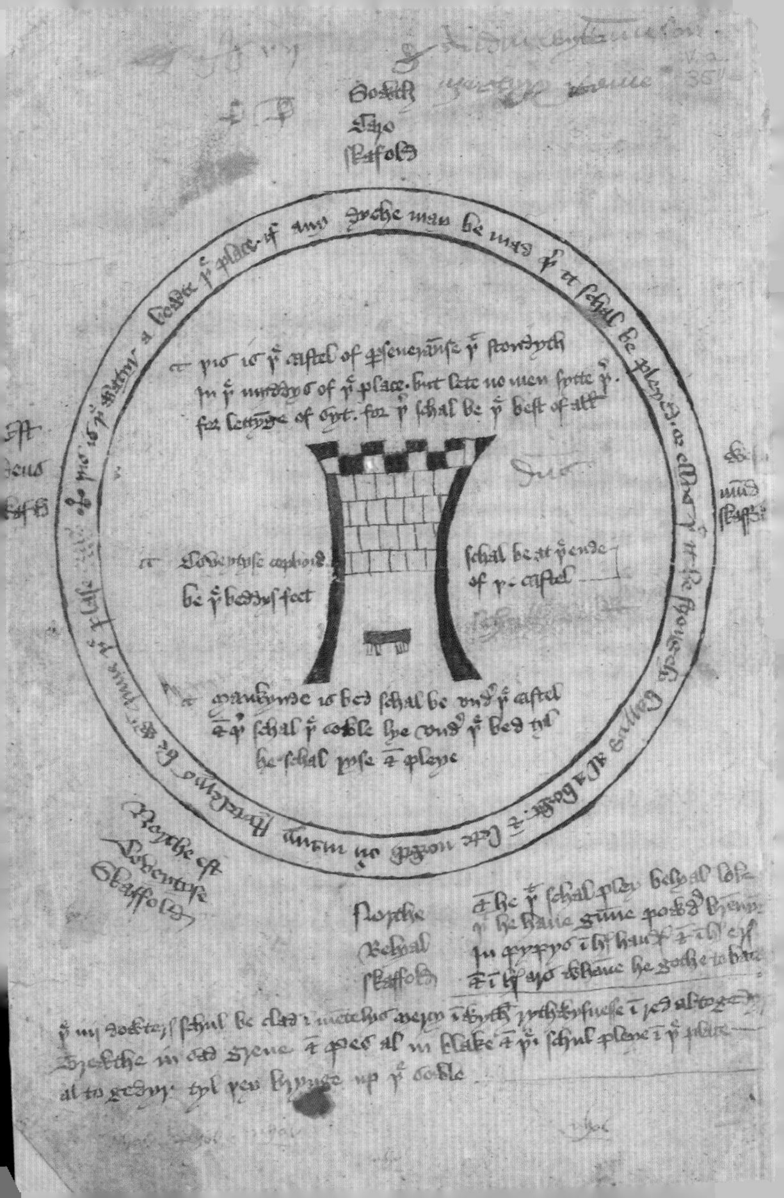

V.a. 354
Sowth Caro skaffold
This is þe watyr abowte þe place, if any dyche may be mad þer it schal be pleyed, or ellys þat it be strongly barryd al abowte, & lete nowth ouyr many stytelerys be wythinne þe plase.
This is þe castel of perseueraunse þat stondyth in þe myddys of þe place. but lete no men sytte þer. for lettynge of syt. for þer schal be þe best of all
Coveytyse copbord be þe beddys feet schal be at þe ende of þe castel
Mankyndeis bed schal be vndyr þe castel & þer schal þe sowle lye vndyr þe bed tyl he schal ryse & pleye
Est Deus skaffold
West Mundus skaffold
Northe est Coveytyse skaffold
Northe Belial skaffold
& he þat schal pley Belyal loke þat he haue gunne powdyr brennynge in pypys in hys handys & in hys erys & in hys ars whanne he gothe to batayl
þe iiii dowterys schul be clad in mentelys, Mercy in wyth, rythwysnesse in red altogedyr, Trewthe in sad grene, & Pes al in blake, & þei schul pleye in þe place altogedyr tyl þey brynge up þe sowle

Hym dare not wene well that euyl doth
A gilour shal euer begyled be
And god that sit in high mageste
Saue al this companye grete and smale
Thus haue I quyt the Myllere his tale

Here endith the Reuys tale .
And begynneth the cokis prolog .

The cok of london whyle the Reue spak
For ioye he thoughte he clawid hym on ye bak
A ha quod he for cristis owen passion
This Myllere hath a sharp conclusion
Vp on his argument of herbegage
Wel sayde Salamon in his langage
Ne preesse not euery man in thy hous
For herborwynge be nyght is perlous
Wel ought a man auisid forto be
Whom that he brynge in to his pryuite
I prey to god so yeue me sorow and care
Syn euyr that I highte hogge of ware
Herd I Myllere bet y set a werk
He hadde a Jape of malice in the derk
But god forbede that we stynten here
And therfore yf ye vouchesauf to here
A tale of me that am a poure man
I wol you telle as wel as I can
A lityl Jape that fyl in our cyte
Our ost answerd & sayde I graunte it the
Now telle on Rogger loke that it be good
For many a pasty hast thou lete blood
And many a iacke of douyr hast thou sold
That had be twis hoot and twis cold
Of many a pilgrym hast thou cristis curs
For of thy persely yet fare they the wers
Now tel on gentil roger be thy name
But I pray the be not wroth for game
A man may say ful soth in game and pley
Thow saist soth sayde Roger be my fey
But soth pley quade pley as the flemyng saith
And therfore harry bally be thy feyth
Be thow not wroth ar we departen here
Though that my tale be of an hostillere
But nathelesI wil not telle it yet
But or we departe Jwis thou shalt be quyt
And therwith al he lowgh and made chere
And sayde his tale as ye shul aftir here

Here endith the cokis prolog .
And begynneth his tale .

A Prentis whilom duelt in our cyte
Of craft of vitaillers was he
As gaylard he was as goldsmyth in ye shawe
Broun as a bery a proper felawe
With lokkis I kembid ful fetously
Daunce he coude wel and iolily
Than he was clepid Perkyn Reuelour
He was as ful of loue and paramour
As is the hyue ful of hony swete
Wel was the wenche yt with hym mighte slepe
And at euery bridale wolde he synge & hoppe

When the Folger purchased the collection of the late English newspaper publisher Sir Robert Leicester Harmsworth in 1938, the scope of its holdings expanded greatly to include politics, science, exploration, and many other aspects of the early modern age—most of them decidedly nonliterary. Harmsworth's interest in early English printing, however, had also led him to collect some of the great English incunables. (The term, from the Latin for cradle, refers to books printed before 1501.)

Among the earliest of these is the 1477 edition of Geoffrey Chaucer's Canterbury Tales. *An uncompleted set of poems written by Chaucer in the late 1300s, the "tales" are recounted by a varied and sometimes testy group of pilgrims on their way to Canterbury. Collectively, they are considered the great masterpiece of Middle English. Popular in manuscript form from Chaucer's day onward, the tales were an immediate and logical choice for the first English printers.*

William Caxton produced this volume in England's first printing shop, located in Westminster at the Sign of the Red Pale. Only ten known copies, including the Folger volume, have survived, in addition to two fragments. Printing was still so new at this time that Caxton and other printers continued to follow the old manuscript tradition of "rubricating"—literally, rendering in red—the large ornamental initial letters, a task performed by hand after the body of the text was printed. The pages shown here begin the "Cook's Tale," an unfinished story offered by the group's unsavory cook, whom Chaucer describes in the prologue as having an open sore on his shin.

Geoffrey Chaucer, *Canterbury Tales* / 1477

Unlike many collectors, Henry and Emily Folger liked to acquire books that had been marked up over the centuries; they believed that the comments of previous owners added to the scholarly value, if not the beauty, of a given work. In 2001, the Folger exhibition The Reader Revealed *displayed several of the more notable examples of such annotated copies. Among them was this folio-sized edition of Euclid's* Elements, *printed in Venice in 1482.*

The book itself, a showpiece of the library's Continental collection, is considered to be the first full-length printed book with extensive mathematical illustrations. In a dedicatory preface, the printer Erhard Ratdolt appears well aware of his place in history; the text explains that he set out to meet the challenge, which had defeated others, of incorporating a large number of printed diagrams. Initially believed to be woodcut images, these are now thought to have been produced with metal lines.

The extensive marginalia, written in brown ink in both Latin and Greek and in several different hands, reveal that for its owners, this was a hardworking textbook. Reader after reader through the years evidently studied the words and pictures, working out proofs in the margins along the way. Long before the halfway point in this edition, however, the industrious note taking dwindles to a halt. The study that began so promisingly for each reader was apparently never continued to its conclusion.

Euclid, *Preclarissimus liber elementorum* / 1482

trianguli.c.b.k.& angulus.b.b.k.e maior angulo.c.b.k. erit p.24.primi basis .b. k.maior basi.k.c.cadē rōne.k.c.maior erit.k.d.& k.d.maior.k.c. & hoc e tertium ¶ Qd si due linee.k.g.& k.e.nō sunt equales erit altera maior:sitq3.k.g. de q̄ sumam.k.l.equalem.k.c.& producā.b.l.quousq3 secet circūferentiam in puncto.m. & q: per ypothesim angulus.g.k.f.e equalis angulo.f.k.e.erit per.13.primi:angulus.l.k.b.equalis angulo.c.k.b.& duo latera.l.k.& k.b.trianguli.l.k.b. sūt equalia duobus laterib⁹.c.k.& k.b.trianguli.c.k.b.ergo p.4.primi basis.b.l. est equalis basi.b.c.& q:.b.m.est equalis.b.c.erit.b.m.equalis.b.l.qd e impossibile.sunt ergo due linee.k.g.& k.e.equales qd est nostrū propositum.quartum

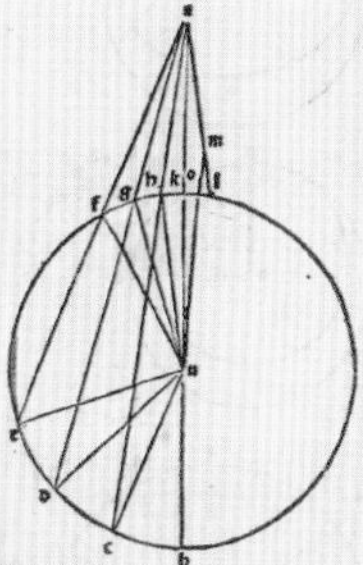

Propositio .8.

Si extra circulum puncto signato ab eo ad circumferentiam linee plurime ducantur circulum secando.que super centrum transierit omnium erit longissima. ¶ Centro autem propinquiores ceteris remotioribus lōgiores. ¶ Linee vero partiales ad circūferentiā extrinsecus applicate:ea quidem que diametro in directum adiacet omnium est minima. eiq3 propinquiores remotioribus breuiores. ¶ Due vero que linee breuissime vtrūq3 eque propinquāt equales sunt.

¶ Sit vt in puncto.a.assignato extra circulū.b.c.d.cuius centrum sit.n. ducātur plurime linee ad circūferentiam secando circulum que sint.a.k.n.b.a.b.c.a.g.d.&.a.f.e. Dico q.a.b.transiens per centrum omniū erit longissima.& q.a.c.e maior.a.d.& a.d.maior.a.c.& q.a.k.e omniū breuissima extrinsecarū: & q.a.b. est minor.a.g.& a.g.minor.a.f.& dico q si ducatur.a.l.ita q ipsa &.a.b. equalit distent ab.a.k.hoc est q angulus.k.a.b.sit equalis angulo.l.a.k.ipse erūt equales ¶ Producā eni a cētro.n.lineas.n.c.n.d.n.e.n.f.n.g.& n.b.erūtq3 per.20.primi duo latera.a.n.& n.c.trianguli.a.n.c.maiora.a.c.& q: ipsa sunt equalia linee.a.b erit.a.b.maior.a.c.cadē ratione erit maior omnibus alijs qd est primum.& quia duo latera.a.n.& n.c.trianguli.a.n.c.sunt equalia duobus lateribus.a.n.& n.d. trianguli.a.n.d.& angulus.a.n.c.est maior angulo.a.n. d. erit per.24.primi:basis.a.c.maior basi.a.d.& cadē rōne erit.a.d.maior.a.c.qd est scdm. ¶ Itēq3 quia in triāgulo.a.n.b.duo latera.a.b.& n.b.sunt maiora.a.n.per.20.primi.& b.n. e equalis.n.k.erit per cōmunē sciam.a.b.maior.a.k.eadem rōne quelibet extrinsecus applicatarū maior erit.a.k.qd est tertiū. ¶ Item quia per.21.primi:due linee a.b.& b.n.sunt minores duabus lineis.a.g.& g.n.& b.n.est equalis.g.n.erit per communem scientiam.a.g.maior.a.b.eadem rōne erit.a.f.maior.a.g.qd e quartum. ¶ Qd si.a.l.non sit equalis.a.b.cum ipse sint equaliter distātes ab.a.k .erit altera maior:sitq3.a.l.ponam ergo.a.m.equalem.a.b.& producam.n.o.m. quia ergo duo latera.m.a.& a.n.trianguli.m.a.n.sunt equalia duobus laterib⁹. b.a.& a.n.trianguli.b.a.n.& angulus.m.a.n.est equalis angulo.b.a. n.erit per.4.primi:basis.m.n.equalis basi.n.b.& quia.m.o.est equalis.n.b.erit.n.o.equalis .n. m. pars videlicet toti qd est impossibile & hoc est quintū

Propositio .9.

Si intra circulū puncto signato.ab eo plures q3 due linee ducte ad circūferentiam fuerint equales.punctū illud centrum circuli esse necesse est.

¶ Sit vt a puncto.a.signato intra circulū.b.c.d.ducte sint.3.linee.a b.a.c.a.d.ad circūferentiā quas pono ēe equales dico punctum.a. esse centrū circuli. Producā enim duas lineas.c.b.& d.c.& diuidā vtrāq3 earū p eqlia.c.b.quidem in puncto.e.& d.c.in puncto.f.& producam.e.a.& f.a. quas applico circūferentie ex vtraq3 parte.eritq3 per.8.primi vterq3 angulorū qui sunt.a. d.e.eql' alteri.igit p.13.vterq3 erit rect⁹.Silr quoq3 p eādē vterq3 angulorū q sūt.a d.f.rectus:ergo per corelariū prime huius.quia.a.e.diuidit.c.b.per equalia & orthogonaliter ipsa transit per centrū.similiter quoq3.a.f.transit per centrum. qua diuidit .d.c .per equalia & orthogonaliter.quare.a.e centrū qd est propositum

Propositio .10.

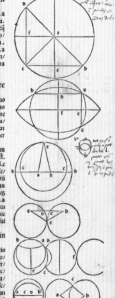

Si circulus circulum secet.in duobus tantum locis secare necesse est.

¶ Sint si possibile est duo circuli secantes se in pluribus q3 in duobus locis super .3.puncta.a.b.c.producam lineas.a.b.& a.c. quas diuidam per equalia in punctis.d.&.e.& producam a puncto.e.lineam.e.f.per pendicularem super lineam.a.c.& a puncto.d.lineam.d. f. ppendicularem super lineam.a.b. & secent se due linee.e.f.et.d.f.i puncto. f. eritq3 per corelariū prime huius punctū.f.centrum circuli vtriusq3 qd est impossibile. per 5.huius.

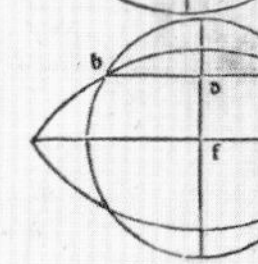

Propositio .11.

Si circulus circulum contingat.lineaq3 per centra eorum transeat.ad punctum contactus earū applicari necesse est.

¶ Si enim linea transiens per centra duorum circulorum.e.c.et.d.c sese contingentium intra vl' extra.nō vadit ad locum contactus secet circūferentiam vtriusq3:sitq3.a.centrum circuli.c.d.et.b. centrū circuli.e.c.et ducatur linea recta.a.b.c.d.secans circūferentiam vtriusq3: et ducantur linee a puncto.c.qui sit locus contactus ad centra que sint. c.a.c.b. eruntq3 in cōtactu interiori.p.20.pmi due linee.c.b.& b.a.longiores.c.a.q̄re longiores.a d.est enim.a.centrū circuli.c.d.& qm̄.b.c.est equalis.c.b.qm̄ .b.est centrum circuli.e.c.erit.c.a.longior.a.d.qd est impossibile. ¶ In cōtactu vero exteriori erūt due linee.a.c.& c.b.longiores.a.b.quare.a.d.& c.b.maius erūt q tota.a.b.qd est falsum.

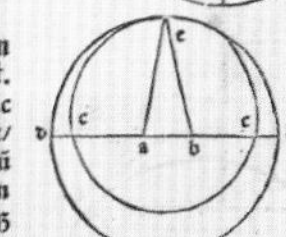

Propositio .12.

Si circulus circulum contingat siue intrinsecus siue extrinsecus.in vno tantum loco contingere necesse est.

¶ Si eni fuerit possibile.vt circulus circulū cōtingat in duob⁹ locis intra vl' extra cōtingat circulū.a.b.c.d.circulus.a.b.e.interi⁹ i duobus pūctis.a.b.vel exteri⁹ circulus.c.d.f.i duob⁹ pūctis.c.d.Cū ergo ducemus lineā rectā ab.a.ad.b.si ipsa cadat extra circulū .a.b.e. interiorē accidet ꝯtrariū secūde hui⁹. Qd si ipsa cadat intra ipsū:cū diuiserimus ipsā p equalia & eduxerim⁹ a pūcto diuisionis ppendicularē ad ipsā.fueritq3 applicata circumferentie ex vtraq3 pte ipsa trāsibit p centrū ambor circulorū.quare accidet cōtrarium premisse. ¶ In circulo vero cōtingente exteri⁹ in pūctis.c.d.si ducam⁹ lineā rectā a puncto.c.ad punctū.d.necesse est accidere ꝯtrariū sc̄e h⁹.quare vtrūq3 ipossibile

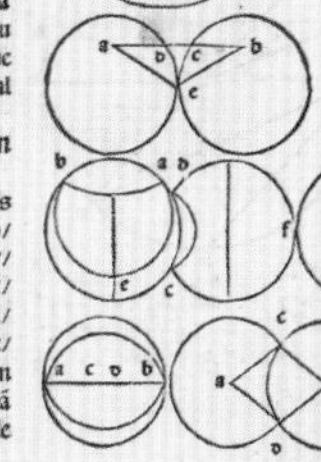

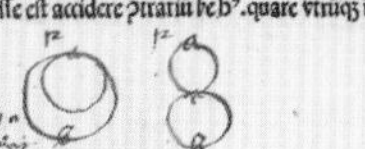

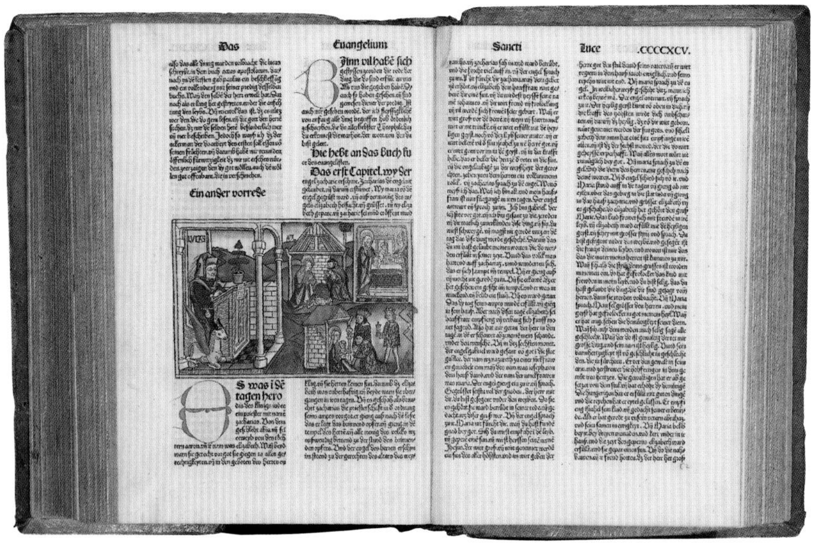

Der Geschopf .V.

Hie hebt sich an. Genesis das erst buch der
fünff bucher moysi. Das erst Capitel ist võ
der schöppfung der werkt vnd aller creaturen.
vnd von den wercken der sechs tag.

IN dem anfang
hat got beschaf
fen hymel vnd
erden. aber dye erde was
eytel vnd lere. vnd die vinsternus warn auff dẽ ant-
litz des abgrunds. vnd der
geist gots swebet oder ward getragen auff dẽ
wassern. Vñ got der sprach. Es werde dz liecht
Vñ das liecht ist worden. vñ got sahe dz liecht
das es gutt was. vnd er teylet das liecht võ der
vinsternus. vnd das liecht hyeß er den tag. vnd
die vinsternus die nacht. Vñ es ward abent vñ
morgen eyn tag. Vnd got der sprach. Es werde das firmament in dem mittel der wasser. vñ
tayle die wasser võ dẽ wassern. Vñ got machet
das firmament. vnd teylet die wasser. dy do wa
ren vnder dem firmament. von dẽ dy do waren
ob dem firmament. vnd es ist also geschehen
vnd got hieß das firmament den hymel vnd es
ist der abent vñ der morgẽ der ander tag wordẽ
vñ got sprach aber. Es sullẽ gesamelt werdẽ dy
wasser. die vnder dem hymel seynd. an eyn statt.
vñ erscheyne die durre. vnd es ist also geschehẽ
Vñ got hieß die dürre dz ertreich. Vñ dy sam
nungen der wasser. hieß er die mere. vnd got sa
he das es was gut. vnd sprach. Die erde gepere
grunendt krawt. das do bringe den samen. vnd
dy öpfelbawm. dz holtz. dz do bringe dy frucht
nach seym geschlecht. des same sey in ym selbs
auff der erde. vnd es ist also geschehen. vnd die
erd bracht grunend kraut. vnd bringenden sa-

Of the nearly 500 books in the Folger's collection that were printed before 1501, more than 100 bear imprints from Germany, the birthplace of printing in the West. This 1483 German Bible, often called the Biblia Germanica, was among the earliest to be published in vernacular German, appearing less than three decades after Gutenberg's own Latin Bible. The language change indicated a growing effort on the part of some to make the Scriptures available to laymen as well as to the clergy—a movement that would accelerate with the Reformation.

The Biblia Germanica was also the first text with illustrations to be printed by the Nuremberg firm of Anton Koberger, which ten years later produced the Nuremberg Chronicle, an illustrated history of the world. In this copy of the Bible, all 109 woodcuts have been hand-colored. In the New Testament, all four Gospels—including the Book of Luke, at far left—begin with a depiction of the Gospel's author in the act of writing; Luke is accompanied by his traditional symbol, a winged bull. Additional images of Christ's birth in the stable, the arrival of the three wise men, and the infant's presentation in the Temple at Jerusalem offer a visual preview of the text that follows. God appears twice at one time in the scene from Genesis at near left, removing a rib from Adam to create Eve and simultaneously looking down on the event from above. As in earlier, manuscript Bibles, the initial capital letters of the Biblia Germanica are inked in blue and red, and in some sections are illuminated in gold.

Biblia Germanica / 1483

A notis discipulis cito derelict⁹ A iudeis traditus venditus afflictus .ān. Adoram⁹ te christe ꝛ benedicim⁹ tibi. Quia per sanctam crucem tuam redemisti mundum.

Oremus

Domine iesu christe fili dei viui pone passionem crucem et mortem tuam inter iudicium tum ꝛ animas nostras nūc ꝛ in hora mortis nostre: largire digneris viuis misericordiam ꝛ gratiam/ defūctis requiē ꝛ veniā/ ecclesie tue sctē pacem ꝛ cōcordiam/ et nobis peccatoribus vitam et gloriam sempiternam. Qui cum patre et spiritusancto viuis et regnas deus. Per omnia secula seculorum. Amen. Gloriosa passio domini nostri iesu christi eruat nos a dolore tristi et perducat nos ad gaudia paradisi.

Matris cor virgineū trina totum triuit. Quando suum filium nocte captum sciuit. Ductum ad pretorium mane cum audiuit. Frequens dans suspiriū sepe singultiuit. ān. Te laudamus et rogamus mater iesu christi. Ut intendas ꝛ defendas nos a morte tristi. Orō

Domine sancte iesu fili dulcis virgis marie: qui pro nobis mortem in cruce tolerasti fac nobiscum misericordiam tuam: et da nobis et cunctis compassionē tue sanctissime matris deuote recolentibus eius amore huius vitam in presenti gratiosam: et tua pietate gloriam in futuro sempiternam. In qua viuis et regnas deus. Per omnia secula seculorū. Amen. Tremosa compassio dulcissime dei matris perducat nos ad gaudia summi celi patris Amen. Benedicamus domino. Deo gratias.

+

Ad primam.

madam I pray yow Remember me in yowr prayers yowr mistres

Elysabeth R

From the beginning, the Folger collection has been rich in what are called association copies, books that are all the more valued because of the identity of those with whom they were once associated, whether through ownership or some other connection. Displayed here and on the pages that follow are some especially notable examples linked directly to English royalty. In 1991, a number of these special treasures were displayed in the Royal Autographs *exhibition, which coincided with the visit to the Folger of Queen Elizabeth II.*

The marriage of Elizabeth of York, who wrote in this book, to Henry VII launched the Tudor dynasty and ended England's Wars of the Roses, the struggle between the houses of Lancaster and York that furnished so much material for Shakespeare's history plays. The Book of Hours shown here, however, relates more to the private sphere than to such causes of state. Such a book was meant for private devotions and contained prayers to be recited at hours laid down by the church. It was not uncommon to find a Book of Hours in a home that had no other books.

All printed editions or manuscript copies included a calendar of fixed religious festivals, an almanac giving the date of Easter, and the hours of the Virgin; the hours, however, were frequently interspersed with verses and responses that varied with local custom. These variations were called the "use" and were often named according to the region in which they occurred. The Sarum or Salisbury use was the most common in England and is the basis for this book, a handsome 1498 edition with hand-colored illuminated lettering. The right-hand page of those shown here bears the inscription by Elizabeth of York: "Madam j pray yow Remember me in yowr good prayers yowr mastras Elysabeth R." The R *stands for "regina," or queen.*

Book of Hours / 1498

Few of the royal association copies at the Folger relate to so young a figure as this copy of Cicero's writings from 1502, boldly inscribed "Thys boke is myne Prince Henry" by the boy who would become Henry VIII. Although the writing is undated, Henry would have been about eleven—then considered a fine age to study Cicero—when the book was new. Annotations and glosses in two hands, identified by some as the writing of Prince Henry and his tutor, the poet John Skelton, appear on other pages of the book as well.

Cicero and other classic Roman prose writers formed the crux of the sixteenth-century curriculum, and were almost certainly studied some decades later by young William Shakespeare in the village grammar school at Stratford-upon-Avon. (His opinion of the era's dry, laborious process of instruction may be inferred from the description in As You Like It *of "the whining schoolboy . . . creeping like snail unwillingly to school.") In their compositions, which were also in Latin, students were encouraged to aspire to Ciceronian purity of language. Cicero's writings have left their mark to this day on the study of ethics, political thought, oratory, logic, and rhetoric, and his works remain a valuable source of historical information on Roman life and times.*

Cicero, *Commentū familiare in Ciceronis officia* / 1502

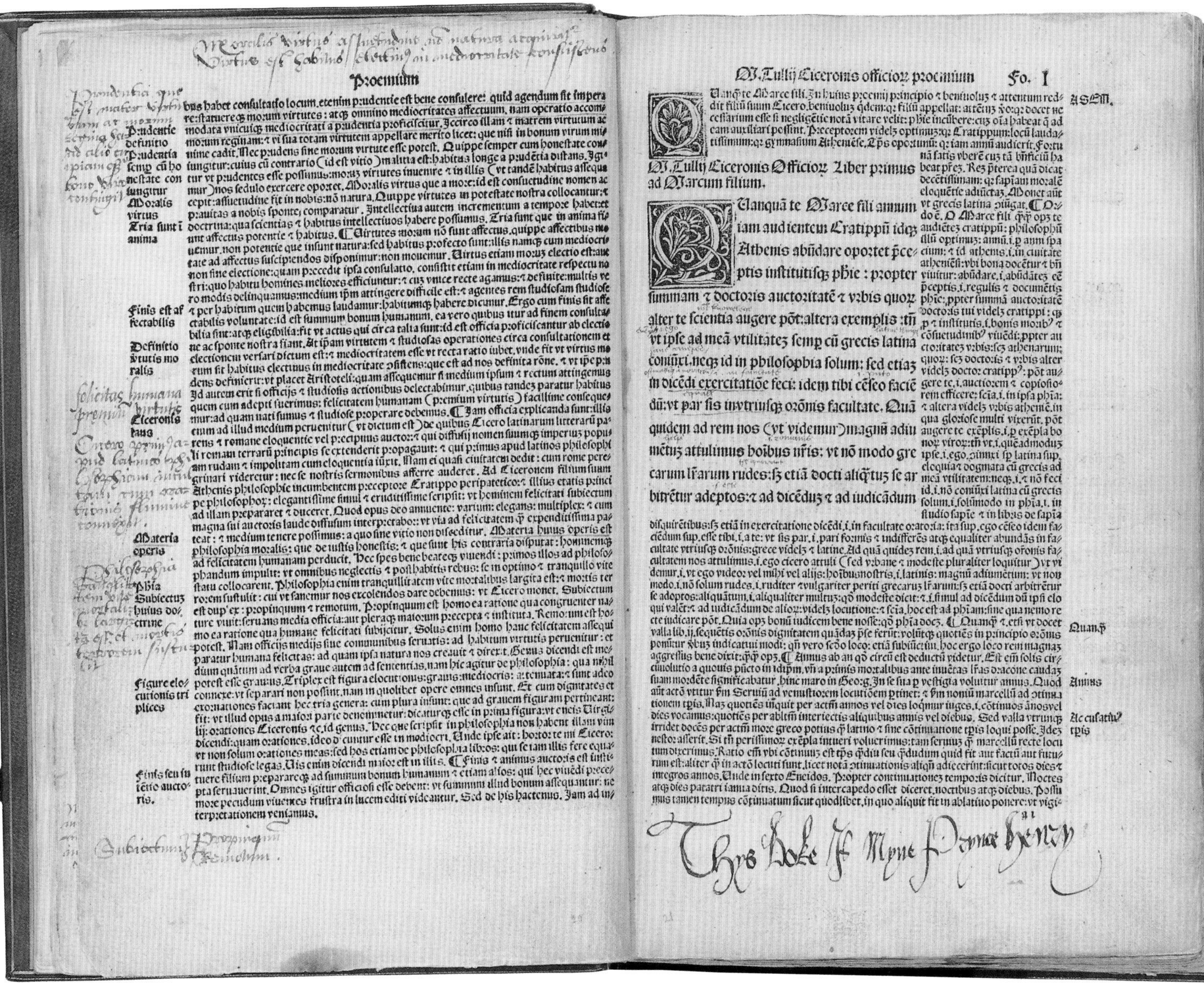
Procemium

M. Tullij Ciceronis officioꝝ procmium Fo. I

M. Tullij Ciceronis Officioꝝ Liber primus ad Marcum filium.

Quanquā te Marce fili annum iam audientem Cratippū idq3 Athenis abūdare oportet pceptis institutisq3 phie: propter summam & doctoris auctoritatē & vrbis quoꝝ alter te scientia augere pōt: altera exemplis: tñ vt ipse ad meā vtilitatē semp cū grecis latina coniūxi. neq3 id in philosophia solum: sed etiā in dicēdi exercitatiōe feci: idem tibi cēseo faciē dū: vt par sis in vtriusq3 orōnis facultate. Quā quidem ad rem nos (vt videmur) magnū adiumētū attulimus hoībus nr̄is: vt nō modo grecarum lr̄arum rudes: sȝ etiā docti aliqtū se arbitrētur adeptos: & ad dicēduȝ & ad iudicādum

Thys boke ys myne Prynce Henry

This uniquely inscribed Book of Hours was presented to Henry VIII by his fourth wife, Anne of Cleves, an amiable but—in Henry's view—utterly unattractive woman whom he rejected within four months of their arranged marriage in 1540. Anne readily granted him a divorce and lived in comfort on the settlement in England until her death in 1557. Given the tragic history of Henry's other marriages, she is often considered the luckiest of his six wives.

Partly obscured when the book was rebound, the inscription in Anne's hand reads (in modernized English), "I beseech Your Grace humbly when you look on this remember me, your Grace's assured Anne, the daughter of Cleves." Anne's signature, one of only three surviving examples, is undated, but the title "daughter of Cleves" has suggested to at least one researcher that the gift must have come after the couple divorced, a period during which they remained on friendly terms.

Printed in vellum in Paris in about 1533—seven years before the short-lived marriage—the volume was then beautifully decorated and illuminated by hand, making it indeed a gift fit for a king. In the image shown here, Mary, pregnant with Jesus, is greeted by her cousin Elizabeth, herself soon to be the mother of John the Baptist. Mary's reply to Elizabeth's greeting is the canticle of praise known as the Magnificat.

Book of Hours / 1533 (?)

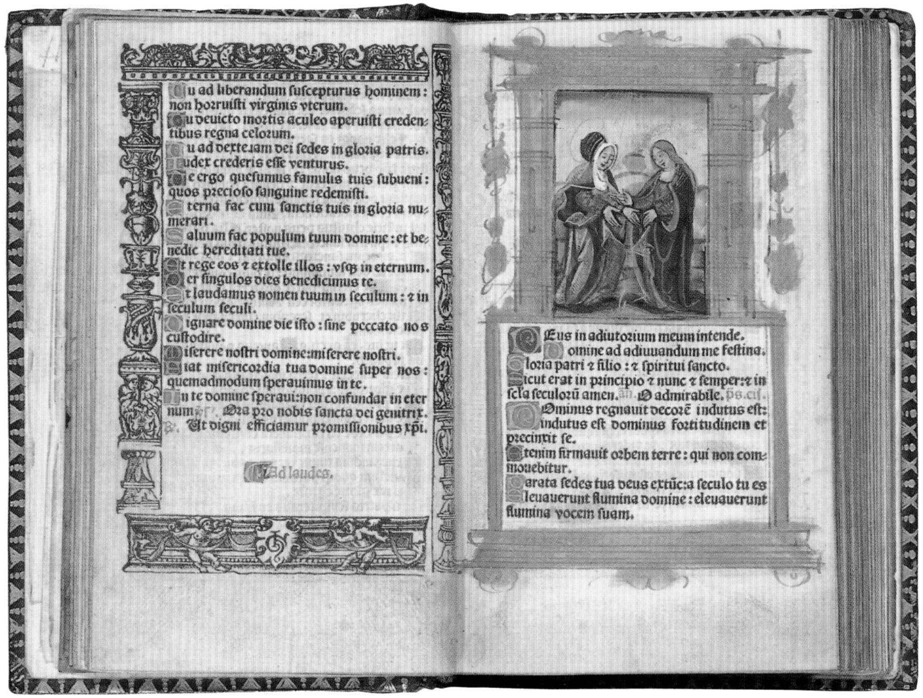

u ad liberandum suscepturus hominem: non horruisti virginis vterum.
u deuicto mortis aculeo aperuisti credentibus regna celorum.
u ad dexteram dei sedes in gloria patris.
udex crederis esse venturus.
e ergo quesumus famulis tuis subueni: quos precioso sanguine redemisti.
terna fac cum sanctis tuis in gloria numerari.
aluum fac populum tuum domine: et benedic hereditati tue.
t rege eos ⁊ extolle illos: vsq₃ in eternum.
er singulos dies benedicimus te.
t laudamus nomen tuum in seculum: ⁊ in seculum seculi.
ignare domine die isto: sine peccato nos custodire.
iserere nostri domine: miserere nostri.
iat misericordia tua domine super nos: quemadmodum sperauimus in te.
n te domine speraui: non confundar in eternum. Ora pro nobis sancta dei genitrix.
Ut digni efficiamur promissionibus xpi.

Ad laudes.

Eus in adiutorium meum intende.
omine ad adiuuandum me festina.
loria patri ⁊ filio: ⁊ spiritui sancto.
icut erat in principio ⁊ nunc ⁊ semper: ⁊ in scl'a seculorū amen. an. O admirabile. ps. xcij.
ominus regnauit decorē indutus est: indutus est dominus fortitudinem et precinxit se.
tenim firmauit orbem terre: qui non commouebitur.
arata sedes tua deus extūc: a seculo tu es
leuauerunt flumina domine: eleuauerunt flumina vocem suam.

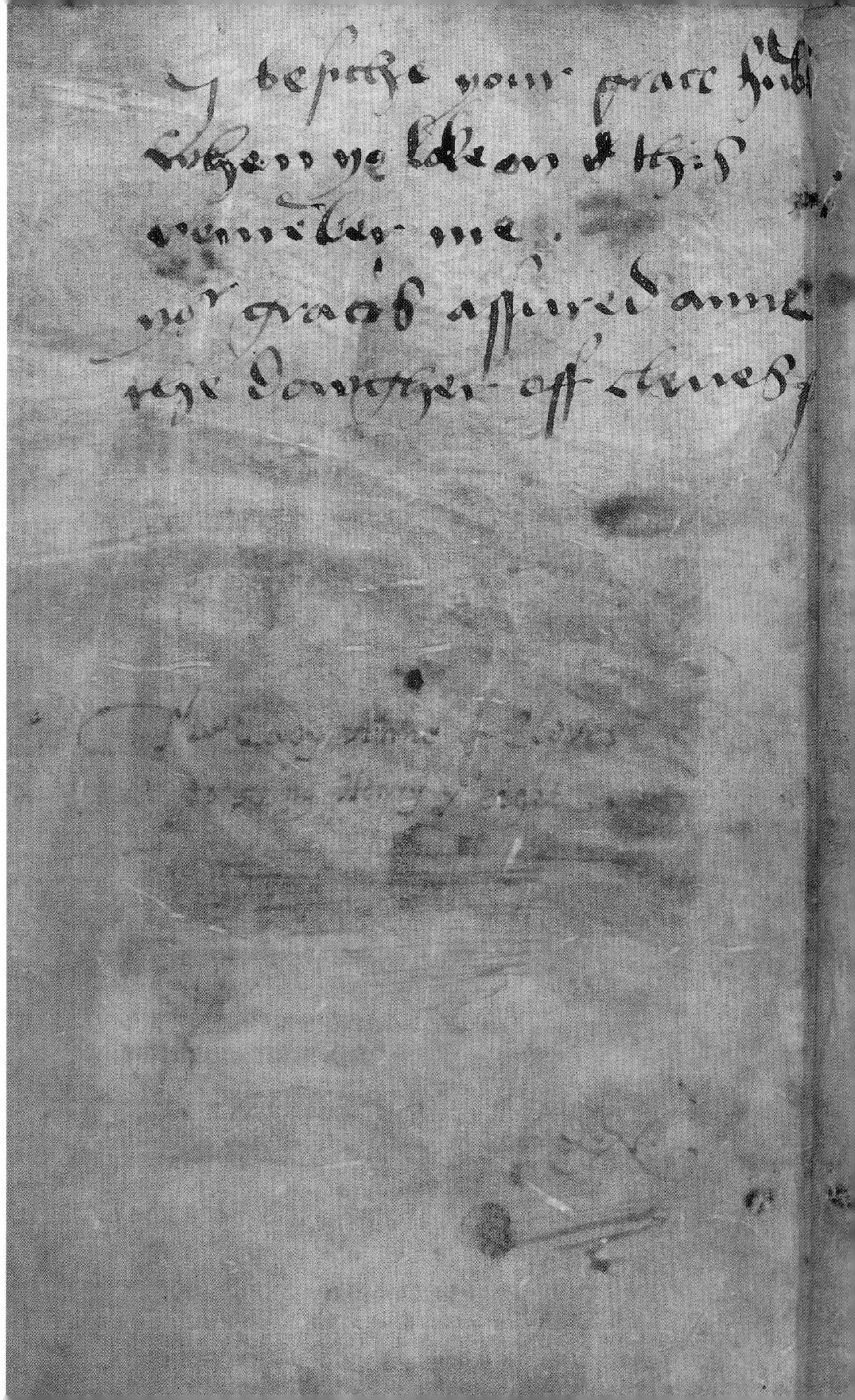

I beseche your grace hu[m]bly
when ye loke on this
remember me.
yor graces assured anne
the dowghter off cleves

Shakespeare's queen, Elizabeth I, holds a special place at the Folger. Her coat of arms is mounted at one end of the Exhibition Hall, and a docent dressed as Elizabeth, farthingale and all, often presides ceremonially over festive and educational occasions. In 1958, a large scholarly conference—at that time, a rare undertaking for the library—was held to celebrate the 400th anniversary of her accession to the throne; in the years since, a wealth of seminars and symposia on the queen and her reign has followed. Letters bearing Elizabeth's signature and in some cases written in her own hand, letters written to her from important figures, and literary and artistic portraits depicting her are all among the prizes of the collection. Drawn to these materials, researchers have come to the Folger for work on such monumental projects as Queen Elizabeth's Wardrobe Unlock'd *(1988) and* Elizabeth I: Collected Works *(2000).*

One of the more remarkable items collected by Henry and Emily Folger and associated with Elizabeth I is the book shown here, the queen's own pulpit copy of the first issue of the 1568 Bishops' Bible (a revision edited by the archbishop of Canterbury and eight other bishops). Bound in crimson velvet over oak boards, this unique royal copy is decorated with silver clasps and bosses bearing the letters EL *and* RE, *her coat of arms, and Tudor roses. In the interior pages at right, a one-page history of the world from its creation to the year 1568 precedes the opening of the Book of Genesis.*

Bishops' Bible (pulpit copy of Elizabeth I) / 1568

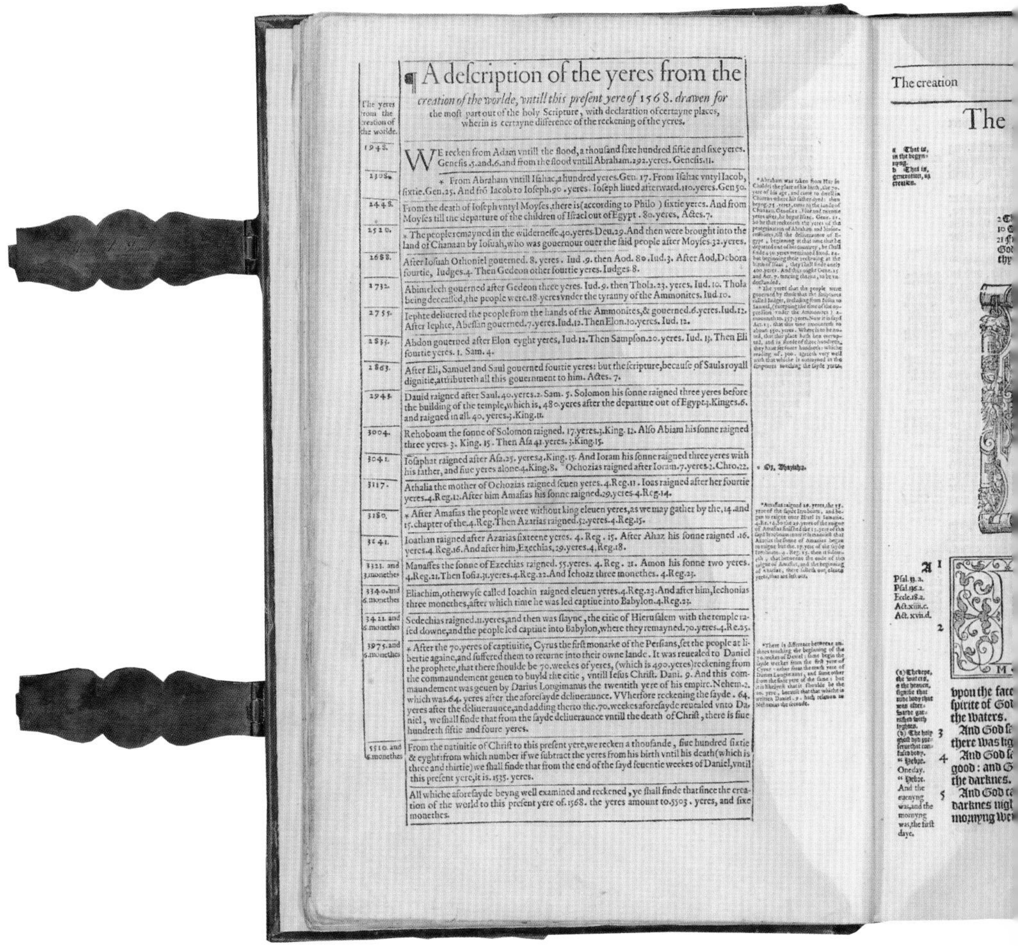
¶ A description of the yeres from the creation of the worlde, vntill this present yere of 1568. drawen for the most part out of the holy Scripture, with declaration of certayne places, wherin is certayne difference of the reckening of the yeres.
The yeres from the creation of the worlde.
1942. WE recken from Adam vntill the flood, a thousand sixe hundred fiftie and sixe yeres. Genesis.5.and.6.and from the flood vntill Abraham.292.yeres. Genesis.11.
2108. * From Abraham vntill Isahac, a hundred yeres.Gen. 17. From Isahac vntyl Iacob, sixtie.Gen.25. And frō Iacob to Ioseph.90 .yeres. Ioseph liued afterward.110.yeres.Gen 50.
2448. From the death of Ioseph vntyl Moyses, there is (according to Philo) sixtie yeres. And from Moyses till the departure of the children of Israel out of Egypt . 80. yeres, Actes.7.
2520. * The people remayned in the wildernesse.40.yeres.Deu.29.And then were brought into the land of Chanaan by Iosuah, who was gouernour ouer the said people after Moyses.32.yeres.
2688. After Iosuah Othoniel gouerned. 8. yeres . Iud .9. then Aod. 80 .Iud.3. After Aod, Debora fourtie, Iudges.4. Then Gedeon other fourtie yeres. Iudges.8.
2732. Abimelech gouerned after Gedeon three yeres. Iud.9. then Thola.23. yeres. Iud.10. Thola being deceassed, the people were.18.yeres vnder the tyranny of the Ammonites. Iud.10.
2755. Iephte deliuered the people from the hands of the Ammonites, & gouerned.6.yeres.Iud.12. After Iephte, Abessan gouerned.7.yeres.Iud.12. Then Elon.10.yeres. Iud. 12.
2833. Abdon gouerned after Elon eyght yeres, Iud.12. Then Sampson.20. yeres. Iud. 13. Then Eli fourtie yeres. 1. Sam. 4.
2863. After Eli, Samuel and Saul gouerned fourtie yeres: but the scripture, because of Sauls royall dignitie, attributeth all this gouernment to him. Actes. 7.
2943. Dauid raigned after Saul. 40. yeres.2. Sam. 5. Solomon his sonne raigned three yeres before the building of the temple, which is, 480. yeres after the departure out of Egypt.3.Kinges.6. and raigned in all. 40. yeres.3.King.11.
3004. Rehoboam the sonne of Solomon raigned. 17.yeres.3.King. 12. Also Abiam his sonne raigned three yeres. 3. King. 15 . Then Asa 41.yeres. 3.King.15.
3041. Iosaphat raigned after Asa.25. yeres.4.King. 15. And Ioram his sonne raigned three yeres with his father, and fiue yeres alone.4.King.8. *Ochozias raigned after Ioram.7.yeres.2.Chro.22.
3117. Athalia the mother of Ochozias raigned seuen yeres. 4.Reg.11 . Ioas raigned after her fourtie yeres.4.Reg.12. After him Amasias his sonne raigned.29.yeres.4.Reg.14.
3180. * After Amasias the people were without king eleuen yeres, as we may gather by the.14.and 15.chapter of the.4.Reg. Then Azarias raigned.52.yeres.4.Reg.15.
3241. Ioathan raigned after Azarias sixteene yeres. 4. Reg . 15. After Ahaz his sonne raigned .16. yeres.4.Reg.16. And after him, Ezechias, 29.yeres.4.Reg.18.
3321. and 3.monethes Manasses the sonne of Ezechias raigned. 55.yeres. 4. Reg . 21. Amon his sonne two yeres. 4.Reg.21. Then Iosia.31.yeres.4.Reg.22. And Iehoaz three monethes. 4.Reg.23.
3340.and 6.monethes Eliachim, otherwyse called Ioachin raigned eleuen yeres.4.Reg.23. And after him, Iechonias three monethes, after which time he was led captiue into Babylon.4.Reg.23.
3421. and 6.monethes Sedechias raigned.11.yeres, and then was slayne , the citie of Hierusalem with the temple rased downe, and the people led captiue into Babylon, where they remayned.70.yeres.4.Re.25.
3975.and 6.monethes * After the 70.yeres of captiuitie, Cyrus the first monarke of the Persians, set the people at libertie againe, and suffered them to returne into their owne lande . It was reuealed to Daniel the prophete, that there shoulde be 70.weekes of yeres, (which is 490.yeres) reckening from the commaundement geuen to buyld the citie , vntill Iesus Christ. Dani. 9. And this commaundement was geuen by Darius Longimanus the twentith yere of his empire. Nehem.2. which was.64. yeres after the aforesayde deliueraunce. VVherfore reckening the sayde . 64. yeres after the deliueraunce, and adding therto the.70.weekes aforesayde reuealed vnto Daniel , we shall finde that from the sayde deliueraunce vntill the death of Christ , there is fiue hundreth fiftie and foure yeres.
5510. and 6.monethes From the natiuitie of Christ to this present yere, we recken a thousande , fiue hundred sixtie & eyght: from which number if we subtract the yeres from his birth vntil his death (which is three and thirtie) we shall finde that from the end of the sayd seuentie weekes of Daniel, vntil this present yere, it is. 1535. yeres.
All whiche aforesayde beyng well examined and reckened , ye shall finde that since the creation of the world to this present yere of.1568. the yeres amount to.5503 . yeres, and sixe monethes.
The creation
The

E R
TVTTO VEDO &
MOLTO MANCHA
SEMPER EADEM
SÆNCHO RIPO
SO& RIPOSATO
AFFANO 1579

Known as the "sieve" portrait because it is the earliest of several paintings that show Elizabeth I holding a sieve, this magnificent portrait was painted by George Gower in 1579, just two years before he was appointed Elizabeth's Serjeant Painter. Considered one of the finest portraits of the queen executed in her lifetime, it is, like other works of the period, rife with allegory. In classical times the sieve was a symbol of the Roman vestal virgin Tuccia, who proved her chastity by carrying water in a sieve; here, it represents Elizabeth's status as the Virgin Queen. The globe to the monarch's right, with the inscription "I see everything and much is lacking," signifies her leadership in imperial expansion. Other elements, however, suggest the weight of the crown; at the time of the portrait, Elizabeth was forty-six and had been queen for twenty-one years. Under the royal coat of arms is an inscription taken from Petrarch, "Weary I rest and, having rested, I am still weary."

The Folger received the portrait in 1997 as a bequest from Francis T. P. Plimpton after the death of his widow, who had retained it during her lifetime with a loan to the Folger for one earlier exhibition. An important addition to the Folger's painting collection, the gift also reaffirmed long-standing ties between the Folger, the Plimpton family, and the trustees of Amherst College, who administer the library under the terms of Henry Folger's will. At the 1932 dedication ceremony, it was Francis's father, George Plimpton, head of the Amherst board, who received the key to the library from Emily Folger. Francis's younger brother, Calvin Plimpton, was president of Amherst from 1960 to 1971. Francis himself continued the family's involvement in Folger affairs, serving as chairman of the Amherst board's Folger Library Committee from 1967 to 1972.

Soon after its arrival at the Folger, the painting was digitally recorded for use in the Seven Ages of Man *multimedia exhibition. The resulting image was subsequently made available as one of the Folger's first online art facsimiles through the Hamnet catalog, sharing the painting with the international public as well.*

"Sieve" portrait of Elizabeth I / 1579

Of all the men who attended Elizabeth at court, Robert Dudley, earl of Leicester, was her favorite. The two had first met when they were children, and the attraction seems to have been mutual. When Elizabeth came to the throne in 1558, she made Leicester Master of the Horse and a member of her Privy Council, and over the years settled various licenses and manors on him that brought him great wealth. In the early years of her reign, rumors circulated of an affair between the two, and if she had married anyone, it probably would have been he. One initial obstacle was his marriage to Amy Robsart, but she died rather mysteriously from a fall at home in 1560.

In 1578, realizing that the queen would never take him as a husband, Leicester married Lettice Knollys, countess of Essex. His friendship with the queen continued, however, as is evidenced by this letter written on August 3, 1588, one of the last he ever sent to her. It is addressed from the royal camp at Tilbury, where Leicester was organizing the defense of Britain against the Spanish Armada. Twice in the letter he puts eyebrows over the double o *in* moost, *and at the end, he draws two eyes by his signature. These are a kind of coded in-joke with the queen, who had once nicknamed him her "Eyes."*

A month after writing this letter, Leicester died on September 4, 1588, at about the age of fifty-six. By then, he had had his day in the sun, riding down the lines at Tilbury with the queen in mid-August when she reviewed her troops and gave her famous speech, "I know I have the body but of a weak and feeble woman, but I have the heart and stomach of a king."

This is one of a group of important letters, including several from the earl of Essex to the queen, that the Folger acquired in 1997 through the generosity of Dorothy Rouse-Bottom. It was exhibited in the year 2000—along with the "sieve" portrait of Elizabeth (page 66)—in a special exhibition entitled A Decade of Collecting.

Earl of Leicester, letter to Elizabeth I / 1588

I am lothe my most dere La. to trowble yo
yo wt out some juste cause, wch at this tyme
god be thanked there ys none touching yor army
here but all things as well as possyble & as
forwardly bent to yor service as any soldiers
or subjects in ye world cā be. but yet
I may not forgett upon my knees to yeld
to yor most swete matie, all humble & dutyfull
thanks for ye great comfort I rec. eved fro
yor owne swete self. I am sorry that
I cā wryte yo not no newes, yet most
glad yt I may hold up my hands to god.
for ye mercyfull dealing for safely towards
yo, for by the advises we here, he sheweth
for yo & yor enemyes fall before yo.
shall all honor prayse & glory be given him
therfor, & whose most gracious be. any occasion
he geveth yo agaynst his enemyes & yors.
This renegate hath passed yor camp here
& came now to my L. of ormond & with
Stanhopp [illegible] & they walke among the
people wch are as sorry to be here as any in
christendome I think. may yt please yor [illegible]
& surely so punishment must follow, I shale
wryte in my lr of so of the offenders wch are to
many as [illegible], god evermore preserve
my most dere La. that she may to ye comfort of
her people & ours end in peace as she hath begon
[illegible]. in so hast fro Tylbury this saturday

by yor most faythfull & most
obedient [illegible]

R. Leycester

Ordinarily, a sovereign's correspondence was in the handwriting of confidential secretaries, and that is true of many of Elizabeth I's letters—but not this one, which seems to come right from the heart. Instead, Elizabeth wrote the letter to Henry IV of France in her own hand (and in French). Like other royal correspondence, it was then folded into a thin strip that was closed with the royal seal in red wax. The double-sided letter, probably written in 1595, dates from the last decade of Elizabeth's reign, a period that was the focus of a large NEH-funded Folger Institute conference in 1991 and of a subsequent volume of essays edited by John Guy.

In this letter, the topic at hand is the enduring and violent religious strife between French Catholics and the Huguenots, who were Protestants. Six years earlier, the assassination of the Catholic king Henry III had brought to the throne the Protestant Henry of Navarre, who became Henry IV. Reaching Paris only after four years of fighting, he officially converted to Catholicism, allegedly remarking that "Paris is worth a mass." But as Spain's King Philip II continued to stir up Catholic opposition to his reign, Henry looked to England's Protestant Queen Elizabeth for advice and support.

Having encountered religious unrest upon her own accession to the throne, Elizabeth in her letter counseled Henry to follow a course of restraint. "Perhaps you will despise this advice coming from a—from the heart of a woman," runs a partial translation, "but when you remember how many times I have not shown too much fear in my breast of pistols and swords which have been prepared for me this idea will pass away." The letter ends with her elegant signature, Elizabeth R.

Elizabeth I, letter to Henry IV of France / ca. 1595

que telle doubte Car a mon juge si l'en
usse de le verrois ou plustost
que couard Mais trop de expériance
en ayant faict exemplaire assurance
de Vostre invincible magnanimité
de vous conduire par tout ce que ayés
le mieulx ou vous vous respectés
non comme prince Souldart ains comme grand prince peult estre que
nous en jugerions le contraire con-
gardant d'un coeur paoureuse de fem-
me quant il vous souviendra p-
combien de fois j'en ay monstré trop
de crainte auparavant de vostres
choses qui ont esté preparé ceste
pièce passera estant faulte de
qui me recognois coulpable attribués
le pourtant a mon seule affection en
vostre endroict Et croyés que je ne
pourrois riens voir de mieulx que de
m'en avoir part. Cest escript ne
peult passer [illegible] sans vous
impartir la grande diligence et
esprit soing de ce Gentilhomme qui
ne laisse a soliciter vos causes
comme un très vif Serviteur Que dieu
vous en donne de les establir. Je prie
ausi bon de vous donner bon advis
et vous conduire la grace de prendre
tousjours le meilleur. Vostre très asseurée
Chère en tous vos fidelle bonne sœur
entreprises et non [illegible] comme
[illegible] comme La premiere
de ses [illegible]

Elizabeth R

En [illegible] de dieu rabaisse [illegible]
[illegible] tambouriers a quoy sert [illegible] en Chalerie com[illegible] ce Gentilhomme

[illegible] by the grace of God kinge of England Scotland ffraunce and Ireland defender of the faith &c. To
our trust[illegible] beloved Sir George More knight our lieutenant of our Tower of London greeting. Whereas
Sir [illegible] knight having been heretofore by order of our lawes [illegible] and attainted of high treason, by
[illegible] to us and our State, since which tyme through our princely [illegible] forbearing to execute upon him
[illegible] have notwithstanding continued him prisoner in our said Tower, where he still remaineth as
prisoner [illegible] of you our lieutenant there. And whereas [illegible] under our Signett to you our said
lieutenant [illegible] directed, wee commanded you to suffer the said Sir Walter Raleigh to goe abroad with his
keeper in our City of London, or elsewhere, which accordingly you have done as wee are informed, and which wee
well [illegible] of and approve by these presents. Now wee out of our princely commission being graciously pleased
that the said Sir Walter Raleigh shalbe noe longer continued prisoner in our said Tower, but forthwith be fully
enlarged and delivered out of the same, in hope he will [illegible] and [illegible] to us and our State. Wee therefore
will and commaunde you our said lieutenant of our said Tower, immediately upon the receipt of these presents, fully and
wholly to [illegible] deliver out of our said Tower, and set at libertie, the said Sir Walter Raleigh, the aforesaid
conviction, attaindor, condemnation, or judgement given and passed against him, or any commandement, order or direction
from us or our Privy Councell, or otherwise concerning the same, to the contrary thereof in any wise notwithstanding.
And these presents shalbe your sufficient warrant and discharge in this behalf. In witnes whereof wee have
caused these our letters to be made Patents. Witnes our self at Westm the thirtieth day of January in the fourteenth
yeare of our reigne of England ffraunce and Ireland and of Scotland the fiftieth. Coppin
per breve de privato sigillo

The Folger's diverse collection of manuscripts includes a number of historic legal documents, among them this royal warrant from James I. Written on vellum and authenticated with the king's Great Seal, it authorizes the release of Sir Walter Raleigh from the Tower of London on January 30, 1617. Raleigh had been one of Elizabeth I's many favorites and is best known for financing and directing the first colonization of Virginia, a colony named for the Virgin Queen. But shortly after her death and James I's accession to the throne, Raleigh was unjustly accused and convicted of involvement in a plot "to surprise the Kings person." On the day before he was to be executed, he was given a reprieve and imprisoned in the Tower of London. There he remained a prisoner from 1603 to 1617, during which time he wrote his monumental History of the World. *With this warrant, James authorized Raleigh's release based upon the promise that Raleigh, now sixty-five years old, would undertake another voyage to the New World and bring back half a ton of gold ore in exchange for his liberty.*

The voyage was unfortunate from the start. Storms scattered the fleet, sinking and disabling many ships. They were driven by a hurricane, then caught in the doldrums for forty days. Short of water and prey to scurvy and fever, many of Raleigh's crew members died. Finally landing in Guiana (now Venezuela), they set off in search of a Spanish gold mine. The attempt to win the mine ended in disaster, including the death of Raleigh's own son. As a man of honor, Raleigh returned to England to imprisonment in the Tower. Spanish anger over this last adventure then led to a reinstatement of the order of execution. He was beheaded on October 29, 1618. As Sir Walter Raleigh laid his head on the block, someone objected that he ought to be facing east. "What matter," he answered, "how the head lie, so the heart be right?"

James I, royal warrant / 1617

One of many classical texts rediscovered in the Renaissance was the Geography of the Greek philosopher Claudius Ptolemaeus, commonly known as Ptolemy. Dating from about AD 150, it sums up nearly six centuries of Greek speculation on the shape of the earth and the extent of its habitation, and includes more than 8,000 place-names. Within a century of his death, however, Ptolemy's accomplishment was virtually forgotten. It was not until the fourteenth century that manuscripts of his work, preserved in Constantinople, became better known in Europe.

When the Geography was translated into Latin in the fifteenth century (the first printed edition appeared in 1477), it had a powerful impact on Renaissance cartographers. In the Geography, Ptolemy not only states that the earth is spherical but also demonstrates the use of a coordinate system based on that shape and proposes three methods, or projections, for depicting the spherical earth on a flat surface.

Although much of Ptolemy's text consists of long lists of places and their respective coordinates, no accompanying maps, if they ever existed, have survived. Maps in medieval and Renaissance publications of Ptolemy are actually reconstructions based on these lists and using his coordinate system. The 1513 Strassburg edition of the Geography is considered among the more important of these publications because of twenty new maps attributed to the German cartographer Martin Waldseemüller, many of which incorporate recent discoveries. The maps in the Folger copy were hand-colored at about the time they were issued. In the example shown here, parts of Europe, Africa, and Asia are depicted with surprising accuracy, but gaps in geographical knowledge give rise to such peculiarities as a land bridge from Greenland to Europe.

Ptolemy, *Geography* / 1513

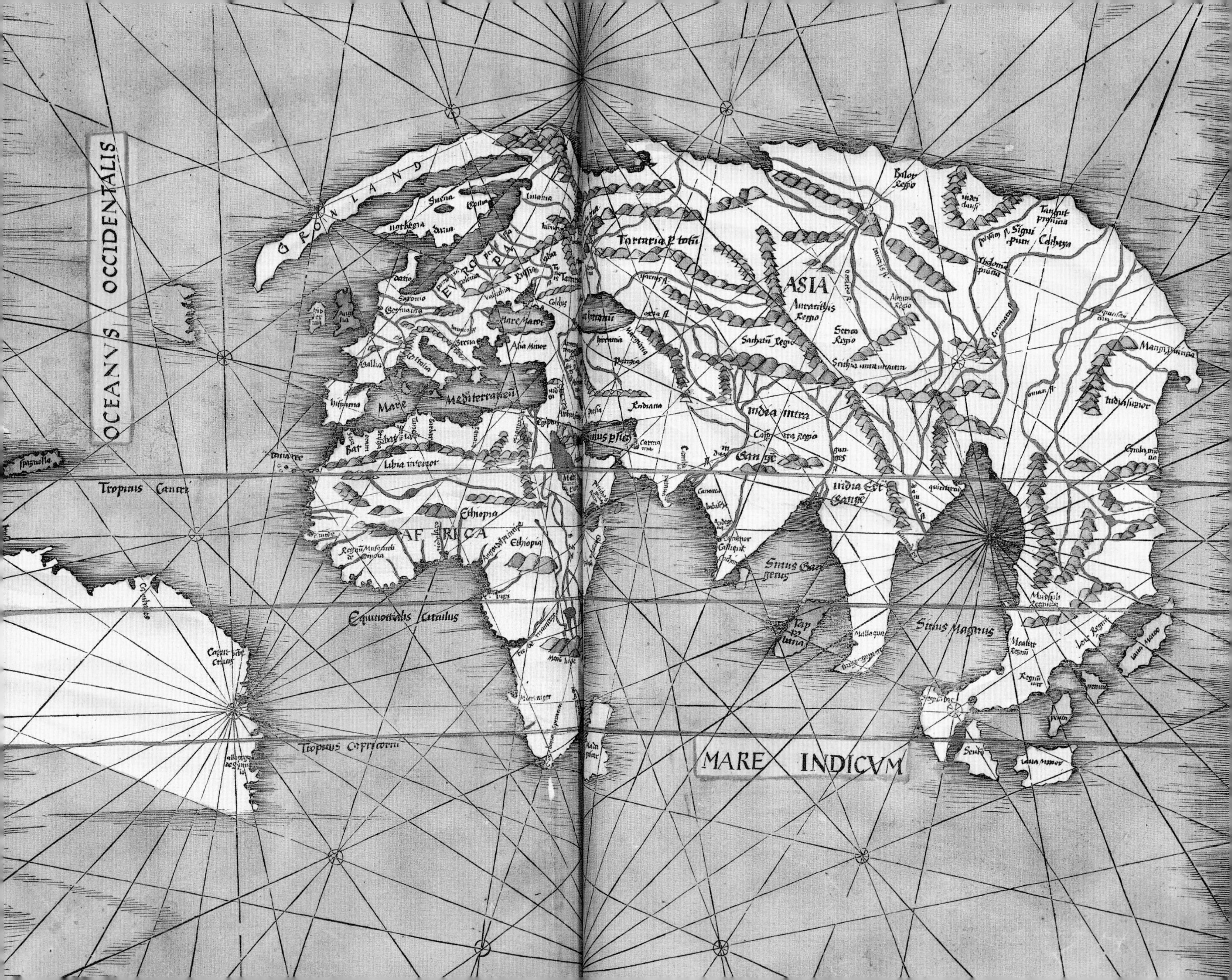
OCEANVS OCCIDENTALIS
GRONLAND
EVROPA
ASIA
AFRICA
Mare Mediterraneu
Asia Minor
Libia interior
Ethiopia
India intra
Sinus Magnus
Tropicus Cancri
Equinoctialis Circulus
Tropicus Capricorni
MARE INDICVM

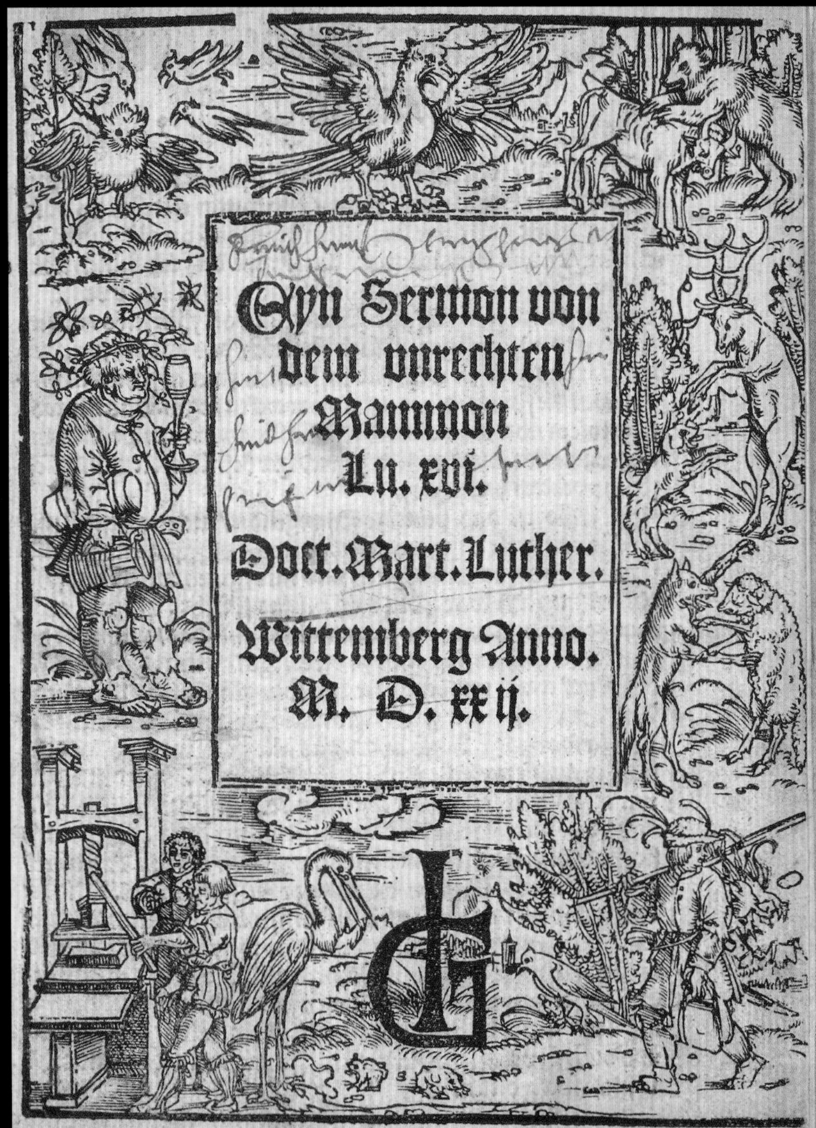

Eyn Sermon von
dem unrechten
Mammon
Lu. xvi.

Doct. Mart. Luther.

Wittemberg Anno.
M. D. xxij.

The Folger has long been one of the best places to study the Protestant Reformation, the subject of a large but relatively little-known collection within its Continental holdings that has been built up over a period of years. In 1977, the library added 850 items when it purchased the Reformation collection of the Swiss writer and scholar Emanuel Stickelberger. Among the reformers represented are Luther, Calvin, Erasmus, Melanchthon, and Zwingli.

This title page from a 1522 Luther sermon on "unrighteous Mammon" is a fine example of the many quartos in the Stickelberger collection, several of which, like this one, were marked up by their early readers. The richly detailed woodcut by Lucas Cranach the Elder includes a picture of a printing press at lower left, a visual acknowledgment of the vital role that printing played in spreading the Reformation across Europe. Cranach's other images include a battling wolf and sheep, evoking the common early Protestant accusation that some priests behaved more like wolves than shepherds toward their flocks.

In 1983, the Folger joined forces with the University of Maryland, the Lutheran Council of America, and its own Lutheran neighbor across East Capitol Street, the Church of the Reformation, in a six-day "Martin Luther Jubilee" commemorating the 500th anniversary of Luther's birth. Among the many events was the opening of a special exhibition of many of the Folger's Luther holdings, including a rare first edition of Luther's 1518 pamphlet Resolutiones disputationem de Indulgentiarum virtutate*—a discussion of his ninety-five theses—and the unique recorded American copy of Luther's prayerbook,* Ein Betbüchlin, *published in Wittenberg in 1531.*

Martin Luther, *Eyn Sermon von dem unrechten Mammon* / 1522

cellencye in musicke, chose Midas for their judge. VVho being corrupted vvyth partiall affection, gaue the victorye to Pan vndeserued: for vvhich Phœbus sette a payre of Asses eares vpon hys head &c.

Tityrus) That by Tityrus is meant Chaucer, hath bene already sufficiently sayde, & by thys more playne appeareth, that he sayth, he tolde merye tales. Such as be hys Canterburie tales. vvhom he calleth the God of Poetes for hys excellencie, so as Tullie calleth Lentulus, Deum vitæ suæ .s. the God of hys lyfe.

To make) to versifie. O vvhy] A pretye Epanorthosis or correction.

Discurtesie) he meaneth the falsenesse of his louer Rosalinde, who forsaking hym, hadde chosen another.

Poynte of worthy wite] the pricke of deserued blame.

Menalcas] the name of a shepheard in Virgile; but here is meant a person vnknowne and secrete, agaynst vvhome he often bitterly inuayeth.

vndersonge] vndermynde and deceiue by false suggestion.

Embleme.

You remember, that in the fyrst Æglogue, Colins Poesie vvas Anchora speme: for that as then there vvas hope of fauour to be found in tyme. But novve being cleane forlorne and reiected of her, as whose hope, that was, is cleane extinguished and turned into despeyre, he renounceth all comfort and hope of goodnesse to come. vvhich is all the meaning of thys Embleme.

Ægloga septima.

ARGVMENT.

THis Æglogue is made in the honour and commendation of good shepeheardes, and to the shame and disprayse of proude and ambitious Pastours. Such as Morrell is here imagined to bee.

Thomalin. Morrell.

Is not thilke same a goteheard prowde,
that sittes on yonder bancke,
Whose straying heard them selfe doth shrowde
emong the bushes rancke?

Morrell.

What ho, thou iollye shepheards swayne,
come vp the hyll to me:
Better is, then the lowly playne,
als for thy flocke, and thee.

Thomalin.

Ah God shield, man, that I should clime,
and learne to looke alofte,
This reede is ryfe, that oftentime
Great clymbers fall vnsoft.

The Folger copy of Edmund Spenser's Shepheardes Calender, *acquired in 1997, is one of only seven extant copies of the first edition, and the only one with the final quire in an early uncorrected state. Upon its publication in 1579, the book established Spenser's poetic genius among his contemporaries. Presented in twelve eclogues, it is a poetic tour de force. Each eclogue is written in a different meter, and all are in a deliberately archaic English of Spenser's own creation, meant in part to honor the medieval poet Geoffrey Chaucer.*

Like all of Spenser's works, the poem is highly allegorical. At one level, it tells the story of Colin Clout, a lovelorn shepherd who laments ill treatment by his beloved Rosalind. But the poem's many shepherds also represent the pastors of the English Protestant Church, and a character named Elisa is surely Elizabeth I. In the month of July, which begins on the right-hand page of the opening shown here, the shepherds Morrell and Thomalin debate whether to take to the hills to avoid the "cruell scortching heate" of high summer. Morrell, seated on a small hill, represents "proude and ambitious Pastours," a preamble explains; while the more worthy Thomalin prefers the plains below.

Spenser, who died in 1599 before completing all twelve projected books of The Faerie Queene, *was buried at Westminster Abbey near his literary hero Chaucer, establishing the tradition of the Poets' Corner. On Spenser's monument is carved the verdict of his contemporaries: "The Prince Of Poets In His Tyme."*

Edmund Spenser, *The Shepheardes Calender* / 1579

Although other Renaissance geographers created important maps, some of them physically very large, it was left to Abraham Ortelius to produce the first manageable and uniform modern atlas of the world in 1570 with his Theatre of the Whole World, *or* Theatrum orbis terrarum. *A Dutchman who served as geographer to King Philip II of Spain, Ortelius explains in his preface that he reviewed all the modern maps he could find, selected the best, and then had them rendered to his specifications on a scale small enough to fit into the book. Crediting the original cartographers by name, Ortelius acknowledges some eighty-four individuals in the 1570 first edition, including Ptolemy and Mercator; in the 1595 edition shown here, published three years before his death, the list has grown to 170, reflecting a similar increase in the number of maps.*

In 1998, a Folger exhibition entitled Mapping Early Modern Worlds *and a Folger Institute conference on the same theme both took up the work of Ortelius as well as other early figures who created important atlases and maps. During the conference, the Folger Consort early music ensemble added to the collaboration by presenting a "Map of the World" concert built on the framework of "Missa 'Ayo visto de la mappa mundi.'" Composed by the fifteenth-century Spanish composer Johannes Cornago in honor of another early world map, the piece is still more evidence of cartography's vital importance at this time.*

The engraving of the Pacific Ocean shown here is interesting not only for the greatly oversized land mass of New Guinea (Australia was not yet known to Europeans) but for the details of the Americas, from the shape of the Florida and California coastlines to such early settlements as Cuba and Hispaniola in the Caribbean and Peru, Chile, and Patagonia to the south. At left, the map includes a distorted but recognizable depiction of China, the Philippines, and Japan, along with a note in Latin on the growing number of Christians in the region, a result of Jesuit missionary efforts.

Abraham Ortelius, *Theatrum orbis terrarum* / 1595

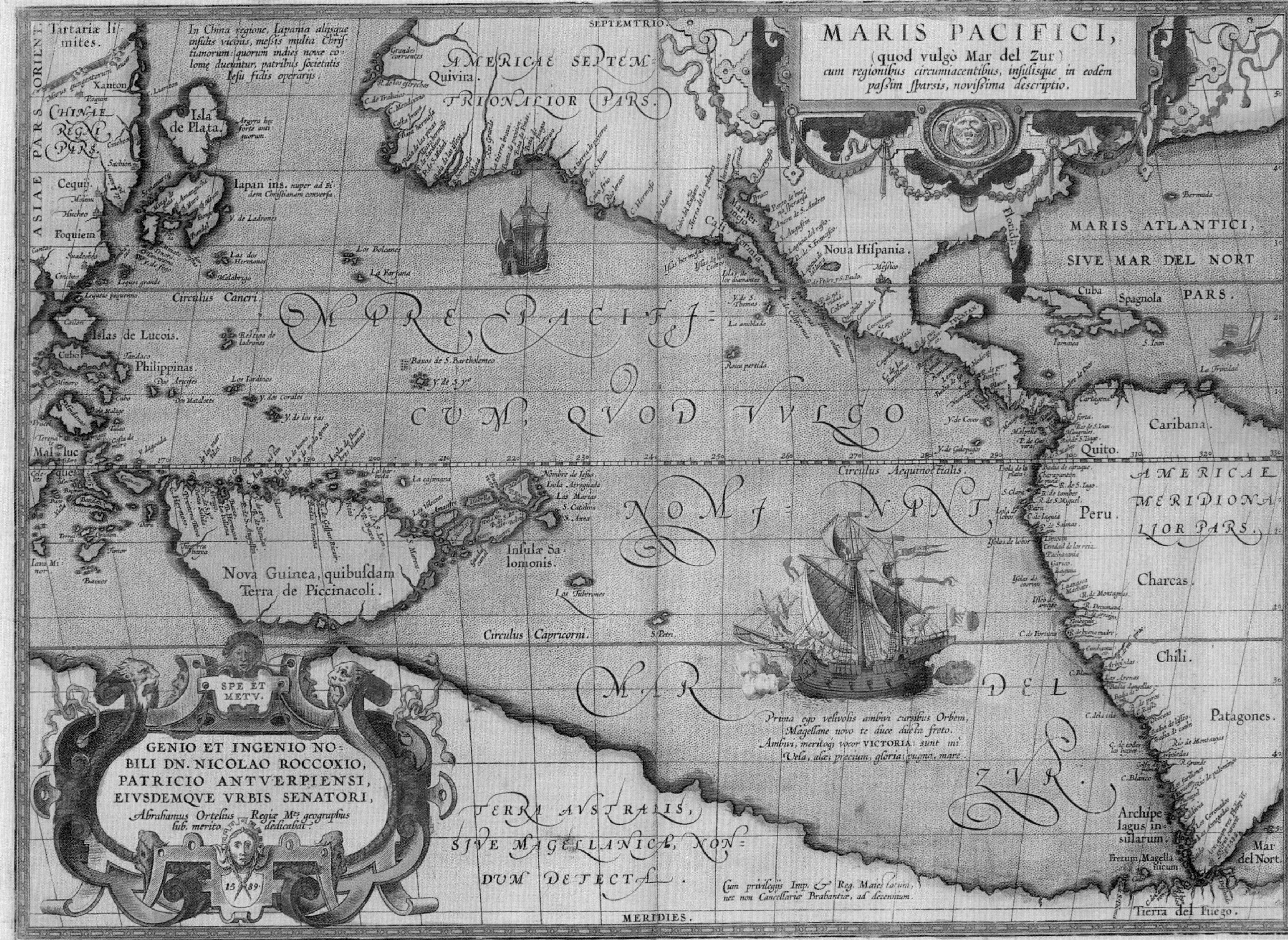
MARIS PACIFICI,
(quod vulgò Mar del Zur)
cum regionibus circumiacentibus, insulisque in eodem
passim sparsis, novissima descriptio.
SEPTEMTRIO.
MERIDIES.
In China regione, Iapania alijsque insulis vicinis, messis multa Christianorum: quorum indies nove colonię ducuntur, patribus societatis Iesu fidis operarijs.
Tartariæ limites.
ASIAE PARS ORIENT.
CHINAE REGNI PARS.
Xanton
Isla de Plata.
Iapan ins. nuper ad Fidem Christianam conversa.
Cequij.
Huchèo
Foquiem
Islas de Lucois.
Philippinas.
Mal luc
AMERICAE SEPTEMTRIONALIOR PARS.
Quivira.
Mar Vermejo
California
Noua Hispania.
Florida.
Cuba
Spagnola
MARIS ATLANTICI, SIVE MAR DEL NORT PARS.
Circulus Cancri.
MARE PACIFICUM, QUOD VULGO NOMINANT MAR DEL ZUR.
Circulus Aequinoctialis.
Circulus Capricorni.
Nova Guinea, quibusdam Terra de Piccinacoli.
Insulæ Salomonis.
Los Tuberones
S. Petri.
Caribana.
Quito.
Peru.
AMERICAE MERIDIONALIOR PARS.
Charcas.
Chili.
Patagones.
Archipelagus insularum.
Fretum Magellanicum.
Tierra del Fuego.
Mar del Nort.
Prima ego velivolis ambivi cursibus Orbem,
Magellane novo te duce ducta freto.
Ambivi, meritoq; vocor VICTORIA: sunt mi
Vela, alæ; precium, gloria; pugna, mare.
TERRA AUSTRALIS, SIVE MAGELLANICA, NONDUM DETECTA.
Cum privilegijs Imp. & Reg. Maiestatum, nec non Cancellariæ Brabantiæ, ad decennium.
SPE ET METV.
GENIO ET INGENIO NOBILI DN. NICOLAO ROCCOXIO, PATRICIO ANTVERPIENSI, EIVSDEMQVE VRBIS SENATORI,
Abrahamus Ortelius Regiæ Mtis geographus lub. merito dedicabat.
1589.

Sr

If I could fear, yt in so much worthynes as ys in yow there were no Mercy,
or yf these waights opprest onely my shoulders, and my fortunes, and not my
conscience, and hers whose good ys dearer to me by much then my lyfe, I
should not thus troble yow wth my Lrs. But when I see that this storme
hath shakd me at roote in my Lords favor, wher I was well planted,
and have iust reason to fear, that those yll reports wch malice hath
raysd of me, may have trobled her, I can leave no honest way vntryed
to remedy these miseryes, nor find any way more honest then this, out
of an humble and repentant hart for the fault donne to yow, to beg
both yor pardon and assistance in my suite to my L. I should wrong yow
as much agayne, as I did, if I should think yow sought to destroy me.
but though I be not hedlongly destroyd, I languish and rust dan-
gerously. from seeking prefermts abrode, my Love and Conscience restrains
me. from hoping for them here my Lords disgracings cut me of. My Em-
prisonmts, and theyrs whose Love to me brought them to yt hath already
cost me 40li. And the love of my frinds, though yt be not utterly groun-
ded vpon my fortunes, yet I know suffers somewhat in these long and
vncertain disgraces of myne. I therfore humbly beseech yow, to have
so charitable a pitty, of what I have, and do and must suffer, as to take
to yor selfe the Comfort, of having saved from such destruction as
yor iust Anger might have layd vpon him a sorrowfull and honest man.
I was bold in my last letter to beg leave of yow, that I might wright
to yor daughter. Though I vnderstood therupon, that after the
Thursday yow were not displeasd that I should, yet I have not nor
wyll not wthout yor knowledge do yt. But now I beseech yow that
I may: since I protest before god yt is the greatest of my afflic-
tions, not to do yt. In all the world ys not more true sorrow
then in my hart, nor more vnderstanding of true repentance then
in yors. And therfore God, whose pardon in such cases ys never denyed
gives me leave to hope, that yow wyll favorably consider my ne-
cessityes. To his mercifull guiding, and protection I comend yow
and cease to troble yow. 1o Mart: 1601

yors in all humblenes
and dutifull obedience

J Donne.

214

In 1940, the Folger Shakespeare Library made its third purchase from the extraordinary manuscript collection held at Loseley Park in Surrey. The Folger had previously turned to Loseley for the records of the first permanent Master of the Revels, Sir Thomas Cawarden. Now, with the aid of a grant from the Rockefellers, the Folger acquired thirteen letters by the seventeenth-century poet John Donne, constituting about a third of Donne's surviving letters.

In the decades since, the Donne letters have yielded physical clues that have helped date the only extant copy of a poem in his own hand. The letters and other manuscripts have also been useful to researchers in preparing the multivolume Variorum Edition of the Poetry of John Donne.

Far from being routine correspondence, eight of the letters illuminate a crisis in Donne's life triggered by his secret marriage in late 1601 to Anne More, daughter of Sir George More of Loseley Park. By marrying Anne without her father's permission, Donne offended against both the civil and the canon laws. He soon found himself in prison and barred from communication with his bride. Donne responded with an outpouring of eloquent, pleading letters to Sir George More that include the example shown here (dated 1601 according to the "old style," in which the year began on March 25). In it, Donne writes movingly of Anne, "whose good ys dearer to me by much then my lyfe." The poet's appeals were eventually heeded, and on April 27, the court of the archbishop of Canterbury confirmed the marriage. Despite some financial difficulties brought on by the scandal, the marriage was apparently a happy one. When Anne died in 1617, she was survived by her husband and seven children.

John Donne, letter to Sir George More / 1601/1602

In 1999, a Folger exhibition entitled Seeing What Shakespeare Means *showcased a number of books and manuscripts from the collection that have supplied images for the New Folger Library Shakespeare paperback editions of Shakespeare's works. Some of the pictures reinforced and explained references in the plays that are now, to modern eyes, somewhat obscure. Materials in the exhibition illustrated how a man might "cross-garter" his legs with ribbons crossed at the knee, for example, as Malvolio does in* Twelfth Night, *and just what Hamlet is referring to when he mentions a petard (a small military explosive). Others showed more familiar subjects, but from a distinctly Renaissance point of view.*

Among the rare books in the latter category is The Historie of Foure-Footed Beastes *(1607) by the English clergyman Edward Topsell. Topsell's book has been the source of numerous images for the Folger editions, including period representations of a beaver, a lion, an elephant, a greyhound, a water spaniel, a panther, a hedgehog—and this rather ferocious porcupine, which sheds new light on the sign of "the Porpentine" that marks a courtesan's house in* The Comedy of Errors.

In composing this book as well as his earlier Historie of Serpents, *Topsell based his writing and illustrations largely on the work of German naturalist Konrad Gesner, whose* Historiae Animaliam *had been printed in 1585. To Gesner's basic text, Topsell added exhaustive accounts of the prevailing traditions and scientific beliefs of his own age. The result includes not only a few mythical beasts such as the sphinx among the real ones, but also hearsay evidence as well as actual fact. For example, Topsell notes (incorrectly) that porcupines can shoot their quills at pursuers: "The beast stretcheth his skin, and casteth them off, one or two at a time, according to necessity upon the mouths of the Dogs, or Legs of the Hunters that follow her, with such violence that many times they stick into trees & woods." The change in gender is typical of Topsell's descriptive style.*

Edward Topsell, *The Historie of Foure-Footed Beastes* / 1607

the Hebrewes,
: to them: The
at is, *Sus setosa*,
uils which they
eta, villi, pinnæ,
s, rough-haire,
call it *Aduldull*,
ha which by *A*-
Montanus Ericius
thornes vppon
all it *Seanzocha*-
l him *Porco-spi*-
spin, the French
ing therein the
me places call it
ed name in imi-
ardes, French,
is beast is a Sea-
r it be a kind of
tus, Bellunensis,
Porcupine *Erici*-
owne in Europe
by the sight of
to a Hares, but
eares like to the
lerfeete like the
ft, but hollow or
, their groweth
wines, and they
nirable in him,
: hands, armes,
at is partly black
e as a Peacocke
hey stand not in
es, being sharp
kin, and casteth
: Dogs, or Legs
ick into trees &
, *spinis suis sæpe*
vt simul concur-
iniores homines,
hurt both Dogs
e backes which
and near them,

OCTO. XXI.

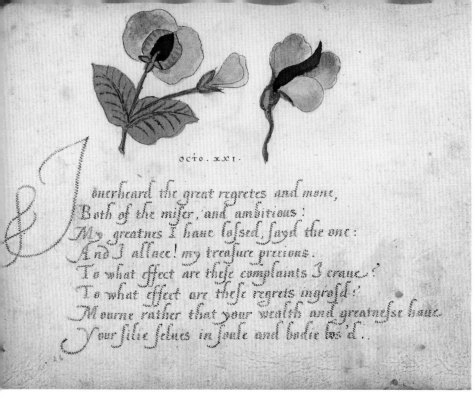

I ouerheard the great regretes and mone,
Both of the miser, and ambitious:
My greatnes I haue lossed, sayd the one:
And I allace! my treasure precious.
To what effect are these complaints I craue?
To what effect are these regrets ingross'd?
Mourne rather that your wealth and greatnesse haue
Your silie selues in soule and bodie los'd.

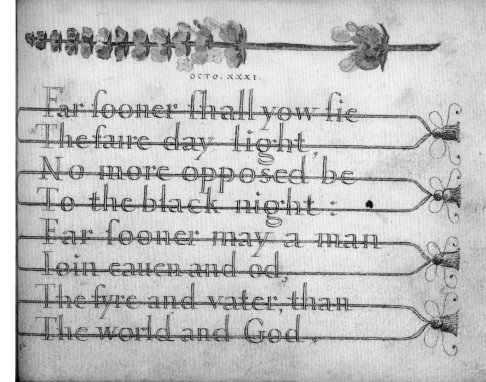

OCTO. XXXI.

Far sooner shall yow see
The faire day light,
No more opposed be
To the black night:
Far sooner may a man
Ioin euen and od,
The fyre and vater, than
The world and God.

OCTO. XXXV.

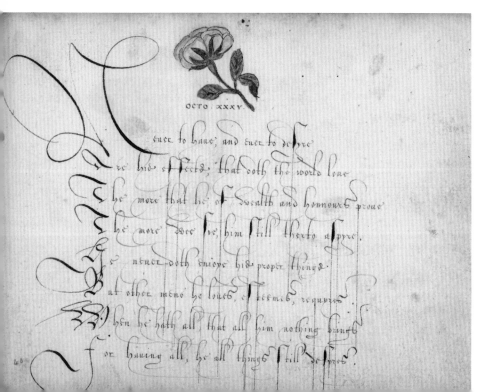

Euer to haue, and euer to desyre
Are his effects, that doth the world loue
The more that he of wealth and honours proue
The more desires him still thereto aspyre,
He neuer doth enioye his proper things
But other mens he loues, esteemes, requyres
When he hath all, that all him nothing bringes
For hauing all, he all things still desyres.

40

OCTO. XLV.

O who is hee that in so happy state is plac'te
Ne neuer of the sweet deceits of sin to taste?
Which man a pris'ner makes while he doth prey on it,
Bewitching so his soule, and blinding both his eyes.
O who is hee that hath by tryall learned witt
T'acknowledge and deserne, the hell that in vyce lyes?
O by what meanes, I saye, may one suche blissinges see?
If not the world in him, though in the world he be.

50

From the late 1500s until her death in 1624, the calligrapher Esther Inglis created more than fifty beautifully crafted manuscript books, which she presented to patrons in England, Scotland, and France, probably with the hope of receiving a "gift" or fee in return. Among the recipients were Elizabeth I, Elizabeth's ministers, and the family of Elizabeth's successor, James I. The daughter of French Huguenot refugees who settled in Edinburgh, Inglis often worked with texts important to Protestants. Today her elegant writing in a great variety of hands, often executed on a very small scale, is still praised for its precision and control.

While calligraphy was an accepted pastime for ladies of culture, the degree to which Inglis pursued it professionally was somewhat unusual for a woman—and was probably at least in part the result of economic necessity. Only one of her manuscript books predates her marriage to Bartholomew Kello, an impoverished Presbyterian cleric who sometimes acted as an overseas agent for the Scottish and English governments. Kello, with whom she had six children, contributed Latin verses in his wife's praise to several of her bound manuscripts and probably delivered some of them to French Protestant patrons during his missions abroad. (Inglis kept her maiden name in her signed works, apparently following the Scottish legal custom of the day.)

The Folger has four of Inglis's manuscripts, among them Octonaries upon the vanitie and inconstancie of the world, of which several pages appear at left. One of Inglis's favorite subjects, the Octonaries consist of forty-seven poems by the French poet Antoine de la Roche Chandieu, each having a verse of eight lines; Kello may have provided the English translation. In this 1607 copy, dedicated to the couple's "freinde and landlord" William Jefferai, Inglis ornamented all but two of the poems with a hand-painted floral design. As in most of her works, the style of writing changes with each poem in what can only be called a virtuosic display. Of the poems shown here, those at upper left and bottom right are variations on lettre frisée (literally, "curled writing"); Octonary 31, the poem at upper right, is written in lettre entrelacée ("interlaced writing"), in which precise horizontal lines weave through each line of the poem; and Octonary 35, at lower left, appears in a mixed hand with extraordinarily long descenders.

Esther Inglis, *Octonaries* / 1607

The pages shown here are among 290 double-sided folios in a bulky manuscript created in 1608 by Thomas Trevelyon. Although little is known about Trevelyon or his unusual book, researchers believe that many of the pictures were meant as embroidery patterns. Today they serve as a remarkable visual record, making Trevelyon's work one of the items at the Folger for which photographs are most often requested.

Among the enormous variety of subjects covered in Trevelyon's book are the kings and queens of Scotland and England, represented here by Mary, Queen of Scots, and Richard III; custom and folk wisdom, as in this dialogue expressing the duties of husband and wife; and designs that include calendars, alphabets and numbers, leaf and flower motifs, and more abstract ornamentation. Other pages depict the relative sizes of the sun, the planets, and the earth; theologians, reformers, and the Lord Mayors of London; pagan, Jewish, and Christian heroes; the nine muses; and the seven deadly sins, among many other topics. Astonishingly, this sprawling work is one of two by Trevelyon. Eight years after creating it at about the age of sixty, he produced a second manuscript containing many of the same images; that work is now in the collection of Sir Paul Getty at Wormsley, England.

For decades, the 1608 manuscript was inaccessible to scholars because of its fragility. In creating his illustrations, Trevelyon used a green pigment called verdigris, made by allowing urine to work on copper; over the centuries, the verdigris gradually ate into many of the pages it once ornamented. Nineteenth-century binders wreaked havoc on the manuscript with indiscriminate patching, and repair attempts in the 1930s and 1940s inadvertently caused inks and pigments to bleed.

Beginning in 1995, in the most ambitious conservation project at the Folger up to that time, senior paper conservator Julia Stevenson and other Folger conservators restored the entire manuscript, reversing the earlier repairs, removing the patches, and strengthening the pages with an ultrathin paper developed and made at the Folger and based on Japanese plant barks. Afterward, every page of the manuscript was digitized from a high-resolution photograph, greatly reducing the need for researchers to work directly with the still-delicate original and making its images accessible to scholars elsewhere as well.

Thomas Trevelyon, commonplace book / 1608

125
marie queene of scotes

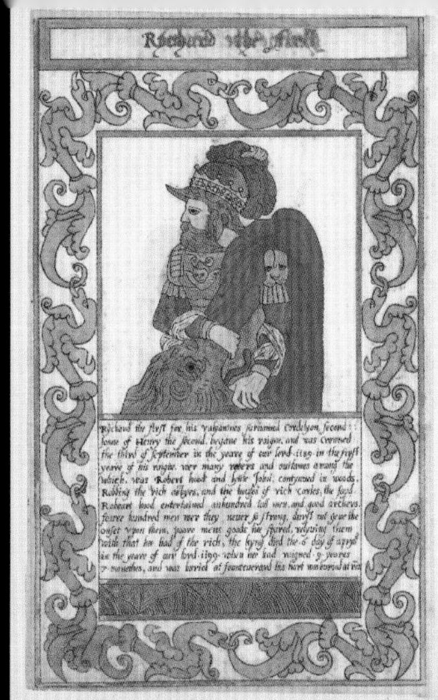
Richard the first

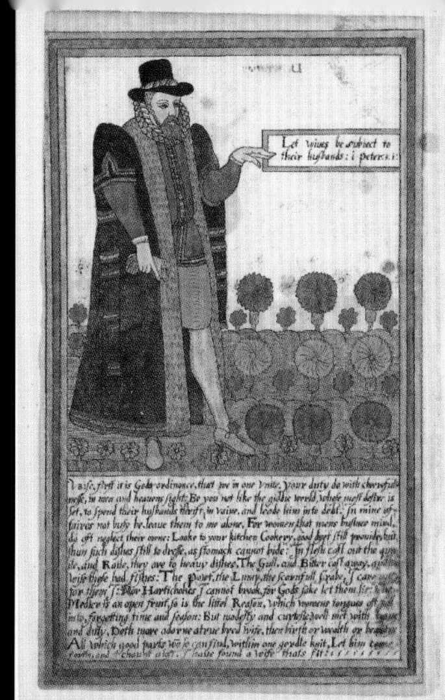
Let wiues be subiect to their husbands: 1 peter 3.1

163
Likewise you husbandes giue honer to the woman, as vnto the weaker vessel: 1 Peter 3.7

A table for the Sondayes letter, and Leape yeare

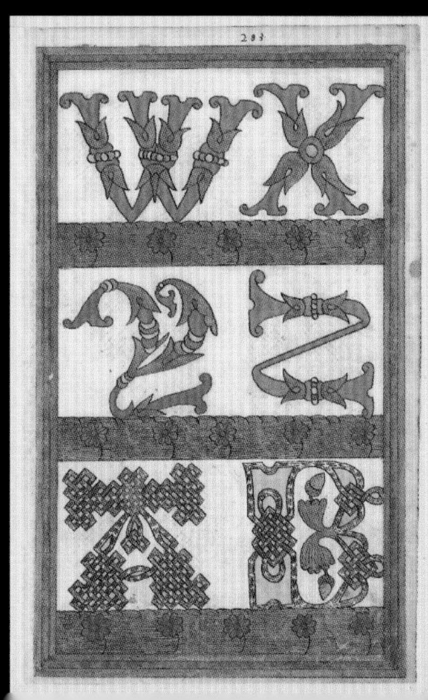

219

The art of depicting aspects of the human anatomy on connected and successive overlays of paper reached its height in the work of Johann Remmelin, a physician whose "pop-up" anatomical atlas Catoptrum Microcosmicum *was first published in 1613 and later reprinted several times. The diagram of a woman at right, one of three large copperplate engravings in the work, is from a 1660 edition. In each of the three engravings, including this one, small printed flaps of paper in superimposed layers may be folded out of the way to reveal the parts of the body that lie beneath. Here the flaps are closed; in the sequence on pages 92 and 93, they are successively folded back to reveal, among many other body parts, the ribs and the lungs (with the trachea tucked neatly out of the way), the heart, and some of the major blood vessels. By the final image, the pieces representing the heart and the lungs have been removed to show the rear wall of ribs.*

Remmelin's book reflects the considerable advances in anatomical knowledge that took place in the Renaissance, and it is absolutely packed with information. Surrounding the central figure are seventeen images of parts of the body as seen from different perspectives, including two with their own printed layers—a skull viewed from below, at lower left, and a posterior view of the stomach, at right. In typical early modern fashion, all of this hard science mingles comfortably on the page with allegorical allusions to a phoenix, a snake, several apples, and, at upper left, a small, grinning skeleton.

With a total of about 120 flaps, Remmelin's book was undoubtedly a nightmare for printers; it is today no easy subject for photographers. Working in a dedicated laboratory, the Folger's photography department handles thousands of requests a year for images, producing meticulously accurate visual records of the collection's rare books and manuscripts as the library has done since its inception. But each assignment poses its own challenge. In this case, since no single photograph could capture the multiplicity of layers, the solution was to plan and shoot a series of images in consultation with a local physician, revealing what structures lie beneath each successive layer in just one of Remmelin's anatomical diagrams.

Johann Remmelin, *Catoptrum Microcosmicum* / 1660

Qui prius respondet quam cognoscat, stultum se esse demonstrat & confusione dignum, Prov. 18, v 13.

Nunquid non paucitas dierum meorum finietur brevi? dimitte ergo me ut plangam paululum dolorem meum, Iob. 10, v. 20.

Occupatio magna creata est omnibus hominibus, &c. in diem sepulturae in matrem omnium, Syr. 40. vers. 1.

Honora Patrem tuum & Matrem tuam ut sis longaevus super terram quam Dominus Deus tuus dabit tibi, Exod. 20, v. 12.

Filium suum unigenitum misit Deus in mundum, ut vivamus per eum, 1. Ioh. 4. v. 9.

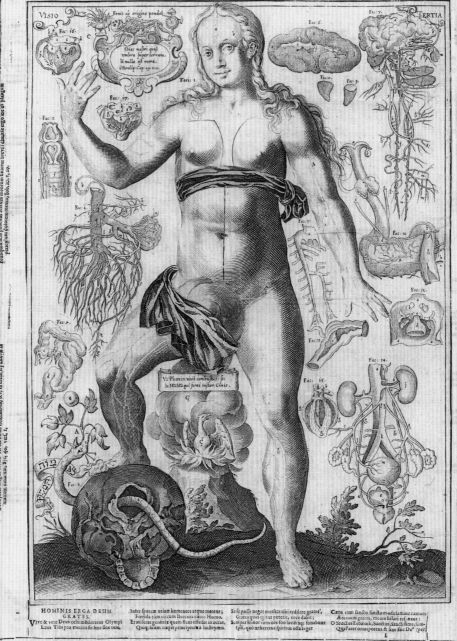

HOMINIS ERGA DEUM GRATES.

Vive & vere Deus celsi moderator Olympi
Laus Tibi pro meritis sit sine fine tuis.
Inter spurcae urinae humentes atque meatus;
Foetida tùm circum stercora natus Homo.
Et miseras genitrix quem flens effudit in auras,
Quiq; suum coepit principium a lachrymis.
Se se posse negat meritas tibi reddere grates',
Grates quas igitur poterit, ecce dabit;
Semper honor tuus ore suo laudesq; sonabunt
Ipsi, quò aethereus spiritus ossa reget
Coetu cum sancto sancto modulamine cantans
Aeternum grates, mente hilari resonans:
O Sanctus Zebaoth, Sanctus, Sanctissime, semper
Qui Pater omnipotens & sine fine De'

L

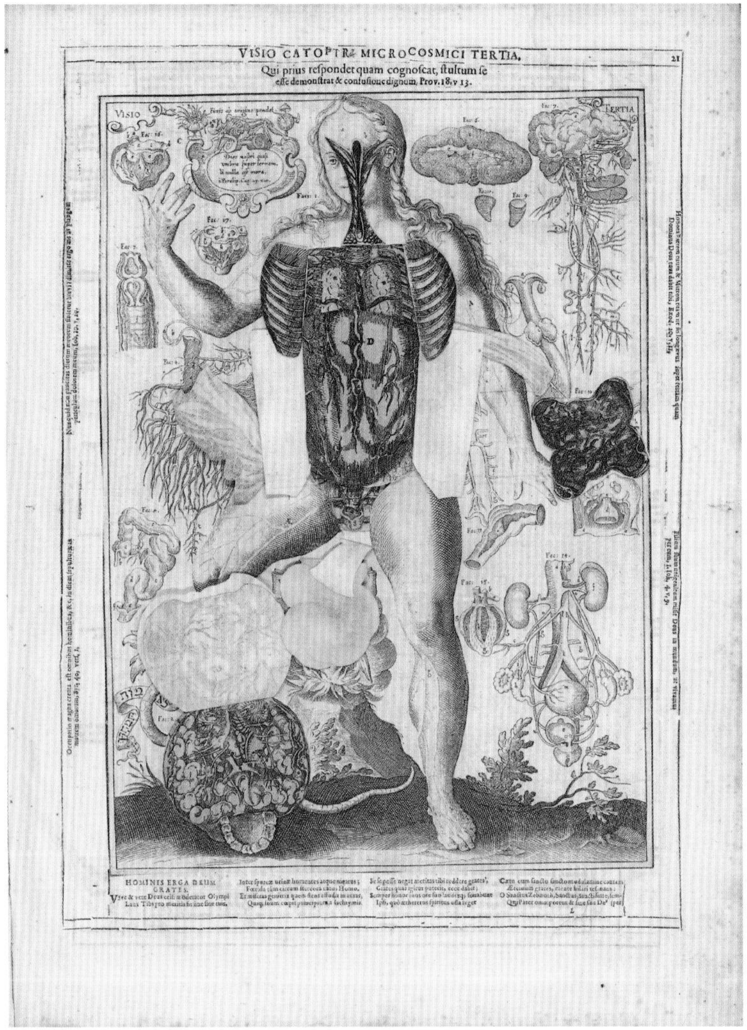

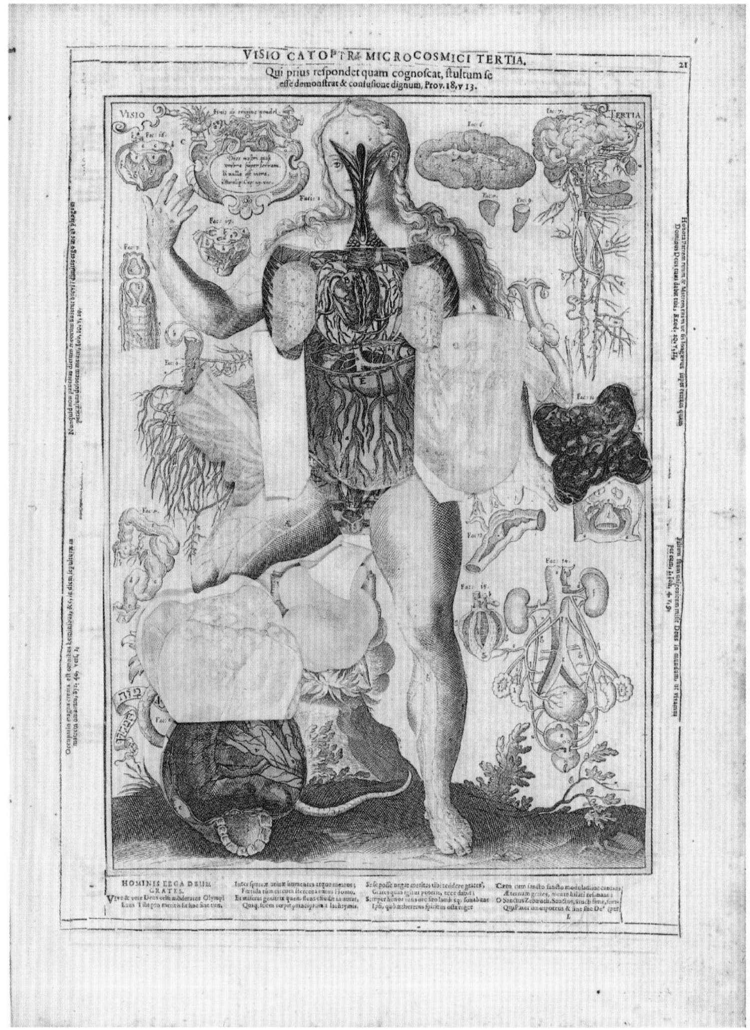

Johann Remmelin, *Catoptrum Microcosmicum* / 1660

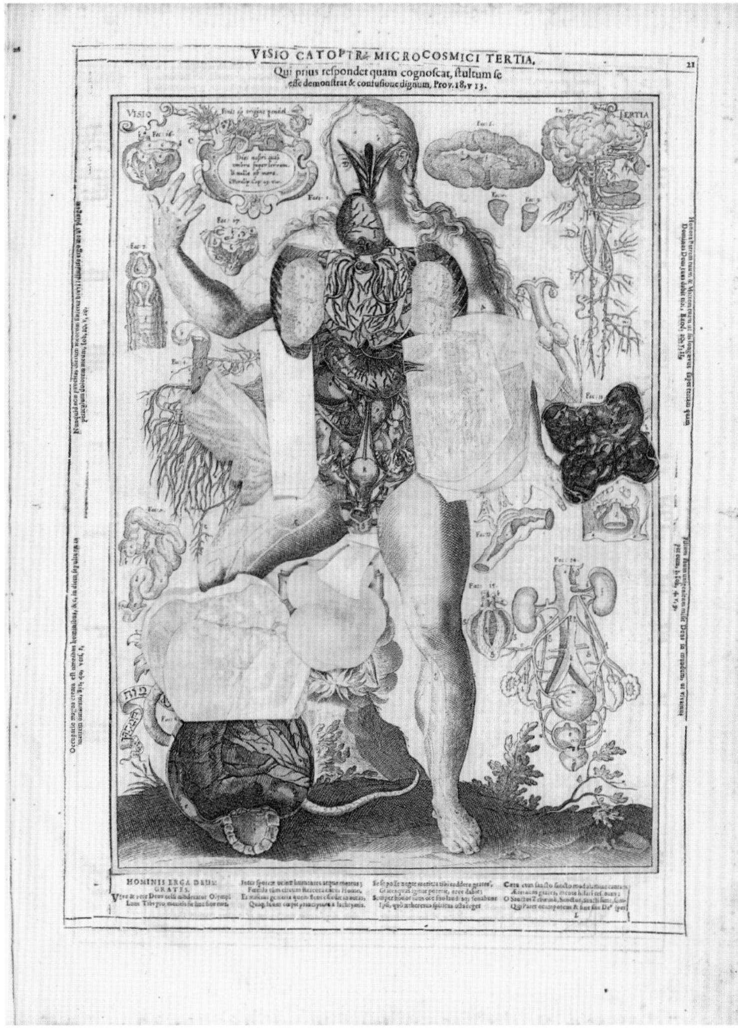
VISIO CATOPTRÆ MICROCOSMICI TERTIA.
21
Qui prius respondet quam cognoscat, stultum se esse demonstrat & confusione dignum, Prov. 18, v 13.
VISIO
TERTIA
HOMINIS ERGA DEUM GRATES.

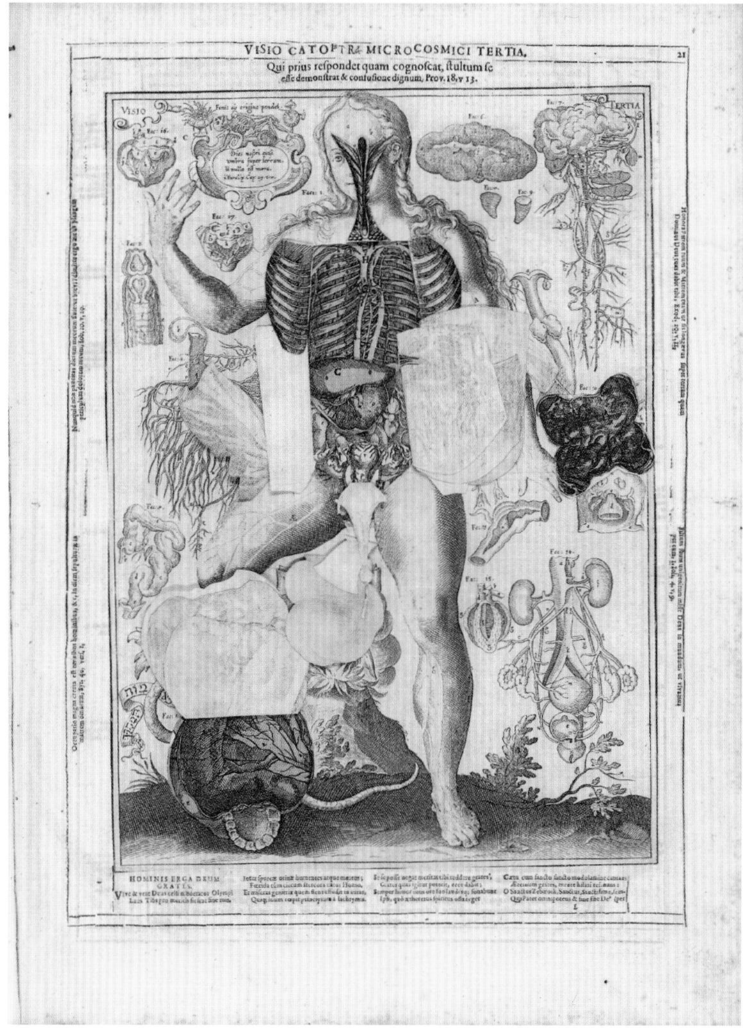
VISIO CATOPTRÆ MICROCOSMICI TERTIA.
21
Qui prius respondet quam cognoscat, stultum se esse demonstrat & confusione dignum, Prov. 18, v 13.
VISIO
TERTIA
HOMINIS ERGA DEUM GRATES.

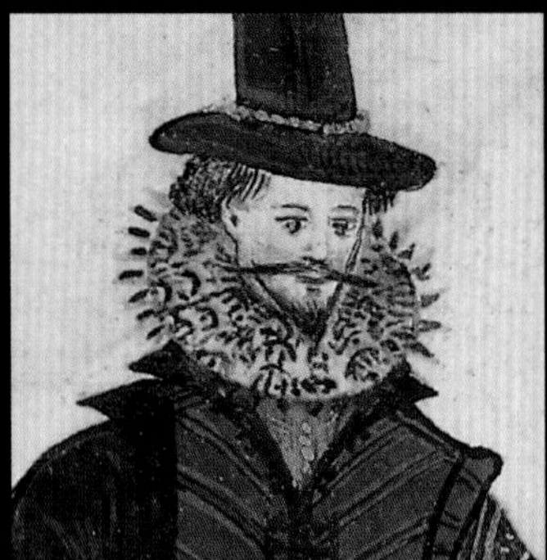

The Folger Shakespeare Library has for many years been one of the world's leading research libraries for Western sixteenth- and seventeenth-century materials, most of which have no particular connection to the Bard. The Folger's expansive early modern collection began with Henry and Emily Folger's own effort to understand the world within which Shakespeare functioned by accumulating materials in such related fields as music, art, and literature. This broadening of interests was dramatically expanded in the 1930s with a series of large acquisitions from private collections, and has gone on to include Continental as well as English holdings.

Today the Folger is the third-largest repository in the world for the books listed in the Short-Title Catalogue, *or STC, which covers works printed in England or in the English language from 1475 to 1640. It is also the sixth-largest holding library for books listed in the Wing catalog, covering the period from 1641 to 1700, and it has some 55,000 rare manuscripts, most of them from the same periods. Continental holdings include more than 30,000 rare books, among them about 1,000 printed Italian plays, in which early Renaissance writers began inventing the more realistic forms of modern drama later employed by Shakespeare and other playwrights. Among other strengths within the collection are holdings related to the New World and its exploration, a wealth of early Dutch and French political pamphlets, printed materials from the Reformation, many etchings and engravings, and an extensive collection of books—many of them the gift of Mrs. H. Dunscombe Colt—commemorating public events and festivities.*

With these early modern materials, a small number of which appear in the following pages, the notion of a "living collection" takes a particularly vibrant form. The details of Renaissance living that they evoke and explain have shaped many a Folger production, exhibition, and family program. Topics such as religion, politics, and domestic life have been at the center of many of the Folger Institute's conferences, seminars, and publications.

The Folger Consort, the institution's resident early music ensemble, also regularly draws on the collection's wealth of printed music. The Consort's performances and recordings help in turn to re-create still another aspect of the past, providing something of an aural equivalent to the wealth of textual and visual detail revealed in the books, manuscripts, and artworks of the Folger collection.

In the era before artificial chemicals, herbs were an essential part of popular culture, vital to almost every aspect of existence from cookery and cleaning to medicine and personal grooming. Among the best records of this side of Renaissance life are the illustrated books known as herbals, which systematically describe plants of all kinds. In 1994, the Folger's collection of herbals was greatly expanded by Mary P. Massey's donation of some 300 herbals, probably the most comprehensive private library of rare and early herbals in the United States.

Among them was the book shown here, Leonhart Fuchs's De historia stirpium *of 1542. Fuchs—for whom both the plant and the color fuchsia are named—was one of the German fathers of botany, and the woodblock illustrations in his work are both accurate and elegant. This hand-colored copy of his work was once owned by the sixteenth-century English naturalist Henry Dingley. Dingley's copious annotations date from the time when Shakespeare was ten years old, and they include some twenty-five plants Dingley saw on the banks of the Avon. Among them was the winter cherry, or Chinese lantern plant, seen here at far right with Dingley's accompanying note, "This growithe in the beare garden at evyssham and in other gardens in evissam and in stradforde vpon avon in grete plente."*

Perhaps as a reflection of his rural background, Shakespeare's own works include innumerable references to herbs and their virtues. In 1989, the Folger paid an unusual tribute to that fact by planting an Elizabethan Garden to the east of the main library building. The garden incorporates a wealth of plants either named in Shakespeare's plays or popular in his day, many of which are to be found in a central knot garden that includes germander, rosemary, lavender, saffron crocus, thyme, and clove pink ("gillyflower" to the Elizabethans). Outside the knot garden, other significant plantings include wild Welsh daffodils (which were sold in abundance in London and are mentioned twice in The Winter's Tale*), the white roses of York, and box hedges, meant to recall the "boxtree" behind which Sir Toby Belch and his friends hide in* Twelfth Night. *A pleasant shaded space amid the city scene, the garden is also educational; regular tours by docents explore how the herbs found there were used for everything from dyeing cloth gold (saffron crocus) to protecting stored linens (lavender).*

Leonhart Fuchs, *De historia stirpium* / 1542

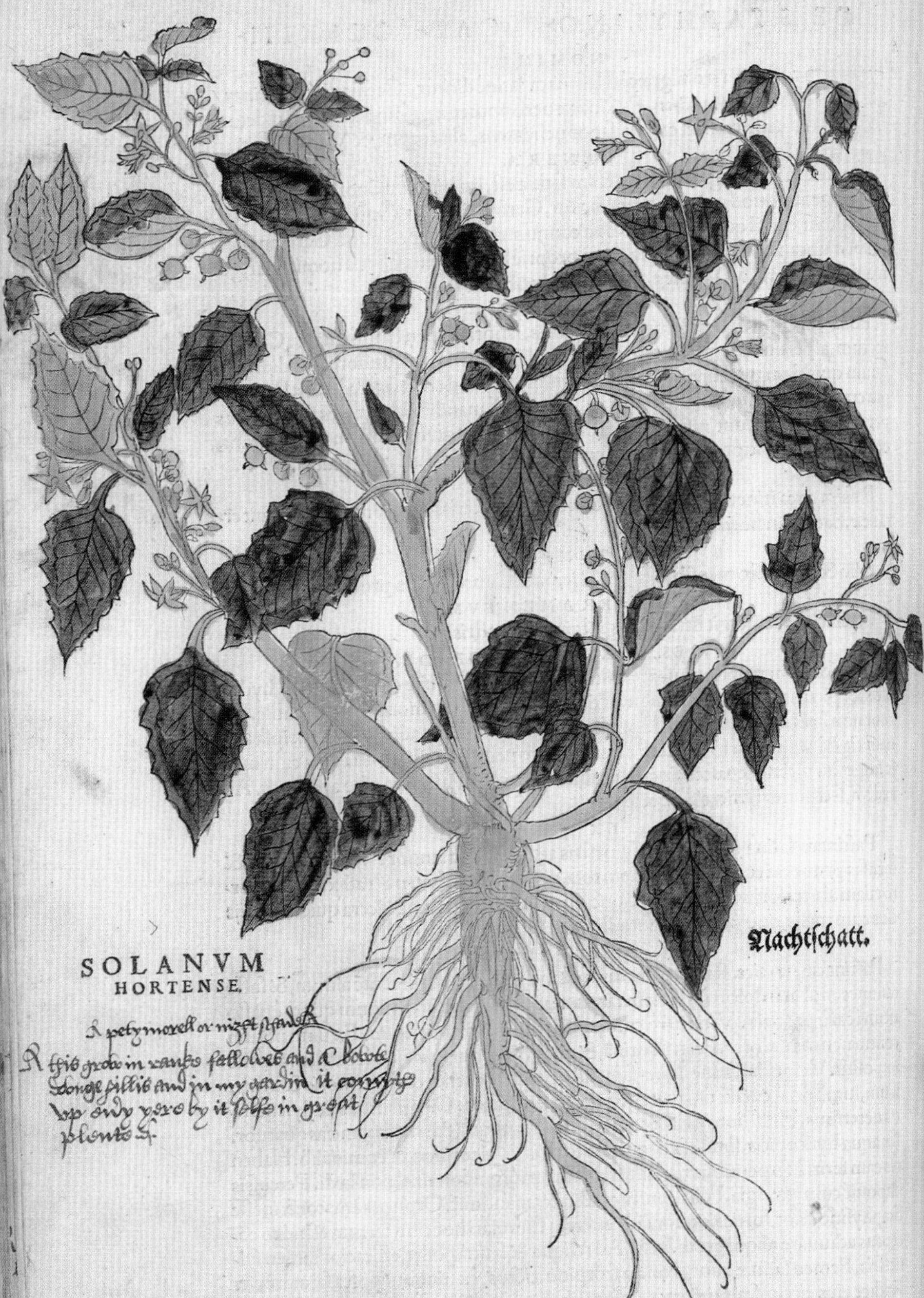

Nachtschatt.

SOLANVM
HORTENSE.

A pety morell or nizht shade

This grow in ranke fallowes and a clowte donge hillis and in my gardin it commys up every yere by it selfe in great plente

HALICACABVM
VVLGARE.

Judendocken.

A wynter cherrys

This growith in the beane garden at Wynsham and in other gardens in Evisham and in Stratford a pon Avon in grete plente

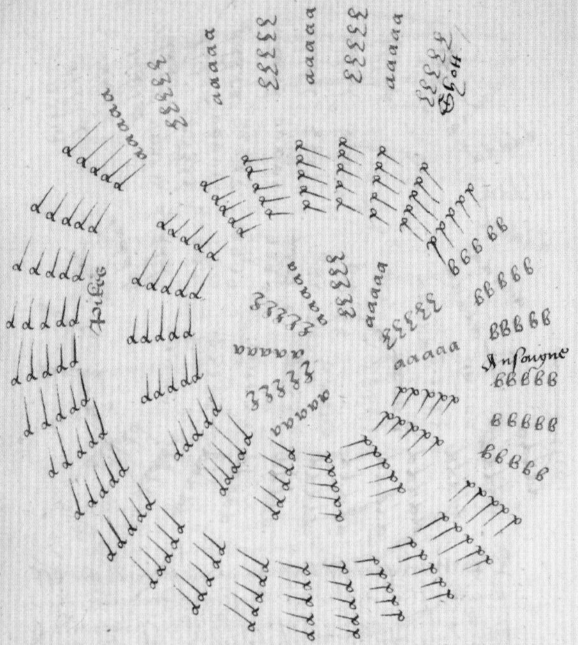

This Fymason or snaile ys not to be used for any intente excepte it be to exercise the array. / Yt bringeth halfe the shott from place of servise and leaveth the Ansaigne open to the enimyes. /

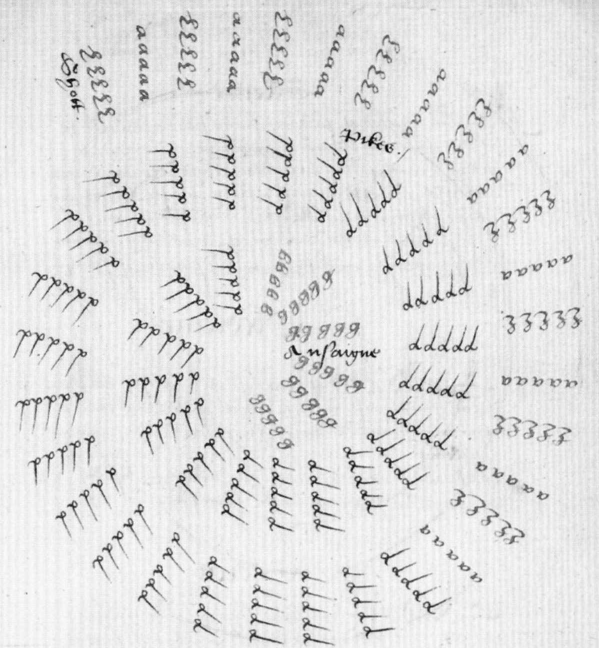

This Fymason may be used upon an extremitie and seme gardable to th'ansaigne. / In makinge ye same bringe the company into a ringe, so yt your shott togethers. / Halberdes wth thensaigne levieth ye marshe to this strengthe: and by the same bringeth themselves within garde of the longe weapons, and beinge forced the shott entreth within the same. /

In the summer of 1970, with the United States still deeply involved in the war in Vietnam, an idealized, almost geometrical version of warfare from a very different age made the cover of the Folger's annual Acquisitions Report. The black and red spiral of marching troops came from a newly acquired manuscript, A breife booke unto private captaynes leadinge footemen, *written in 1562 by one Henry Barrett, of whom little is known.*

The manuscript, which exists only in the Folger copy, was meant as a training manual for use by amateur captains of local militia companies at a time when most Englishmen lacked military experience. As described in a 1978 article by John Hale, author of the popular 1961 Folger Booklet The Art of War and Renaissance England, *Barrett's handbook explains in detail how to form 200 or so raw recruits into an infantry company and prepare them to become part of a larger army should the need arise. Included are forty-four diagrams of formations, including the instances of a curled marching drill shown here.*

Beautifully copied and bound, Barrett's manuscript may have been meant as a presentation copy. But the final pages noted in its list of contents were never added, and the manuscript did not become widely known. For the time being, practical resources on military subjects remained scarce in England; it would be some years before the gap was filled by translations of European texts like the one that appears on page 105.

Henry Barrett, *A breife booke unto private captaynes* / 1562

John Foxe's massive and influential Actes and monumentes, *more familiarly known as the Book of Martyrs, is fundamental to almost any study of the English Reformation. First published in 1563, it recounts the fate of 300 English Protestants put to death during the restoration of Catholicism under Queen Mary, sometimes called Bloody Mary, in a five-year reign that ended in 1558. The book grew in subsequent editions, and the Folger's collection of early Foxe editions has been an essential resource for such programs as the Folger Institute's 1998 NEH summer seminar, "Redefining the Sacred in Early Modern England." Several images from the books were reproduced in the packet of classroom materials that the NEH funded for participants.*

Although Foxe's work is hardly an evenhanded account, it served in its day as an important source of contemporary history. Shakespeare is thought to have drawn on episodes from the Book of Martyrs for the second and third parts of Henry VI *and an incident in* Henry VIII. *Shown here in a woodcut from the second edition of 1570 is one of the acknowledged highlights of the book—the death of Thomas Cranmer, archbishop of Canterbury, who had earlier tried to save his life by agreeing in writing to some aspects of Catholic doctrine. In this scene, Cranmer is burned at the stake at Oxford on March 21, 1556. As the flames rise, a Spanish Dominican friar, Juan de Villagarcia (labeled here as "Fryer Iohn"), waits in vain for Cranmer to once again recant his Protestant beliefs. Instead, Cranmer extends the treacherous right hand with which he signed his early recantations so that it will burn first.*

The two-volume 1570 edition of the Book of Martyrs, of which the Folger owns one of approximately two dozen remaining copies, is more than 2,300 pages long. Like other editions of Foxe's work held at the Folger, it is nearly always in demand, which combined with its thin paper and awkward size has led to gradual wear. In the year 2000, the Foxe scholar John King provided a special gift to support the conservation of this edition. Over the course of a year, senior conservator Linda Blaser and others in the department disassembled the first volume and mended, washed, and dried the individual pages, repairing many through a process known as leaf casting. Once all the pages had been treated, the entire block was then resewn and rebound. The second volume, however, required only a new cover and binding; in a lasting repair, chief conservator Frank Mowery had treated and conserved its contents some twenty years before.

John Foxe, *Actes and monumentes* / 1570

ked deuils in hell, and I see before myne eyes presently either heauen ready to receiue me, or els hell ready to swallow me vp: I shall therfore declare vnto you my very fayth how I beleue, without any colour or dissimulation: for now is no tyme to dissemble, what soeuer I haue sayd or written in time past.

The Archb. declareth the true confession of his fayth without all colour or dissembling.

First, I beleue in God the father almighty, maker of heauen and earth. &c. And I beleue euery Article of the Catholicke faith, euery word and sentence taught by our Sauiour *IESVS CHRIST*, his Apostles & Prophetes, in the new and old Testament.

The Archb. reuoketh his former recantation and repenteth the same.

And now I come to ye great thyng that so much troubleth my consciẽce more then any thing that euer I did or sayd in my whole life, and that is the settyng abroad of a writyng contrary to the truth: which now here I renounce and refuse as thynges written with my hand contrary to the truth which I thought in my hart, and writtẽ for feare of death, and to saue my lyfe if it might be, and that is, all such billes and papers which I haue written or signed with my hand since my degradation: wherin I haue written many thinges vntrue. And for as much as my hand offended, writyng contrary to my hart, my hand shall first be punished therfore: for may I come to the fire, it shalbe first burned.

The Archb. refuseth the Pope as Christes enemy, and Antichrist.

And as for the Pope, I refuse him as *CHRISTES* enemy and Antichrist, with all his false doctrine.

The Archb. standeth to his boke written against Winchester.

And as for the Sacrament, I beleue as I haue taught in my booke agaynst the Bishop of Winchester, the which my booke teacheth so true a doctrine of the Sacrament, that it shall stand at the last day before the iudgement of God, where the Papisticall doctrine contrary therto, shalbe ashamed to shew her face.

The expectation of the papistes deceaued.

Here the standers by were all astonyed, marueiled, were amased, did looke one vpõ an other, whose expectation he had so notably deceiued. Some began to admonish him of his recantation, & to accuse hym of falshode.

Briefly, it was a world to see the Doctours begyled of so great an hope. I thinke there was neuer crueltie more notably or better in tyme deluded and deceiued. For it is not to bee doubted but they looked for a glorious victorie and a perpetuall triumph by this mans retractation. Who as soone as they heard these thynges, began to let downe their eares, to rage, fret, and fume:

The papistes in a great chafe against the Archb.

and so much the more, because they could not reuenge their griefe: for they could now no longer threaten or hurt him. For the most miserable man in the world can dye but once: and where as of necessitie he must needes dye that day, though the Papistes had bene neuer so well pleased: now being neuer so much offended with him, yet could he not be twise killed of them. And so when they could do nothyng els vnto him, yet lest they should say nothyng, they ceassed not to obiect vnto him hys falsehode and dissimulation.

Cranmers answere to the papistes.

Unto which accusation he aunswered: Ah my Masters (quoth he) do not you take it so. Alwayes since I lyued hetherto, I haue bene a hater of falsehode, and a louer of simplicitie, and neuer before this tyme haue I dissembled: and in saying this, all the teares that remained in his body, appeared in his eyes. And when he began to speake more of the Sacrament and of the Papacy, some of them began to cry out, yalpe, and baule, and specially Cole cried out vpon him: stoppe ye heretickes mouth, and take hym away.

Cranmer pulled downe from the stage.

Cranmer led to the fire.

And then Cranmer beyng pulled downe from the stage, was led to the fire, accompanied with those Friers, vexyng, troublyng, and threatnyng him most cruelly. What madnes (say they) hath brought thee agayne into this errour, by which thou wilt drawe innumerable soules with thee into hell? To whom he aunswered nothyng, but directed all his talke to the people, sauyng that to one troublyng him in the way, he spake and exhorted him to get hym home to his study, and apply his booke diligently, saying if he did diligently call vpon God, by readyng more he should get knowledge. But the other Spanish barker, ragyng and fomyng, was almost out of his wittes, alwayes hauyng this in his mouth: Non fecisti? diddest thou it not?

The Archb. brought to the place of execution.

But when he came to the place where the holy Byshops & Martyrs of God, Hugh Latimer and Ridley, were burnt before him for the cõfession of ye truth: knelyng downe, he prayed to God, and not long taryng in his prayers, putting of his garmentes to hys shirt, he prepared hym selfe to death. His shirt was made long downe to hys feete. His feete were bare. Lykewyse his head, when both his cappes were of, was so bare, that not one heare could be sene vpõ it. His beard was long and thicke, couering his face with maruaylous grauity. Such a countenaunce of grauity moued the hartes, both of hys friendes and of his enemies.

Then the Spanish Fryers, Iohn & Richard, of whõ mention was made before, began to exhort hym & play their partes with him a fresh, but with vayne & lost labour, Cranmer with stedfast purpose abydyng in the profession of hys Doctrine, gaue hys hand to certayne old mẽ, and other that stode by, bidding them farewell.

M. Ely refuseth to geue his hand to the Archb.

And when he had thought to haue done so lykewyse to Ely, the sayd Ely drew backe his hand and refused, saying: it was not lawfull to salute heretickes, and specially such a one as falsely returned vnto the opiniõs that he had forsworne. And if he had knowen before that he would haue done so, he would neuer haue vsed hys company so familiarly, and chid those Sergeantes and Citizẽs which had not refused to geue him their hands. This Ely was a Priest lately made, and studẽt in diuinitie, being then one of the fellowes of Brasennose.

The Archb. tyed to the stake.

Then was an yron chayne tyed about Cranmer, whom when they perceiued to bee more stedfast then that he could be moued from his sentence, they commaunded the fire to bee set vnto hym. And when the wood was kyndled, and the fire began to burne neare him, stretching out his arme, he put hys right hand into the flame: which he held so stedfast & immouable (sauing that once with the same hand he wiped hys face) that all men might see hys hand burned before hys body was touched.

Cranmer putteth his right hand which subscribed first into the fire.

Hys body did so abide the burning of the flame, with such constancye and stedfastnes, that standing alwayes in one place without mouing of hys body, hee seemed to moue no more then the stake to which he was bound: his eyes were lifted vp into heauen, and often tymes he repeated, hys vnworthy right hand, so long as his voice would suffer hym: and vsing often the wordes of Steuen, *Lord IESVS receiue my spirite*, in the greatnes of the flame, he gaue vp the ghost.

The last wordes of Cranmer at his death.

This fortitude of mynd, which perchaunce is rare and not vsed among the Spaniards, when Frier Iohn saw, thinking it came not of fortitude but of desperation (although such maner examples which are of the like constancy haue bene common here in England) ran to the Lord Williams of Tame, crying that the Archbishop was vexed in mynd, and dyed in great desperation.

The Fryers lying report of Cranmer.

But he which was not ignorant of the Archbishops constancy, being vnknowen to the Spaniards, smyled onely, and (as it were) by silence rebuked the friers folly. And this was the end of this learned Archbishop, whom, lest by euill subscribing he should haue perished, by well recanting God preserued: and lest he should haue lyued longer with shame and reprofe, it pleased God rather to take him away, to ye glory of his name and profit of his church. So good was the Lord both to his church in fortifying the same with the testimony and bloud of such a Martyr: and so good also to the man, wyth this crosse of tribulation to purge hys offences in this world, not only of his recantation, but also of hys standing against Iohn Lambert, and M. Allen, or if there were any other wyth whose burning & bloud his handes had bene before any thing polluted. But especially hee had to reioyce, that dying in such a cause, he was to bee numbred amongst *CHRISTES* Martyrs, much more worthy the name of S. Thomas of Caunterbury then he whom the the Pope falsly before dyd Canonise.

¶The

¶The burning of the Archbishop of Cant. D. Tho. Cranmer, in the Towndich at Oxford, with his hand first thrust into the fire, wherewith he subscribed before.

Lord receaue my spirite.
Fryer Iohn.

The Martyrdome of Doct. Tho. Cranmer Archbyshop of Canterb. at Oxford. An. 1556. March. 21.

And thus haue you the full story concerning the life and death of this reuerend Archbishop and Martyr of God Thomas Cranmer, and also of diuers other the learned sort of *CHRISTES* Martyrs burned in Queene Maries tyme, of whom this Archbishop was the last, being burnt about the very middle tyme of the raygne of that Queene, and almost the very middle man of al the Martyrs which were burned in al her raygne besides.

Archb. Cranmer the middle Martyr of all the Martyrs burnt in Queene Maryes tyme.

Now, after the life and story of this foresaid Archbishop discoursed, let vs adioyne withall hys letters, beginning first wyth hys famous letter writtẽ to Queene Mary, which he wrote vnto her incontinent after hee was cited vp to Rome by bishop Brokes and hys fellowes, the tenour whereof here followeth.

¶ *Letters of D. Tho. Cranmer Archb.*

¶The Archbishop of Canterburies letter to the Queenes hyghnes.

A writing or letter of the Archb. sent to Q. Mary.

IT may please your Maiesty to pardon my presumption, that I dare be so bold to wryte to your highnes. But very necessity constrayneth me, that your Maiestye may know my mynde rather by myne own writing, thẽ by other mens reportes. So it is that vpon wednesday being the .xx. day of this moneth, I was cited to appeare at Rome, the .lxxx. day after, there to make aunswer to such matters as should be obiected against me, vpon the behalfe of the kyng, and your most excellent Maiestye: which matters the Thursday following were obiected against me by Doctor Martyn, and Doct. Story your maiesties Proctours, before the bishop of Glocester, sittyng in iudgement by commission from Rome. But (alas) it can not but greeue the hart of a naturall subiect, to be accused of the kyng and Queene of hys own realme: and specially before an outward Iudge, or by authority comming from any person out of thys Realme: where the kyng and Queene, as they were subiectes within theyr own Realme, shall complayne, and require iustice at a straungers hands against their own subiect, being alredy condemned to death by their own lawes: As though the kyng and Queene could not do or haue iustice within their own realmes, agaynst their own subiectes, but they must seeke it at a straungers handes in a straunge land: the like whereof (I thinke) was neuer seene.

The king & Queene make thẽselues no better then subiectes complayning of their owne subiect vnto the Pope.

I would haue wished to haue had some meaner aduersaries: and I thinke that death shall not greue me much more, then to haue my most dread and most gracious soueraygne Lord and Ladye, to whom vnder God I doe owe all obedience, to bee myne accusers in iudgement, within their own Realme, before any straunger and outwarde power. But for as much as in the tyme of the Prince of most famous memory king Henry. VIII, your Graces father, I was sworne neuer to consent, that the bishop of Rome should haue or exercise any authority or iurisdiction in this realme of England, therefore lest I should allow hys authoritie contrary to myne oth, I refused to make aunswer to the bishop of Glocester sitting here in iudgement by the Popes authority, lest I should runne into periury.

The first cause why the Archb. would not make answere to the Popes delegate, is to auoyde periury.

An other cause why I refused the Popes authority is this, that hys authority, as he claymeth it, repugneth to the crowne imperiall of this Realme, and to the lawes of the same: which euery true subiect is bound to defend. First, so that the Pope sayth, that all maner of power, as well temporall as spiritual, is geuen first to him of God, and that the tẽporall power he geueth vnto Emperours and kings to vse it vnder hym, but so as it be alwaies at hys commaundement and becke.

The 2. cause is, that the Popes lawes are contrary to the crowne and lawes of England.

But contrary to this clayme, the Emperiall crowne and iurisdiction temporal of this realme is taken immediatly from God, to be vsed vnder hym onely, and is subiect vnto none, but to God alone.

The oth of the king & Iustices, and the duty of subiectes.

Moreouer, to the Emperiall lawes and customes of thys realme, the King in hys Coronation, and all Iustices when they receaue their offices, be sworne, and al the whole realme is bound to defend and mayntayne. But contrary hereunto the Pope by his authoritye maketh voyde, and commaundeth to blot out of our bookes, all lawes and customes being repugnant to hys lawes, and declareth accursed all Rulers and Gouernours, all the makers, writers & executors of such lawes or customes: as it appeareth by many of the Popes lawes, whereof one or two I shall rehearse. In the decrees Distinct. 10. is written thus: Constitutiones contra Canones & decreta præsulum Romanorum vel bonos mores, nullius sunt momenti. That is: the constitutions or statutes enacted against the Canons and decrees of the bishops of Rome or their good customes, are of none effect. Also, Extra, de sententia excommunicationis, nouerit: Excommunicamus omnes hæreticos vtriusque sexus, quocunq; nomine censeantur

Dist. 10. Constitutiones.

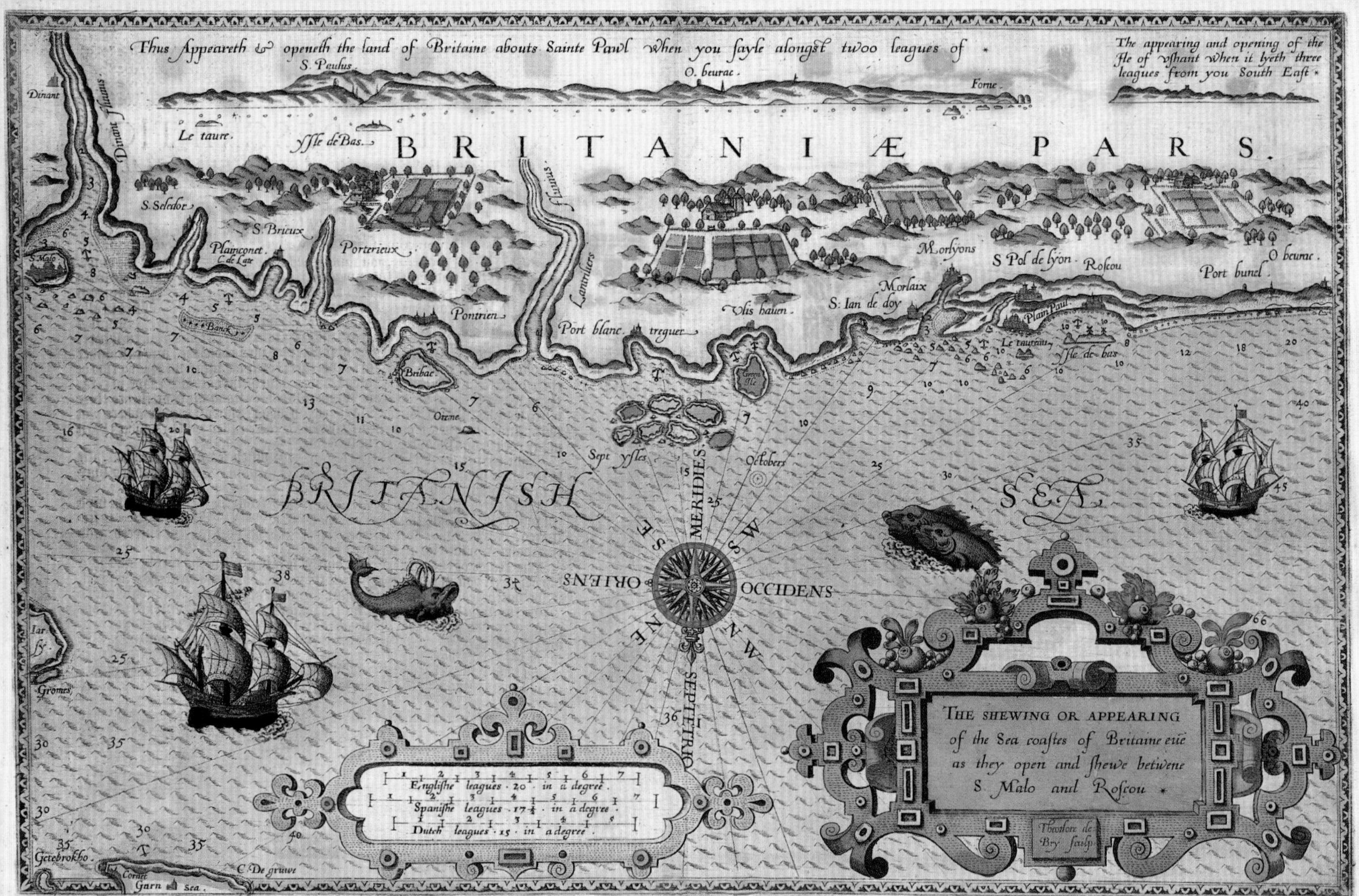
Thus Appeareth & openeth the land of Britaine abouts Sainte Pawl when you sayle alongst twoo leagues of
The appearing and opening of the Ile of vshant when it lyeth three leagues from you South East
S. Paulus
O. beurac
Forne
BRITANIÆ PARS.
Dinant
Dinant flumius
Le taure
Ysle de Bas
S. Seledor
S. Brieux
Plainconet
C. de Late
Porterieux
Pontrien
Lantrillers
flumius
Port blanc
treguer
Vlis hauen
S. Ian de doy
Morlaix
Morlyons
S Pol de lyon
Roscou
Port bunel
O beurac
Plain Paul
Le taureau
Ysle de bas
Banck
Bribac
Oiene
Sept ysles
Octobers
BRITANISH
SEA
MERIDIES
OCCIDENS
ORIENS
SEPTETRIO
SE
SW
NE
NW
Iarsy
Gromes
Getebrokho
C. De gruwe
Garn
Sea
Englishe leagues 20 in a degree
Spanishe leagues 17½ in a degree
Dutch leagues 15 in a degree
THE SHEWING OR APPEARING of the Sea coastes of Britaine eue as they open and shewe betwene S. Malo and Roscou
Theodore de Bry sculp

Unlike the atlases of his countryman Abraham Ortelius, the Spieghel der Zeevaerdt, *or* The mariners mirrour, *of Lucas Waghenaer was meant as a guide for those navigating ships along the crowded coasts of western Europe and the British Isles. The book proved so popular that its author's name gave rise to a whole category of handbook, the "waggoner." Summarizing in one place all the contemporary astronomical and mathematical knowledge necessary to position finding,* The mariners mirrour *also includes a wealth of charts showing channels, harbors, and other coastal features from a shipboard perspective. Its publication in 1585 in the Netherlands was soon followed by this English translation, dating from about 1588. In the coastal profile of Brittany shown here, the mouth of a river is among several prominent features of "the Sea coastes of Britaine" between "S. Malo and Roscou."*

Like some other books of its day, however, the Folger's brilliantly hand-colored copy of The mariners mirrour *has not lasted well. The vivid green so characteristic of its illustrations comes from verdigris, the same highly acidic pigment found in the Trevelyon manuscript (pages 88–89). For decades, the copy at the Folger has been unbound and its pages stored separately, so that verdigris on one page cannot eat through those beside it; it remains so fragile that it is normally off-limits to researchers. A limited number of images from the colorful guide, including those shown here, have been recorded photographically, however, and have served over the years as a source of lively graphic ornaments for Folger books, pamphlets, and even Web pages.*

Lucas Janszoon Waghenaer, *The mariners mirrour* / 1588 (?)

While Elizabethan England lacked much firsthand experience in ground combat, its Continental neighbors were not so fortunate, enduring a series of wars that led in turn to advances in military science. For the English, therefore, European texts became the primary source of knowledge about emerging methods of warfare. Several such books from Italy were included in the Folger's 1993 exhibition The Elizabethan View of Italy, *among them this beautifully hand-colored book, a 1588 translation by Cyprian Lucar of Niccolò Tartaglia's* Quesiti et inventioni diverse, *first published in 1546.*

A mathematician and a natural philosopher, Tartaglia was himself wounded as a boy during the 1512 attack on Brescia, and was left with a permanent speech impediment and the self-assigned nickname Tartaglia, "the stammerer." Although he translated Euclid's Elements *and published two treatises on mechanics by Archimedes, he is best known today for his writings on the technology of war.*

Much of Tartaglia's text offers such practical advice for the gunner as the type of gunpowder to use. He also uses mathematical principles to explain trajectories. The pages shown here instruct the reader in how to aim a mortar to shoot "fireworks or great stones" over a wall or other obstacle. For greater clarity, the scenario is depicted first as a realistic drawing at left, and then diagrammatically at right, including a label neatly indicating the "fort to be burned or beaten downe."

Niccolò Tartaglia, *The arte of shooting* (Cyprian Lucar translation) / 1588

ket must alwayes bee somewhat lesse than the diameter and circumference in the bore of his Musket,& that a fit pellet of lead for his Musket wayeth two ounces $\frac{3}{4}$ of an ounce,one dramme & six graines of *auer de poize* waight,and that six fit pellets & $\frac{134}{191}$ of one fit pellet of lead for his Musket doe waie iust one pound of *auer de poize* waight.

4 Also he ought to learne how he shall in a commendable maner charge his peece,and how he shall afterwardes(when need shall require)lay it to his cheeke.

5 Hauing learned to charge, he ought also to know how hee should shoote in the saide peece at randon,and likewise how he should shoote in that peece at a marke within the leuell of the same peece,and how vppon a small stay in march or skirmish hee should charge and discharge speedily his peece.

6 Also he ought to prooue before hee hath vrgent cause to vse his peece,whether it bee good and meete for his purpose or like to breake.

7 And in a skirmish made only for practise or sport,let him take heed that hee doe not charge his peece with any bullet whereby any person may be maymed or put in hazard of his life or limmes.

8 Also for diuers reasons which are not meete to be expressed in this booke,let no person at any time vse to shoote out of his peece any pellet of lead after hee hath chawed it in his mouth,and bitten it with his teeth.

The 75 Chapter.

How to mount a morter peece for to shoote out of the same fireworks or great stones ouer walles or other high places into cities,townes,or camps,to burne and beate downe houses,tents, and lodgings within the same places.

IT behooueth him which will shoote out of a morter peece any fireworke or great stone for to haue it fall right downe vppon the appointed place to know these 3 things. The waight of the shot how much ground his peece wil shoote at the best of the randon,& how far the place which he would burne or beate downe is from him. The said three things being knowne,he may easily by this example following learne to doe as he intended.

Example.

The peece will shoote the fireworke, or the great stone at the best of the randon 800 paces.and the place to be burned or beaten downe is distant from that peece 600 paces, therefore that peece must be mounted for to doe this exploit at 48 degrees and $\frac{1}{2}$ degree. But if the fireworke or the great stone will flie at the best of the randon 900 paces,and the place to bee burned or beaten downe bee distant from the peece sixe hundred paces, then the saide peece must bee mounted at fortie one degrees and almost $\frac{1}{2}$ of a degree.

And

And when the fireworke or stone will flie at the best of the randon 1000 paces, and the space betweene the peece and the said place doth containe 600 paces,the said peece must be mounted at sixe & thirtie degrees and $\frac{1}{2}$ part of a degree,but for the better vnderstanding hereof marke well this figure following.

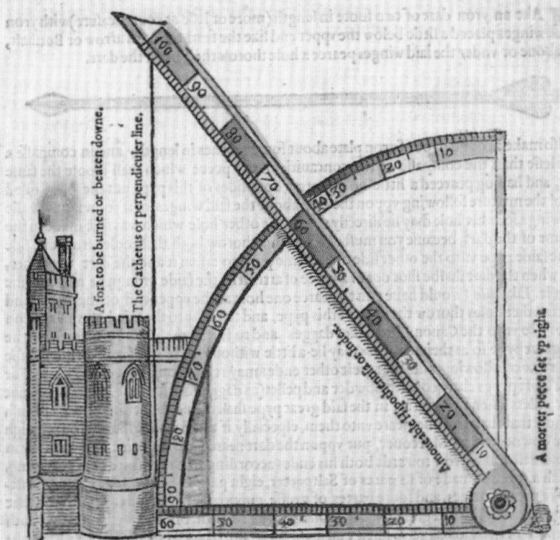

In the said figure there is a Quadrant,and vppon the same with a moueable Hipothenusa or Index a right angled triangle is fashioned. The base of that triangle representing the space betweene the peece & the marke ought to bee diuided into so many equal partes as the said distance betweene the peece and the marke doth containe paces, Likewise the said Hipothenusa or Index representing the way of the shot would be marked with so many of such like equall partes as may shew the number of paces which the peece wil shoote at the best of the randon to be numbred from the center downewardes. Now when a fireworke or a great stone is to be shot out of a morter peece vnto an appointed place, the gunner hauing in a readinesse such a Quadrant,and knowing how much ground his said peece wil shoote at the best of the randon,& also what distance is betweene the peece & the place to be Burned or beaten downe, must mooue vpwardes or downewardes the said Hipothenusa or Index vntill that part of the Hipothenusa which is equall to the number of paces which the peece will shoote at the best randon doth touch the Cathetus or perpendiculer line of the said triangle : And thē he must note the degree vpon the Quadrāt which is touched with the fiduciall line of the sayde Hipothenusa or Index , and mount the sayd morter peece to that degree for to shoote the fireworke or the great stone to the appoynted place.

The

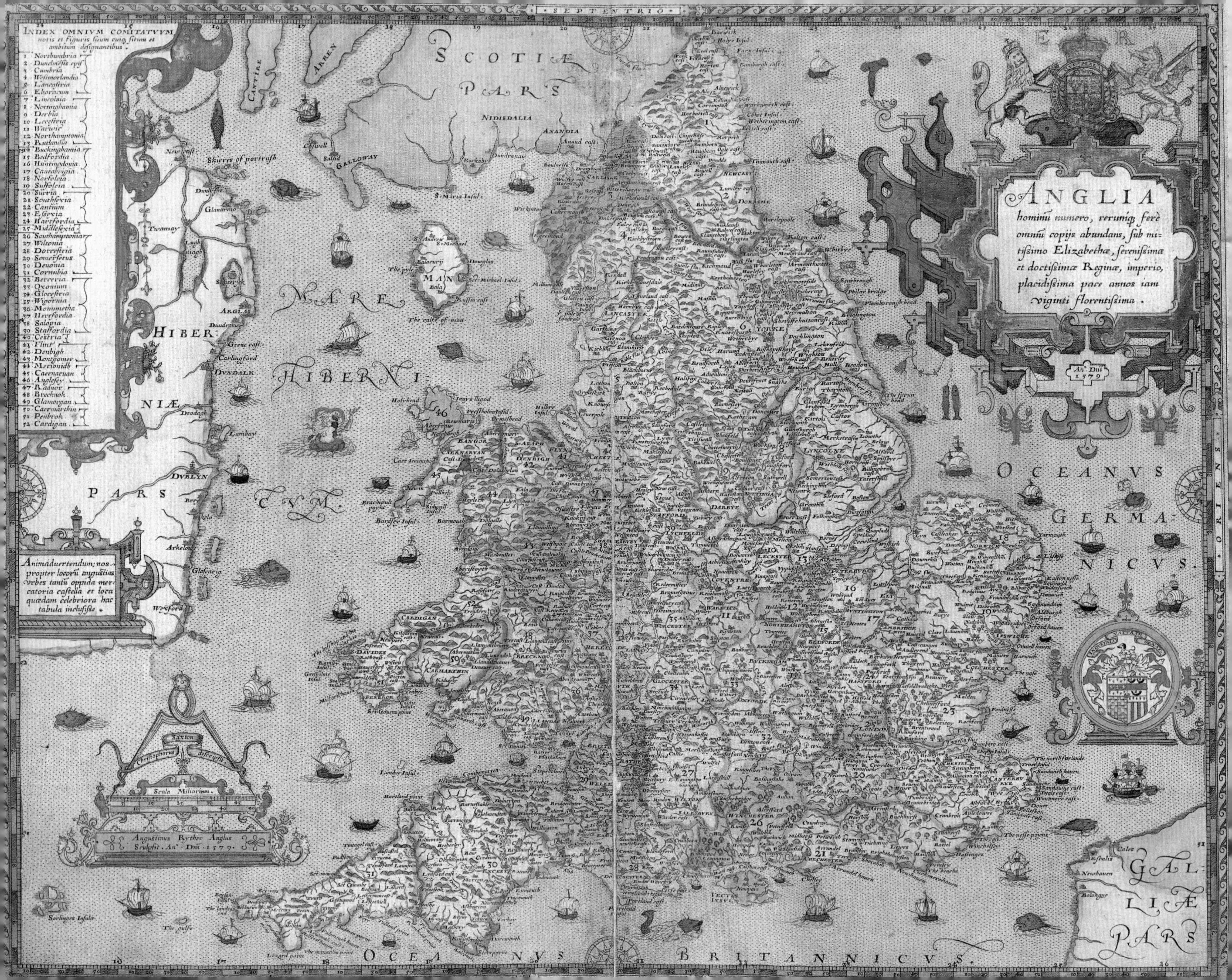
SEPTENTRIO
INDEX OMNIVM COMITATVVM notis et figuris suum cuiq; situm et ambitum designantibus.
1 Northumbria
2 Dunelmēsis epis
3 Cumbria
4 Westmorlandia
5 Lancastria
6 Eboracum
7 Lincolnia
8 Nottinghamia
9 Derbia
10 Leicestria
11 Warwic
12 Northamptonia
13 Rutlandia
14 Buckinghamia
15 Bedfordia
16 Huntingdonia
17 Cantabrigia
18 Norfolcia
19 Suffolcia
20 Surria
21 Southsexia
22 Cantium
23 Essexia
24 Hartfordia
25 Middlesexia
26 Southamptonia
27 Wiltonia
28 Dorcestria
29 Somersetus
30 Deuonia
31 Cornubia
32 Berceria
33 Oxonium
34 Glocestria
35 Wigornia
36 Monumetha
37 Herefordia
38 Salopia
39 Staffordia
40 Cestria
41 Flint
42 Denbigh
43 Montgomer
44 Merionidh
45 Caernaruan
46 Anglesey
47 Radnor
48 Brecknok
49 Glamorgan
50 Caermarthin
51 Penbrok
52 Cardigan
ANGLIA hominū numero, veruniq; ferè omniū copijs abundans, sub mitissimo Elizabethæ, serenissimæ et doctissimæ Reginæ, imperio, placidissima pace annos iam viginti florentissima.
Anº Dñi 1579
Animaduertendum; nos propter locorū angustias vrbes tantū oppida mercatoria castella et loca quædam celebriora hac tabula inclusisse.
Christophorus Saxton descripsit.
Scala Miliarium.
Augustinus Ryther Anglus Sculpsit. Anº Dñi 1579.
SCOTIÆ PARS
HIBERNIÆ PARS
MARE HIBERNICVM
OCEANVS GERMANICVS
OCEANVS BRITANNICVS
GALLIÆ PARS
LONDON
YORKE
CARLISLE
LANCASTER
CHESTER
STAFFORD
LECESTER
COVENTRE
WORCESTER
OXFORDE
BATH
WINCHESTER
CANTERBVRY
NORWICH
IPSWICHE
COLCHESTER
LYNCOLNE
DVBLYN
DVNDALK
MAN

While seafarers were exploring previously unknown lands abroad, an English surveyor named Christopher Saxton pursued a project that was, in its own way, equally daunting—the mapping, for the first time, of an entire nation. This feat was achieved in 1579, with the publication of an atlas by Saxton that charted the towns, rivers, and other features of all of the counties of England and Wales, with the omission of the roads.

Saxton's project, commissioned by Queen Elizabeth's Privy Council, began so quietly that historians are uncertain just when it started, although one tradition suggests the middle of 1573. Certainly it was a multiyear commission, undertaken with the full backing of the government. An official letter Saxton carried into Wales asked local mayors and justices to make sure he was "conducted unto any tower, castle, high place, or hill to view that country," further requesting that he be aided by "two or three honest men such as do best know the country" in each locality. Through a combination of such new survey work and the judicious use of partial existing maps, Saxton created some thirty-four meticulously detailed maps, twenty-five of single counties and others consisting of combinations of counties. After all the counties were completed, he then created an overview map of England and Wales, shown here from an issue of the atlas dating from about 1590. Unlike a modern map, this charming Renaissance image fills the otherwise empty space of the seas with ships, the heads of large swimming animals, and a male figure holding a trident and hugging a mermaid.

Saxton's atlas was not only a cartographic but also a commercial success, selling well and encouraging others to enter the field. John Speed, John Norton, and Michael Drayton—all of whom, like Saxton, were represented in the Folger's 1998 mapping exhibition—were among the many mapmakers who built on and added to Saxton's work, helping to forge Britain's emerging identity as a nation in the process.

Christopher Saxton, Atlas of England and Wales / 1590 (?)

In 1992, on the 500th anniversary of Columbus's arrival in the Americas, the Folger organized *New World of Wonders*, one of the more ambitious exhibitions in its history. Funded by the NEH, the exhibition explored early European images of the Americas and their inhabitants as they were portrayed not only by writers, artists, and engravers, but onstage and in public displays such as masques. In addition to rare books and manuscripts from the Folger's collection, the exhibition included numerous borrowed objects, such as a set of Native American artifacts preserved since the 1600s in a cabinet of curiosities at a library in Paris. Supplementing the display were public lectures (including one, with samples, on the history of chocolate), gallery talks, workshops, and a staged reading of *The Tempest*, in which Prospero's relationship with Caliban echoes the European treatment of New World peoples.

Among the rarities in the exhibition was the Folger's 1590 first edition of Thomas Hariot's *A briefe and true report of the new found land of Virginia*, acquired in 1938 from the estate of Sir Robert Leicester Harmsworth. A cartographer and mathematician, Hariot served as scientific adviser to the 1585–86 Roanoke Island expedition sponsored by Sir Walter Raleigh. During the expedition, he worked closely with the English artist John White in mapping the region and recording information on its plants, animals, and mineral resources, as well as the local population of southeastern Algonquian Indians. On the expedition's return, Hariot's report was published with engravings by Theodor de Bry based on White's drawings. Here, in Hariot's chapter "Their manner of fishynge in Virginia," an engraving depicts methods of catching fish that include nets, interlocking traps, and, in the shallows, the use of spears. Omitting no detail of the watery environment, de Bry renders crabs, turtles, fish, and eels in exquisite detail below the surface of the water.

Both the text and the pictures of this early glimpse of the mid-Atlantic coast proved so fascinating to English and Continental readers that they were widely copied, reappearing in many other publications. In the year 2000, a Folger Institute summer institute on the founding of Jamestown examined the circulation and impact of such images and words, which helped shape the European understanding of the New World.

Thomas Hariot, *A briefe and true report of . . . Virginia* / 1590

XIII.

Their manner of fishynge in Virginia.

THey haue likewiſe a notable way to catche fishe in their Riuers. for whear as they lacke both yron, and ſteele, they faſte vnto their Reedes or longe Rodds, the hollowe tayle of a certaine fishe like to a ſea crabb in ſteede of a poynte, wehr with by nighte or day they ſtricke fishes, and take them opp into their boates. They alſo know how to vſe the prickles, and pricks of other fishes. They alſo make weares, with ſettinge opp reedes or twigges in the water, which they ſoe plant one within a nother, that they growe ſtill narrower, and narrower, as appeareth by this figure. Ther was neuer ſeene amonge vs ſoe cunninge a way to take fish withall, wherof ſondrie ſortes as they fownde in their Riuers vnlike vnto ours. which are alſo of a verye good taſte. Dowbtleſs yt is a pleaſant ſighte to ſee the people, ſomtymes wadinge, and goinge ſomtymes ſailinge in thoſe Riuers, which are shallowe and not deepe, free from all care of heapinge opp Riches for their poſterite, content with their ſtate, and liuinge frendlye together of thoſe thinges which god of his bountye hath giuen vnto them, yet without giuinge hym any thankes according to his deſarte.
So ſauage is this people, and depriued of the true knowledge of god.
For they haue none other then is mentionned before in this worke.

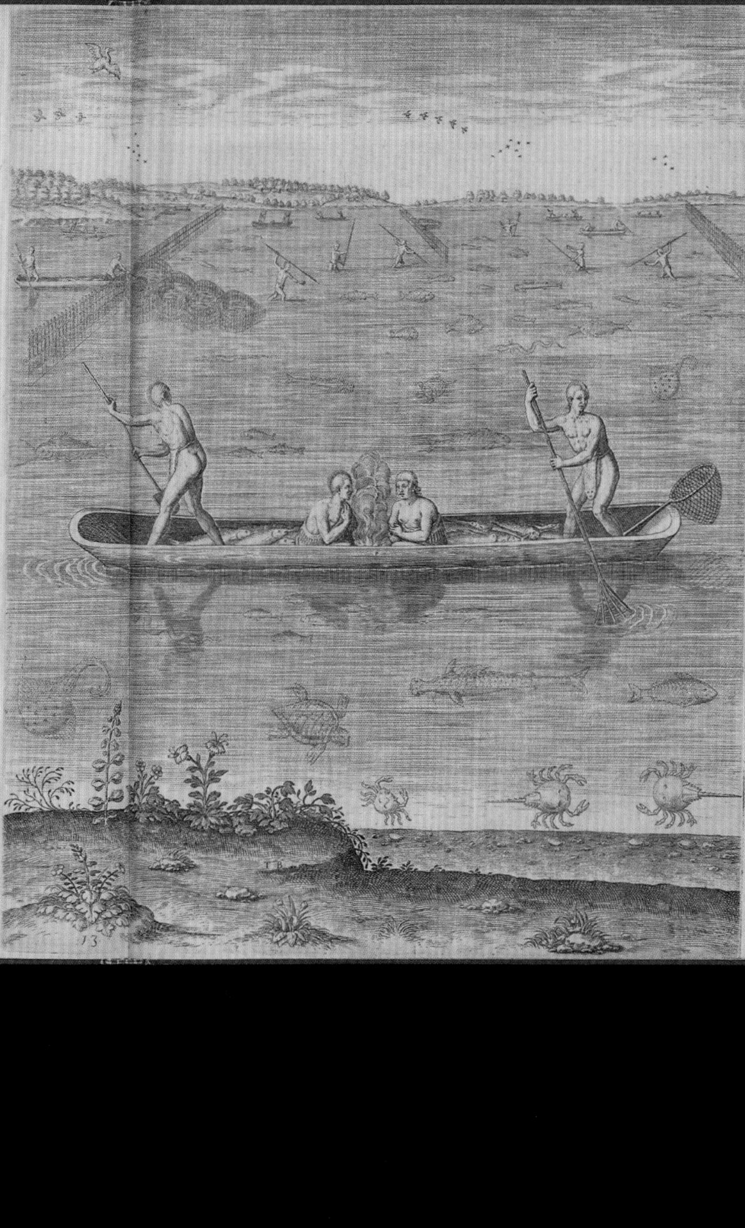

While large, expensive books of the sixteenth and early seventeenth centuries stood a good chance of survival in the private libraries of the wealthy, the printed ephemera of everyday life were both more common and less likely to be preserved. Saved by some chance of history, documents like those shown here—both of which deal with the recurring menace of the plague—are today among the rarities of the Folger's collection.

The bubonic plague was a fact of life in the early modern age, having revisited Europe and the British Isles often since its first appearance in Sicily in 1347. Periodically, it reached crisis proportions. In the twelve months beginning in December 1592, almost 11,000 people died of infection in London, and public life ground to a halt. With the theatres closed, Shakespeare is thought to have written his epic poems Venus and Adonis *and* The Rape of Lucrece *during this time. While no one knew what caused the plague, the government-issued booklet at near right sought to contain it with a variety of regulations. The most severe of these imposed a quarantine on any affected house built close to others, requiring that residents be closed in (with provision for supplies) until five weeks after the last death from plague in that home. Anticipating modern public-health strategies that stress prevention, the booklet also shares "sundry good rules and easie medicines" to ward off the plague, offering a mix of sense and nonsense to modern eyes. Suggestions included improving the air circulation in houses; filling them with fragrant scents; and eating such "medicines" as buttered, vinegar-soaked bread sprinkled with cinnamon.*

The plague bill at far right, an official form filled out by local officials, provides a glimpse of another outbreak seventeen years later. Such weekly bills provided important statistics that gave government leaders a sense of where and how fast the plague was spreading. This one indicates 364 deaths, of which 177 were due to plague, in London in the last week of August 1609—the worst year for plague in the twenty-two-year reign of James I. In that year, actors and playwrights were left with little occupation as the theatres closed once again.

Elizabeth I, *Orders, . . . by her Majestie, and her privie Counsell* / 1592
Bill of mortality, London / 1609

ORDERS, THOVGHT MEETE
by her Maiestie, and her priuie Counsell, to be
executed throughout the Counties of this Realme,
in such Townes, Villages, and other places, as are, or
may be hereafter infected with the plague, for the
stay of further increase of
the same.

Also, an aduise set downe vpon her Maiesties expresse commaundement, by the best learned in Physicke within this Realme, containing sundry good rules and easie medicines, without charge to the meaner sort of people, aswell for the preseruation of her good Subiectes from the plague before infection, as for the curing and ordering of them after they shall be infected.

Imprinted at London by the Deputies
of Christopher Barker, Printer to the
Queenes most excellent
Maiestie.

An. Do. 1592.

1609.

From the 24 [illegible]
to the 31. there
died in London, the Liberties, } 364
the out parishes, & the pesthouse
whereof of the Plague ——— 77
Christned in all those places —— 123
Parishes clear 73 parishes infec. 48
[illegible]

THE THYRDE DAYES *Discourse, of* Rapier *and* Dagger.

Luke.

I Know not certainly, whether it hath been my earnest desire to encounter you, that raisde me earlier this morning than my accustomed houre, or to be assertained of some doubtfull questions, which yester-night were proposed by some gentlemen and my selfe, in discourse

course of armes: for they helde, that although a man learne perfectly the dritta, riuersa, the stoccata, the imbroccata, the punta riuersa, with eche seuerall motion of the body, yet when they hap to come to single fight, where the triall of true valour must ende the quarrell, they vtterly forget all their former practises. Therefore would I request of you, (if you so please) to know your opinion, whether in single fight a man can forget his vsuall wardes, or vse them then with as much dexteritie and courage as he accustomed in play.

V. It is very likely, that many are of this opinion, for there are fewe or none that in cause of quarrell when they come as we tearme it to buckling, but suffer themselues to be ouercome with fury, and so neuer remẽber their arte: such effect choller worketh. And it may be some being timerous and full of pusillanimity, (which is euer father to feare) are so scarred out of their wits, that they seeme men amazed and voide of sence. Or some may be taken in the humor of drinke, or with diuers other occasions, that may enfeeble their vnderstanding. And by these reasons well may they forget in fight, what they learned in play: but in them in whome no such effectes are predominant, neither are assailed with such accidentes, they behaue themselues discreetely, and are not distempered with any such perturbations: and besides this, I haue seen many that being fearfull by nature, through dayly practise haue become couragious, and alwaies so continued. Neither is it possible, but in practise he should obtaine courage and encrease his valour more then before.

L. But to what end doe you teach such skill, if it be scarse secure, and hard to performe.

V.

As the business of printing took off in the 1500s, handbooks of all kinds became increasingly common. One popular subject was fencing—an important social skill for gentlemen, whether or not it was ever required in earnest. The manual shown here is by Vincentio Saviolo, an Italian fencing master who settled in London around 1590. His Practise, *written in 1558 but first translated into English in this 1595 edition, is in effect two books in one. The first part, from which these pages are taken, is written as a dialogue, and deals with the use of the rapier and dagger. The second part, "Of Honor and Honorable Quarrels," is adapted from an Italian work on dueling by Girolamo Muzio.*

Such methods of quarreling and use of the dagger and rapier appear prominently in Romeo and Juliet, *one of Shakespeare's earliest tragedies, which has been dated to the period 1595–96. Writing in* Shakespeare Quarterly *in 1994, Joan Ozark Holmer argued that the technical terminology of rapier fencing does not appear in Shakespeare's plays until after Saviolo's manual was published in translation. Shakespeare also uses more of Saviolo's Italian terminology (including such terms as* passado, punto riverso, *and* alla stoccata*) in* Romeo and Juliet *than in any other play.*

Quite aside from that specific example, duels and stage combat were common enough in Elizabethan drama that Saviolo's book and other manuals were of immediate help to contemporary actors choreographing their own staged fights. Theatre companies have continued to rely on many of the same texts ever since. During the Folger Theatre's 1999 production of Hamlet, *a lobby display by fight director Brad Waller incorporated a wealth of images from Renaissance fencing manuals, a graphic illustration of how images and instruction from the past inform the staged productions of today.*

Vincentio Saviolo, *Vincentio Saviolo his practise* / 1595

The Folger collection has always been rich in sixteenth- and seventeenth-century music, in part because of Henry Folger's own musical bent; a boy soprano who became a baritone, he sang in the Amherst glee club and choir, and later supported amateur choral societies. This interest, combined with the many incidental songs in Shakespeare's plays, led Folger to collect early modern music in both printed and manuscript forms. Later acquisitions, including fifty rare music volumes included in the Harmsworth collection, built on this foundation, forming a useful resource for students and performers of Renaissance music.

One composer especially well represented is the English lutenist John Dowland. This setting of a Fulke Greville sonnet, "Who ever thinks or hopes of love for love," is from the 1597 first edition of Dowland's First Booke of Songes, an immediate success that was reprinted at least four times over the next sixteen years. Like other songs in the book, this one is arranged so it can be sung either by a solo voice and lute or as a four-part air. The parts are oriented in different directions so that the singers and the lutenist can sit around a table; this way of presenting the piece also means that it fits onto two facing pages, avoiding the need to turn the page in midsong.

Dowland was appointed lutenist at the court of the Danish king, Christian IV, in about 1598. Despite this success, however, he was unable to fulfill his consuming ambition to receive a royal appointment from the English court until fourteen years later, in October 1612, when he was made one of King James I's lutenists. By then, the veteran musician had published several other collections of his works, some purely instrumental. His music continues to be printed and enjoyed today.

John Dowland, *The First Booke of Songes* / 1597

II.
CANTVS.
Ho euer thinks or hopes of loue for loue, or who belou'd in Cupids
lawes doth glorie, who ioyes in vowes or vowes not to remoue, who by this light-god
hath not ben made sorry: Let him see me ecclipsed from my son with darke clowdes of an
earth: ij. Quite ouer runne.

Who thinks that sorrowes felte, desires hidden,
Or humble faith in constant honor arm'd,
Can keepe loue from the friut that is forbidden,
Who thinks that change is by entreatie charm'ds
Looking on me let him know loues delights
Are treasures hid in caues, but kept by Sprights.

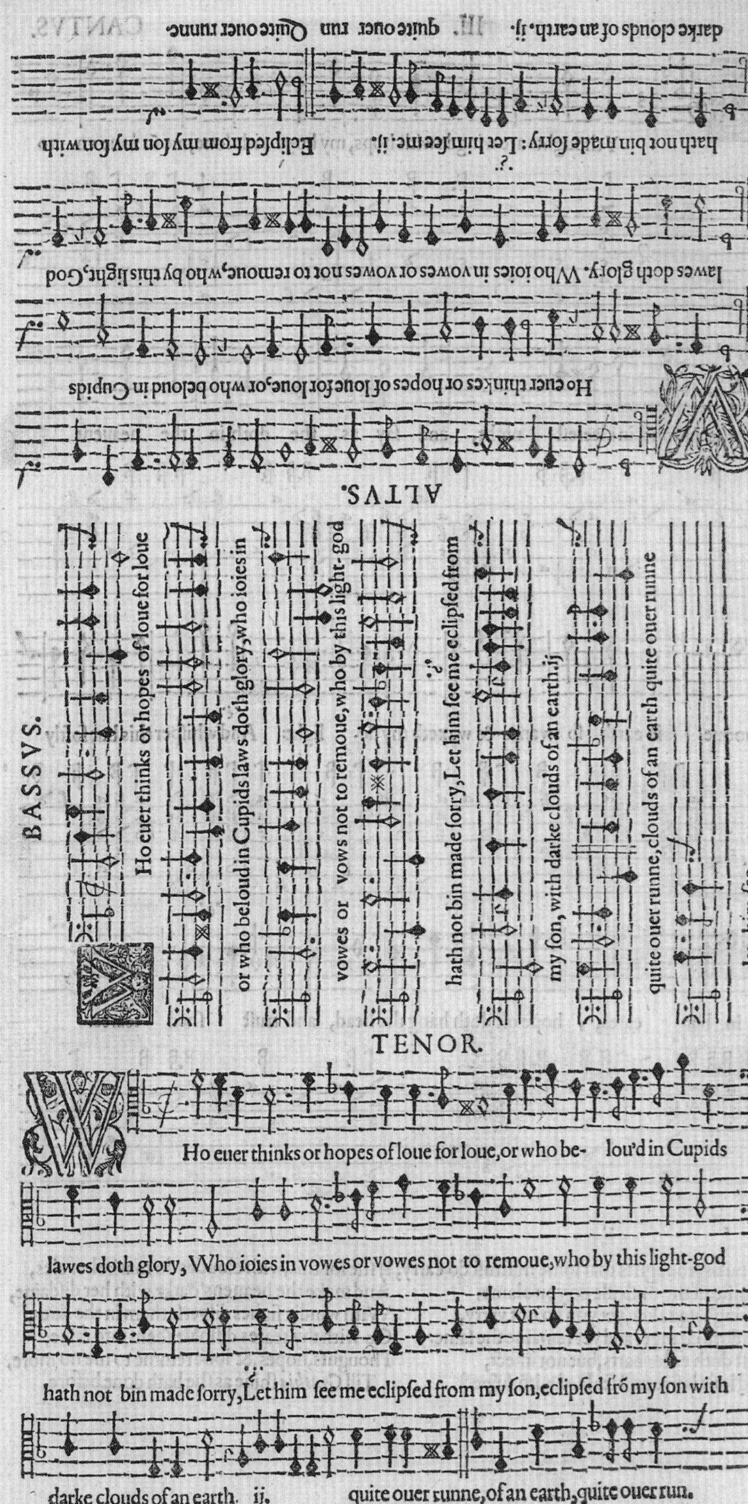
CANTVS.
darke clouds of an earth. ij. III. quite ouer run Quite ouer runne.
hath not bin made sorry: Let him see me. ij. Eclipsed from my son my son with
lawes doth glory. Who ioies in vowes or vowes not to remoue, who by this light, God
Ho euer thinkes or hopes of loue for loue, or who belou'd in Cupids
ALTVS.
BASSVS.
Ho euer thinks or hopes of loue for loue
or who belou'd in Cupids laws doth glory, who ioies in
vowes or vows not to remoue, who by this light-god
hath not bin made sorry, Let him see me eclipsed from
my son, with darke clouds of an earth. ij
quite ouer runne, clouds of an earth quite ouer runne
let him see.
TENOR.
Ho euer thinks or hopes of loue for loue, or who be- lou'd in Cupids
lawes doth glory, Who ioies in vowes or vowes not to remoue, who by this light-god
hath not bin made sorry, Let him see me eclipsed from my son, eclipsed frō my son with
darke clouds of an earth. ij. quite ouer runne, of an earth, quite ouer run.

Built in Padua in 1598, the instrument shown here is a lute from the workshop of Michielle Harton—as one can read, in good light, on the interior of the lute, and as indicated by the initials on the face of the instrument. A beautiful example of both workmanship and design, its construction incorporates thirty-five ribs of shaded yew in alternating brown heartwood and white sapwood. The poplar neck and beechwood pegbox are veneered with ebony and ivory. Inside, vellum strips reinforce the joints.

The lute is one of several instruments in the Folger collection that are of particular interest because they were purchased in late 1930 from Arnold Dolmetsch, a leading figure in the revival of early music performance at the beginning of the twentieth century. Originally, the lute shown here had nine courses—the term course *refers either to paired strings that are played together or to a single string. During its restoration, however, Dolmetsch gave the instrument the ten courses called for in the repertoire of the late Elizabethan period and subsequent eras. Perhaps because of Henry Folger's death earlier that year, the acquisition of the Dolmetsch instruments was considered worthy of a news story in the* New York Times.

Early modern music has been performed at the Folger ever since, becoming a regular feature of the institution in 1977 with the formation of the library's resident ensemble, the Folger Consort. Although the Harton lute is not generally used in actual performance, Consort members employ their own lutes, recorders, harps, violas da gamba, and other period instruments to play music from the Middle Ages to the Renaissance, continuing the dream that Dolmetsch did so much to foster.

Lute / ca. 1598

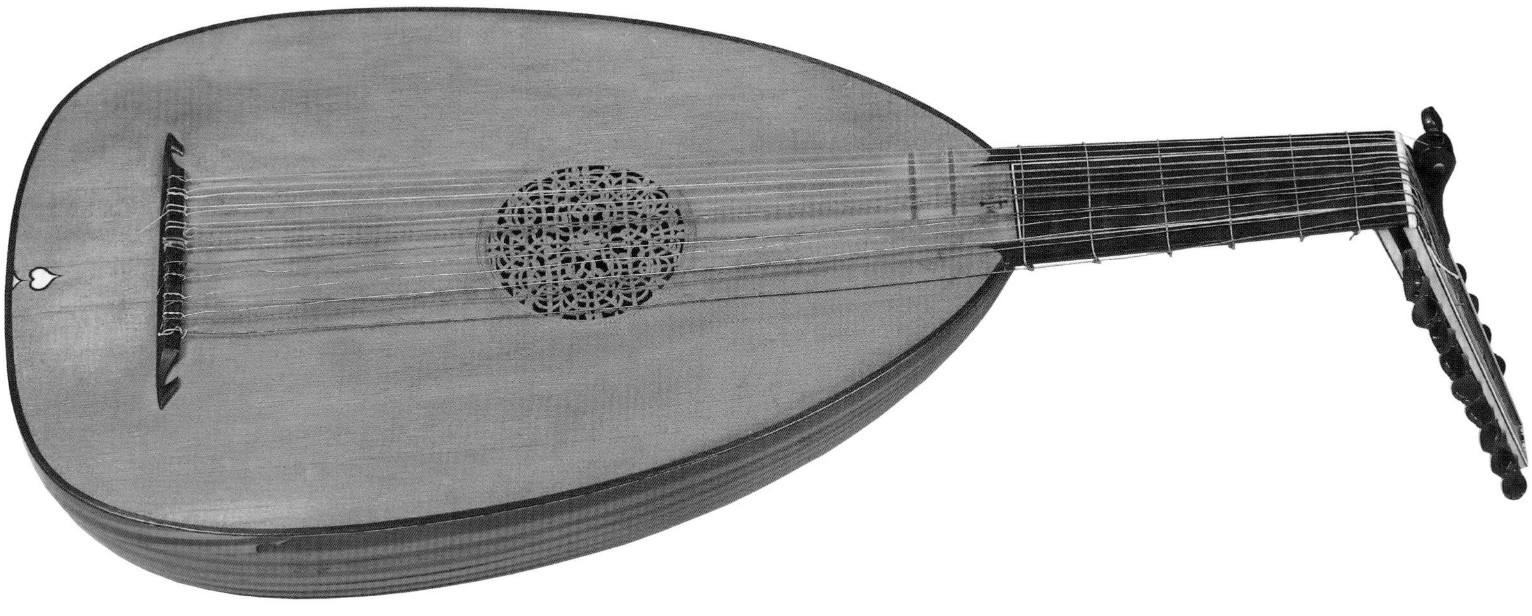

In April 1598, Hugh Alley, a government informer who styled himself a "Citizen and Plaisterer of London," presented to the Lord Mayor an illustrated handwritten account of commercial abuses in the city markets. Entitled A Caveatt for the Citty of London, *it has been seen by many researchers as a manuscript with a mission, and one that was apparently accomplished: a little more than a year later, Alley landed a newly created job as a market overseer.*

Although Alley himself has been called "bumptious and meddlesome" by one modern scholar, his self-righteous booklet offers a comprehensive look at thirteen London markets, each of which specialized in certain goods. Escheape (or Eastcheap) Market, shown here, was a meat market with butchers' shops along both sides of the street, and Alley's depiction suggests that stock was driven there for slaughter. Within the image, a labeled pillar highlights the crime of "engrossing," buying up all or most of a good in order to resell it at a higher price. With each market, Alley included respectful portraits of the officials in charge: in this case, Sir Henry Billingsley, an alderman who as a former mayor was entitled to wear a gold chain, and, to Sir Henry's right, his deputy Robert Thomas.

Privately held and little known before the 1920s, Alley's Caveatt *has come to be appreciated for what it reveals about ordinary life outside the high culture of the court, offering, as one researcher put it, "a new look at what might seem familiar territory." In 1988, a team of scholars, assisted by Folger curator of manuscripts Laetitia Yeandle, reproduced the manuscript in an annotated edition. Seven years later, Alley's manuscript went on display in the* Elizabethan Households *exhibition, held in conjunction with an NEH-sponsored Folger Institute conference on* Material London; *that joint endeavor also produced a packet of images for use in college classrooms, a book of scholarly essays, and a popular exhibition catalog. By the twenty-first century, several of Alley's illustrations were playing a role in the Folger's multimedia exhibition,* Seven Ages of Man.

Hugh Alley, *Caveatt for the Citty of London* / 1598

CANDELWEEKE STREETE

ESCHEAPE MARKET

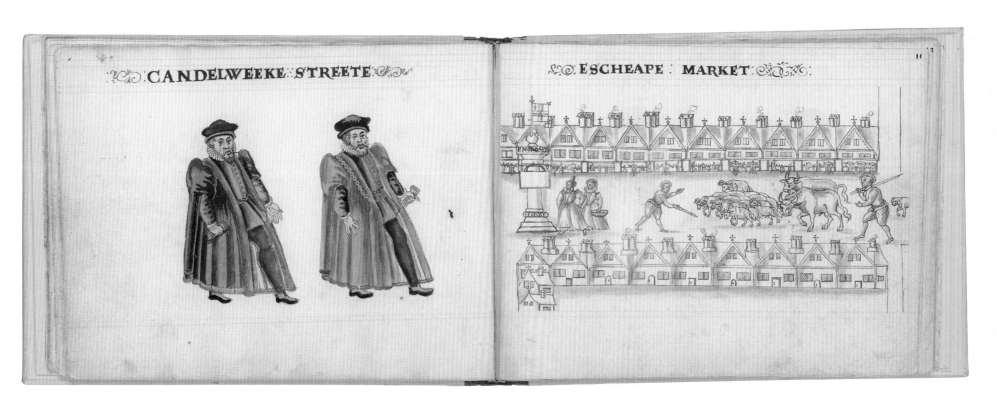

To make a Hagis.

Take a calves Chadarne, and parboile it, when it is cold minsle it fine, with a pound of Beefe suet, a penny-lofe grated, some rose-mary, time, winter-savery, and penyriall, of all a small handfull, a little Cloves, Mace, nutmegge, and Cinamon, one quarter of a pound of Currence, a little sugar, a little salt, rose-water, all these mixt together, wett with 16 yolkes of Eggs, put it in a sheeps panch, and boyle it.

To make Plague water.

Take Cowslip flowers, Redwerte, Roman wormewood, Mugwort, Horshound, Pimpernell, Rice, Sage, Saladine, Mother worte, Wormwood, Burnot, Turmentall, Sorrell, Ellicompaine-rootes, ffeather few, Balme, Dragon, Angelico, Marrigolds, Rose-mary halfe a pound, Broome may weeds, Scabius, Egrimony, Bittony, Cardis, Endiff, Sotherne-wood, The Birch lott, Macthaline, Sinkfall, of each a quarter of a pound, shred them very small, and lay them a steepe 24 hours in 3 quarts of white wine,

Then still them in a Limbick, or still, then save the first as strongest, and soe a 2 and 3 sort.

An Excellent Plaster to keepe a woman from miscarring.

Take of the choisest Mastick 4 drames, gum Elemie halfe an Ounce, Burgandie pitch 3 drames, Benjamin, and Dragons blade, of each 2 drames, melt all these, and straine them, and add to them 2 drames of the Trochises called Alipta Muscata, one drame of Venice Turpintine a little boyled, 3 drames of the plaster of red lead made of Oile of Quinces, halfe an Ounce of Bees-wax, one drame and halfe of Indian Balsome, 2 scruples of Oile of Spike, make these all into one plaster, and spread there of upon your leather, on for the region of yo:r back, and another for the lower Region of the belly.

Sirrope of Violetts.

Take a reasonable quantity of Violetts, and pick them, then weigh them, and take to a quarterne of Violatts halfe a pound of sugar, and halfe a pint of

While the great events of public life are richly documented, the domestic world of the Tudor and Stuart eras can be a more elusive subject. Handwritten and printed "receipt," or recipe, books are one source of important clues to how household affairs were conducted, and the Folger has many examples. The pages shown here are from a particularly early manuscript that has been dated to about 1610. Compiled by Mistress Sarah Longe, a middle-class Elizabethan housewife, the entire book was transcribed into printed form in the 1999 Folger catalog for Fooles and Fricassees, *an exhibition that grew out of a Folger Institute summer seminar two years earlier, "Food History and Food Theories, 1500–1700."*

Longe's book is typical in that it freely mingles culinary and medicinal recipes, reflecting a time when health was still primarily a domestic concern. These pages, for example, include recipes for haggis, preventives against the plague and the risk of miscarriage, and sugared syrup of violets, which was sometimes used medicinally. The haggis recipe calls for sixteen egg yolks, suggesting the scale of cookery in a day when meals had to feed a household of servants as well as the extended family. The book's early date is more unusual, since literacy was an uncommon accomplishment for a middle-class woman in the early 1600s. It is remarkable that a woman of Sarah Longe's background was able to record an entire book. She and some other, unidentified writers—probably, subsequent members of the family, who may have handed the book down—also created three indexes (for preserves and conserves, cookery, and medicine).

Every year, the Folger's education and public programs division organizes a series of highly participatory family programs for local parents and children, and often the workshops are tied to exhibitions or stage productions then under way. In the case of the Fooles and Fricassees *exhibition, docent Frances Owens created a family cooking adventure, in which "foole" (a cooked fruit dessert with cream or custard, served cold) was one of many foods prepared during a Saturday program called "Play the Cook."*

Sarah Longe, recipe book / 1610

In the 1600s, English printers produced a growing number of travel guides to provide Englishmen journeying to the Continent with practical advice; today, these works offer modern researchers a wealth of information not only about the places described but also about English attitudes toward them. Then as now, a traveler's memoir in which the author mocks his own difficulties abroad was a surefire recipe for a hit. One fine example of that approach is the book shown here, Coryats Crudities, *which has been called the first travel guide printed in England. Published in 1611, this popular work offers an insouciant but fact-filled account of Thomas Coryate's journey—largely on foot—through France and northern Italy to Venice, and then back by way of Switzerland, the Rhine valley, and the Low Countries. By his own account Coryate visited forty-five cities in about 140 days.*

Coryate, who called himself the "Odcombian legstretcher" after his provincial hometown of Odcombe, was an adventurer of no mean wit who played a self-mocking part in the inner circle of King James's son Prince Henry. Remarkably, he embarked on his brisk tour of Europe in 1608 with little if any grasp of French, Italian, or German—a fact that sometimes created difficulties. But with Latin and some Greek, he could communicate with any well-educated European. The breakneck speed of Coryate's journey across Europe explains his self-deprecatory title, Crudities, *from the French meaning of the term as a piece of raw food that could, as he notes, be "hastily gobled."*

The title page, engraved by William Hole, effectively captures the tone of Coryate's book, showing the author seasick during the passage to Calais at upper left and, in the detail shown here, pelted with eggs by a Venetian courtesan as he flees in a gondola. Yet Crudities *also provides thorough and comprehensive reports on the towns and cities Coryate visited, from the inscriptions on local monuments to the details of everyday life. Among the latter is the first written English reference to that future British icon, the umbrella—then in use by the Italians as a parasol.*

Thomas Coryate, *Coryats Crudities* / 1611

E
F

CORYATS
Crudities
Hastily gobled vp in five
Moneths trauells in France,
Sauoy, Italy, Rhetia comonly
called the Grisons country, Hel-
uetia alias Switzerland, some
parts of high Germany, and the
Netherlands;
Newly digested in the hungry aire
of ODCOMBE in the County of
Somerset, & now dispersed to the
nourishment of the trauelling Mem-
bers of this Kingdome.

Little is known about the watercolors shown here, which belong to a larger group held at the Folger that has been dated to the time of James I. The artist is anonymous, as is the occasion for this wealth of detail. The costumed figures, as well as the nameless lovers, may have been part of a "friendship album," or album amicorum, *an early variation on the autograph book, into which pictures like these were often copied. Representing Continental as well as English dress and grooming, the pictures have much to tell both social historians and designers of theatrical costumes.*

As the images show, clothing of this period was highly layered. The woman at far left, for example, wears red undersleeves inside her hanging sleeves, while the seated woman has a handsome underskirt, and her companion's doublet and sleeves are slashed to reveal a blue shirt inside. Men and women of the upper and middle classes proclaimed the relative prosperity of the times by wearing materials such as silks and velvets, dyed in a rainbow of colors, often with touches of gold adding to the display. Gold embroidery ornaments the clothes worn by both of the standing figures, and the female lover has a gold purse. Typically for the period, all four figures wear ruffs, in a variety of styles.

Both of the women wear gowns with slimming bodices and padded sleeves; each has her hair dressed over a pad to give it added bulk and structure, and the woman being wooed has a wheel farthingale meant to extend her gown outward at the hips. For their part, the men are dressed in doublets and matching trunk hose with garters at the knee and colored stockings; both have moustaches (the standing figure also sports a beard) and are wearing swords. To emphasize the intimacy of the scene at near left, however, the male lover has removed his hat, something men normally did not do in public—indoors or out—except in the presence of the sovereign.

Details of miniatures from the time of James I / early 1600s

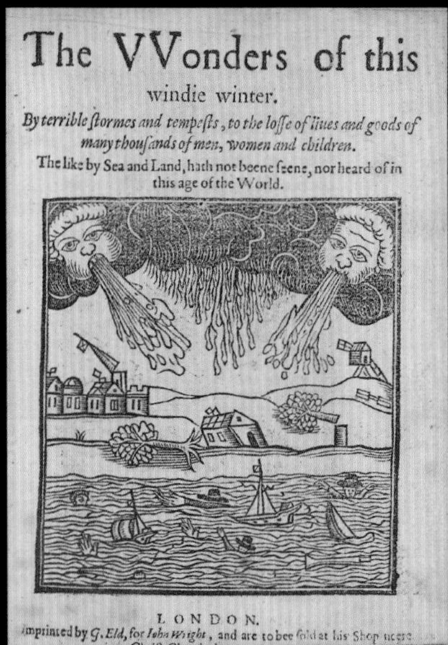

The VVonders of this windie winter.

By terrible stormes and tempests, to the losse of liues and goods of many thousands of men, women and children.

The like by Sea and Land, hath not beene seene, nor heard of in this age of the World.

LONDON.

Imprinted by *G. Eld*, for *Iohn Wright*, and are to bee sold at his Shop neere

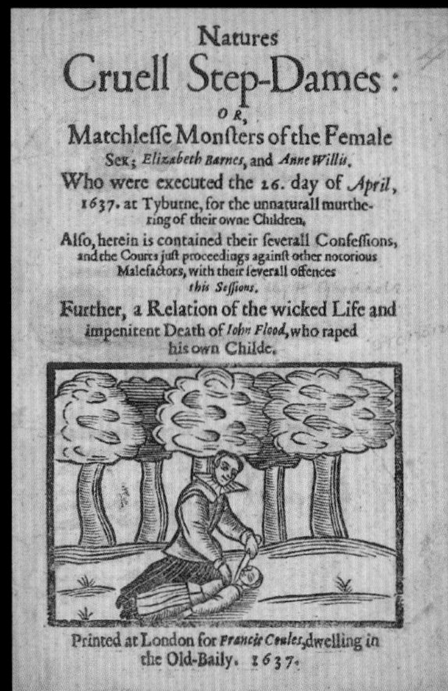

Natures Cruell Step-Dames: *OR,* Matchlesse Monsters of the Female Sex; *Elizabeth Barnes*, and *Anne Willis*.

Who were executed the 26. day of *April*, 1637. at Tyburne, for the unnaturall murthering of their owne Children.

Also, herein is contained their severall Confessions, and the Courts just proceedings against other notorious Malefactors, with their severall offences *this Sessions*.

Further, a Relation of the wicked Life and impenitent Death of *Iohn Flood*, who raped his own Childe.

Printed at London for *Francis Coules*, dwelling in the Old-Baily. 1637.

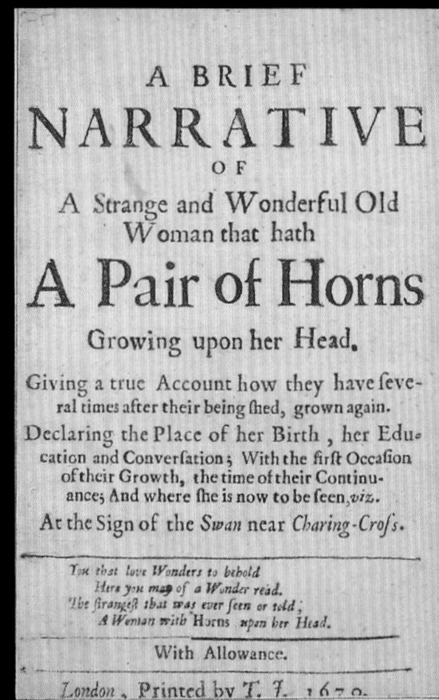

A BRIEF NARRATIVE OF A Strange and Wonderful Old Woman that hath A Pair of Horns Growing upon her Head.

Giving a true Account how they have several times after their being shed, grown again.

Declaring the Place of her Birth, her Education and Conversation; With the first Occasion of their Growth, the time of their Continuance; And where she is now to be seen, *viz.*

At the Sign of the *Swan* near *Charing-Cross*.

You that love Wonders to behold
Here you may of a Wonder read.
The strangest that was ever seen or told;
A Woman with Horns upon her Head.

With Allowance.

London, Printed by T. J. 1670.

A Short and Serious NARRATIVE OF LONDONS Fatal Fire, WITH ITS Diurnal and Nocturnal Progression, From Sunday Morning (being) the Second of SEPTEMBER, *Anno Mirabili* 1666. Until Wednesday Night following.

A POEM.

AS ALSO *Londons* Lamentation to her Regardless Passengers.

With Allowance.

LONDON: Printed for *Peter Dring*, at the Sign of the *Beaver* in the *Strand*, between *Ivy-bridge* and *Durham-Yard*, who formerly lived at the *Sun* in the *Poultrey* in *London*. 1667.

From a horned lady and an assortment of child murderers to winter storms and the catastrophic Great Fire of London, the subjects of the "newsbooks" shown here typify the explosion of domestic news in seventeenth-century England. Small, quickly printed pamphlets that ranged in length from as few as four to as many as forty pages, newsbooks were only one form of popular journalism. In 1996, an exhibition called Yesterday's News *showcased a selection of newsbooks, broadsides, and ballads from the Folger collection in a display that drew considerable attention from modern-day reporters and broadcasters.*

The texts of these and other newsbooks show the predecessors of today's journalists hard at work buttressing their accounts with specific details—the classic who, what, when, where, and why. "It may be, upon the first View of the Title of this short Relation, thou wilt throw it down with all the carelessness imaginable, supposing it to be but an idle and impertinent Fiction," begins the 1678 account of the horned lady, before describing her as the seventy-six-year-old widow of one Henry Davies and providing a London address where doubters might go to see her. Her horns, "in shew and substance much like a Ramms Horns, solid and wrinckled," were a medical misfortune that the anonymous writer attributed to "wearing a straight Hat." The hat, it is reported, led to sores from which horns grew on four separate occasions, for which the years are provided.

Unlike any modern-day journalistic report is Samuel Wiseman's 1667 newsbook on the Great Fire of London, which is presented in rhymed verse. By Monday morning—two days after high winds started the fire—Wiseman writes, "The spreading Flames now conquer all they meet, / And walk in Triumph through the frighted streets, / And finding in their fury such success, / Outragious grew, and become merciless." A final list of statistics—273 acres laid waste inside the city, 130,200 houses burned, 89 parishes and churches burned, 11 parishes remaining—lends point to the horror.

The Wonders of this windie winter / 1613
Natures Cruell Step-Dames / 1637
An account of an old woman with horns / 1678
A Short and Serious Narrative of Londons Fatal Fire / 1667

Householders and other spectators fill the balconies—and a few rooftops—of Cheapside in this splendid hand-colored scene from Jean Puget de la Serre's Histoire de l'entrée de la reyne mere du roy trés-Chrestien, dans la Grande-Bretaigne, *of which a detail is shown on pages 130–131. Published in London in 1639, the French-language book records the visit of sixty-five-year-old Marie de Médicis, the queen mother of France and the mother-in-law of England's Charles I. This copy, bound in red goatskin, bears the arms of its first owner, Cardinal Jules Mazarin, who succeeded Cardinal Richelieu as the de facto ruler of France in 1642.*

In the early modern age, royal visits, births, and funerals were great occasions marked by parades, fireworks, bands, masques, and other festive celebrations. Books like this one helped readers visualize such events before the days of instantaneous television reporting. Today, the details of the illustrations reveal much about the daily life of the period as well. Here, the background offers a good view of London's closely crowded half-timbered houses before the Great Fire of 1666.

The Folger now holds some 55,000 volumes from between 1475 and 1700 that were either printed—like this one—in England, or printed in English on the Continent, making it the third-largest repository for such books in the world, after the British and Bodleian Libraries. At the turn of the millennium, a four-year recataloging project made nearly all of the bibliographic records of the Folger's early English books available online.

Jean Puget de la Serre, *Histoire de l'entrée de la reyne mere . . . dans la Grande-Bretaigne* / 1639

ENTREE ROYALLE DE LA REYNE MERE DU ROY TRES-CHRESTIEN DANS LA VILLE DE LONDRES:

ENTREE ROYALLE DE LA REYNE MERE DV R

RES-CHRESTIEN DANS LA VILLE DE LONDRES:

Perhaps no other artist recorded so many aspects of seventeenth-century English life as Wenceslaus Hollar, a Bohemian who spent most of his forty-year career in England. Prolific and meticulous, Hollar has been compared to a modern-day photojournalist in his careful documentation of the contemporary scene. His works include fashion plates and portraits of prominent figures, landscapes and maps, renditions of ships and buildings, and even crude newsbook illustrations. Some provide the only accurate images of parts of London before the Great Fire, while others are the sole surviving copies of lost works by such artists as Van Dyck, Raphael, and Holbein. The Folger houses more than 1,400 examples of his work.

Although he produced drawings and watercolors, Hollar is known primarily for his carefully detailed etchings, of which some 150 examples were presented in the 1996–97 exhibition Impressions of Wenceslaus Hollar. *Several were works newly attributed to the artist. Etching is a delicate art that was a perfect vehicle for Hollar's fascination with detail. The exhibition included a rolling press, tools, and plates that would have been used in the etching and printing process.*

Among the considerable range of Hollar etchings on display were the three portraits shown here, representative of the growing number of ethnic groups to be found in England and the Continent during the age of exploration. The figure labeled as a twenty-three-year-old American Indian has been identified by researchers as Jacques, a Munsee Delaware man transported from the Dutch colony of New Netherland in 1644, about a year before Hollar etched his portrait. (In a typical usage of the day, the colony is referred to incorrectly as Virginia in the incorporated text.) Hollar's carefully detailed image has been called the first European print from life of a Native American. In the same year that Hollar created it, he also produced this portrait of a young African woman, probably a servant in Antwerp. His etching of a young African man may date from the same year.

Wenceslaus Hollar, *Unus Americanus ex Virginia* / 1645
Wenceslaus Hollar, portrait of a young African man / 1645 (?)
Wenceslaus Hollar, portrait of a young African woman / 1645

Americanus ex
Virginia. Aetat 23
W. Hollar ad vivum
delin: et fecit 1645

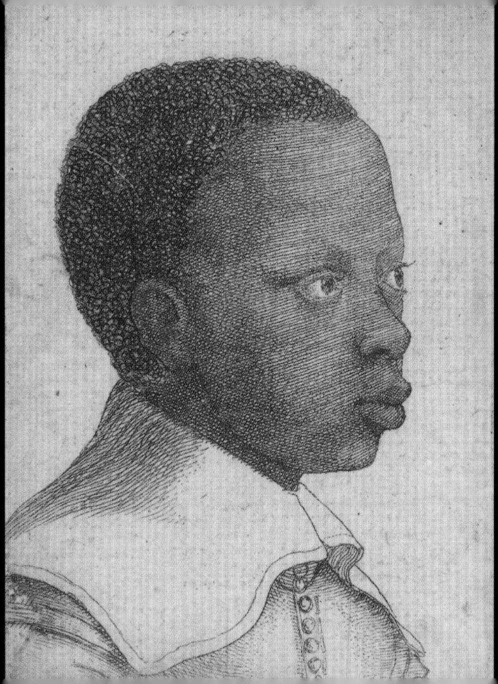

W. Hollar fecit
Antverpie A° 1645

One of the most important volumes in the Folger's holdings of early English scientific thought is this 1687 first edition of Sir Isaac Newton's Philosophiae naturalis Principia Mathematica (Mathematical Principles of Natural Philosophy). *A fundamental work on the laws of motion and gravitation, the* Principia *has been called the greatest work of exact science ever published. Only between 250 and 400 copies of the first edition were printed by England's premier scientific organization of the day, the Royal Society. The Folger's copy is thought to be one of the rarer "first issues" within that group.*

Even that small number of books was produced only through the generosity of the British astronomer Edmund Halley, a man of modest means who underwrote the cost of printing and saw the book through publication. It was also Halley who suggested the use of woodcut diagrams, which could be set on the same page as the text, rather than inconvenient separate plates. In the opening shown here, one such diagram illustrates a proposition on the motion of very small bodies that appears in the first major portion of the book.

In 1972, the same year it acquired the Principia, *the Folger also purchased an extremely rare 1711 edition of* Analysis per quantitatum series, *Newton's explanation of differential calculus. Other Folger holdings of Newtoniana include the definitive 1713 second edition of the* Principia *and the 1730 fourth edition of still another breakthrough book,* Opticks; *the text of the latter is said to incorporate Newton's final revisions for the work, prepared just before his death in 1727. Considerably less central to the scientist's work, but of interest to historians, is* Tables for Renewing & Purchasing of the Leases of Cathedral-Churches and Colleges *(1686). Newton's chief connection with this work may be the printed statement that it was he who checked the accuracy of the tables by means of calculus.*

Sir Isaac Newton, *Principia Mathematica* / 1687

te quam minima O, & ordinatim applicatam $\overline{A+O}|^{\frac{m}{n}}$ resolvo in Seriem infinitam $A^{\frac{m}{n}} + \frac{n}{m} O A^{\frac{m-n}{n}} + \frac{mm-mn}{2nn} O^2 A^{\frac{m-2n}{n}}$ &c. atq; hujus termino in quo O duarum est dimensionum, id est termino $\frac{mm-mn}{2nn} O^2 A^{\frac{m-2n}{n}}$ vim proportionalem esse suppono. Est igitur vis quæsita ut $\frac{mm-mn}{nn} A^{\frac{m-2n}{n}}$, vel quod perinde est, ut $\frac{mm-mn}{nn} B^{\frac{m-2n}{m}}$. Ut si ordinatim applicata Parabolam attingat, existente $m=2$, & $n=1$: fiet vis ut data $2B^0$, adeoq; dabitur. Data igitur vi corpus movebitur in Parabola, quemadmodum *Galilæus* demonstravit. Quod si ordinatim applicata Hyperbolam attingat, existente $m=0-1$, & $n=1$; fiet vis ut $2B^{-3}$ seu $\frac{2}{B\,cub.}$: adeoq; vi, quæ sit reciproce ut cubus ordinatim applicatæ, corpus movebitur in Hyperbola. Sed missis hujusmodi Propositionibus, pergo ad alias quasdam de motu, quas nondum attigi.

SECT. XIV.

De motu corporum minimorum, quæ viribus centripetis ad singulas magni alicujus corporis partes tendentibus agitantur.

Prop. XCIV. Theor. XLVIII.

Si media duo similaria, spatio planis parallelis utrinq; terminato, distinguantur ab invicem, & corpus in transitu per hoc spatium attrahatur vel impellatur perpendiculariter versus medium alterutrum, neq; ulla alia vi agitetur vel impediatur; Sit autem attractio, in æqualibus ab utroq; plano distantiis ad eandem ipsius partem captis, ubiq; eadem: dico quod sinus incidentiæ in planum alterutrum erit ad sinum emergentiæ ex plano altero in ratione data.

Cas. 1. Sunto Aa, Bb plana duo parallela. Incidat corpus in planum prius Aa secundam lineam GH, ac toto suo per spatium intermedium transitu attrahatur vel impellatur versus medium incidentiæ, eaq; actione describat lineam curvam HI, & emergat secundum lineam IK. Ad planum emergentiæ Bb erigatur perpendiculum IM, occurrens tum lineæ incidentiæ GH productæ in M, tum plano incidentiæ Aa in R; & linea emergentiæ KI producta occurrat HM in L. Centro L intervallo

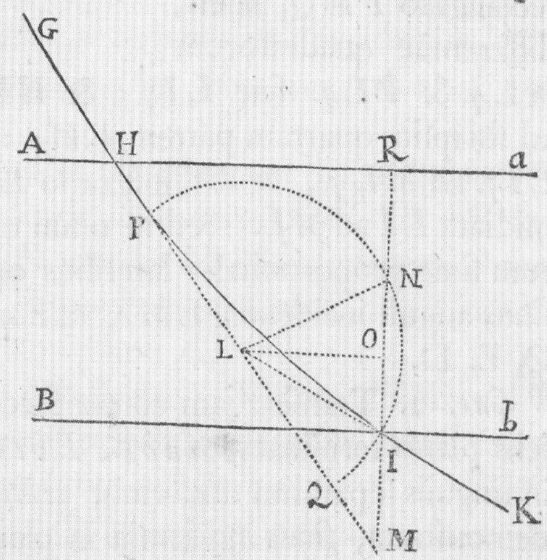

The Folger's Shakespeare collection is the largest in the world. Historically, it was the earliest part of what was to become the library's collection, having been begun by Henry and Emily Folger in the late 1800s. Yet the Shakespeare holdings of the Folger also include some of the institution's most recent archival material. Books, manuscripts, and a variety of items documenting theatrical productions come up to the present, as does the long progression of Shakespeare editions and other materials tracing the impact of Shakespeare in film, television, and other contexts. The Folger holds more than a quarter of a million playbills, dozens of period theatrical costumes, and several hundred promptbooks. Materials related to theatrical families specializing in Shakespeare, among them the Keans, the Kembles, and the Booths, are also well represented in the collection.

In 1991, that family aspect of theatrical history was brought into modern times when Lynn Redgrave—a member of a long dynasty of actors—created and presented for the Folger an evening of Shakespeare inspired in part by her father, Sir Michael Redgrave. The show later became a full-length play, Shakespeare for My Father, *and a Tony Award nominee.*

As that example suggests, Shakespeare and his works give rise to many activities at the Folger, including innovative theatre productions, a wide range of educational programs, and the articles and reviews of Shakespeare Quarterly. *The New Folger Library Shakespeare editions offer readers the plays and poems, reedited and freshly illustrated. The Shakespeare collection remains the focus of research by about a quarter of the library's visiting scholars and is the inspiration for the Folger Institute's Center for Shakespeare Studies.*

In the section that follows, materials related to Shakespeare's life, including two real-estate documents and an early image of the Globe, are succeeded by a variety of portraits (most of them contested) and a few of the original quartos and Folios of Shakespeare's works. The survey then expands to a diversity of materials—art, texts, costumes, photographs, and more—revealing how the Bard and his works have been performed, depicted, and perceived from the early 1700s to the present. Each is drawn from a collection that has become a unique resource for Henry and Emily Folger's modern-day successors—all those in the United States and around the world who share the Folgers' love for Shakespeare and his works.

One of two documents held at the Folger that seem likely to have passed through Shakespeare's own hands, the "Final Concord" of 1602 confirms Shakespeare's title to the second-largest house in Stratford-upon-Avon, known as New Place. A seemingly routine legal record, the document actually marked the conclusion to some horrific events.

In purchasing New Place, a brick-and-timber house with ten fireplaces and extensive gardens, Shakespeare celebrated his improved social standing, resulting in part from his professional success in London. Just two months after he purchased the property from William Underhill in 1597, Underhill was poisoned by his oldest son and heir, Fulke. Fulke was then hanged in 1599, leaving behind a younger brother, Hercules. Once Hercules came of age, Shakespeare prudently protected his title to New Place by paying Hercules to reconfirm the purchase, resulting in the document shown here.

According to the custom of the time, the confirmation document, known as an indenture, consisted of three identical copies on a single piece of vellum, which were subsequently cut apart on wavy lines and distributed to the parties involved. These two pieces, belonging to Underhill and Shakespeare, were brought together by a collector in the early 1700s; the third portion, originally written at right angles to the two, was the court's own copy and remains at the British Public Record Office.

Final Concord for purchase of New Place / 1602

Hec est finalis concordia facta in Curia domine Regine apud Westmonasterium a die sancti Michaelis in unum mensem Anno regnorum Elizabeth dei gratia Anglie Ffrancie et
Hibernie Regine fidei defensoris &c a conquestu quadragesimo quarto coram Edmundo Anderson Thoma Walmysley Georgio Kyngesmyll et Petro
Warburton Justiciariis et aliis domine Regine fidelibus tunc ibi presentibus Inter Willelmum Shakespeare generosum querentem et Herculem Underhill
generosum deforciantem de uno mesuagio duobus horreis duobus gardinis et duobus pomariis cum pertinentiis in Stratford super Avon Unde placitum conventionis
summonitum fuit inter eos in eadem curia Scilicet quod predictus Herculus recognovit predicta tenementa cum pertinentiis esse ius ipsius Willelmi ut illa que
idem Willelmus habet de dono predicti Herculi Et illa remisit et quietumclamavit de ipso et heredibus suis predicto Willelmo et heredibus suis imperpetuum Et preterea
idem Herculus concessit pro se et heredibus suis quod ipsi warantizabunt predicto Willelmo et heredibus suis predicta tenementa cum pertinentiis contra predictum
Herculem et heredes suos imperpetuum Et pro hac recognicione remissione quietaclamancia warantia fine et concordia idem Willelmus dedit predicto
Herculi sexaginta libras sterlingorum.

This Indenture made
Witnesseth
Which said
To have and to holde
And the said
And further
And also
And further
In witnesse whereof

By 1613, Shakespeare had invested in several properties in and around Stratford-upon-Avon, where he is generally thought to have retired by that time. Only one of his real-estate purchases was in London, a property in the Blackfriars district not far from the Blackfriars Theatre. A "gate-house" built partly above a gate in the wall surrounding the district, it came with an enclosed garden plot. The deed of bargain and sale shown here is the one belonging to Shakespeare. Because it was his copy, there was no need for him to sign it.

In the 1960s, Shakespearean biographer S. Schoenbaum became perhaps the first person to study this document since it came into the Folgers' possession some years before the library was founded. As he later recounted the story, Schoenbaum was originally presented with a locked antique wooden box and the news that the key was missing. After a locksmith failed to open the box, a librarian on staff quietly solved the problem with a bobby pin, and the group was next faced with the delicate task of unfolding the large document. Since then, the deed has been both photographed and treated by conservators. Of its subsequent display during the Folger's touring exhibition, Shakespeare: The Globe and the World, *in 1979 through 1982, Schoenbaum wrote, "The Blackfriars Gate-house conveyance has never, I suspect, looked better at any time since it was first drawn up." Visitors to the Kansas City installation of the document, he added, "cluster around and gape at the apparently pristine surface."*

Blackfriars Gate-House Conveyance / 1613

LONDON
S. Paules Church
Bow Churche
Guild Hall
S.Laurens Poultney
The Exchange
Cole harbour
Olde Swan
The Gally fuste
ESIS
FLVIUS
ar. Gardne
The Globe
Winchester howse
South

Although Shakespeare was associated with several London theatres, the playhouse with which he is most closely linked was the Globe, visible in the foreground of this detail from a view of London by the Amsterdam engraver Claes Jansz. Visscher, which appears in full on pages 144–145. The first version of Visscher's engraving was issued in 1616, the year of Shakespeare's death; the Folger's unique, very early copy has been dated to 1625. A full seven feet three inches in width, it consists of multiple pieces of paper. In 1978, Folger conservators removed these separate papers from a binding, mended them, and mounted the engraving into its original contiguous panorama, newly lined with Japanese paper. The work was one of several contemporary images of London examined in a 1987 Folger Institute seminar, "Shakespeare and the Theatres of His Time."

For many years, Visscher's view of London was crucial to theories about the Globe's construction. More recently, it has been shown to be inaccurate in many respects; the Globe, for example, is now thought to have been a many-sided polygon, not the towerlike octagon shown here. On the larger scale, however, the view still offers a useful look at early seventeenth-century London as it may have appeared before the Great Fire of 1666. In the early 1600s, the city probably looked much as it did when Shakespeare first arrived in about the late 1580s—a large, bustling metropolis with the River Thames as its main thoroughfare, and small boats for hire playing much the same role as the taxicabs on modern city streets. Among the many labeled churches is old Saint Paul's Cathedral, later destroyed in the fire and replaced by the familiar domed structure by Christopher Wren. Along the north bank of the river, stairs led to the houses of the great families. Above the river, London Bridge stood absolutely packed with buildings, most of them shops. It is no coincidence that the Globe, as well as other theatres, was located on the south bank of the river, and therefore outside the jurisdiction of the city. Already, the influence of the Protestants known as Puritans was being felt, and the city fathers were unfriendly to stage productions.

Following pages: Visscher's view of London / ca. 1625 (detail at left)

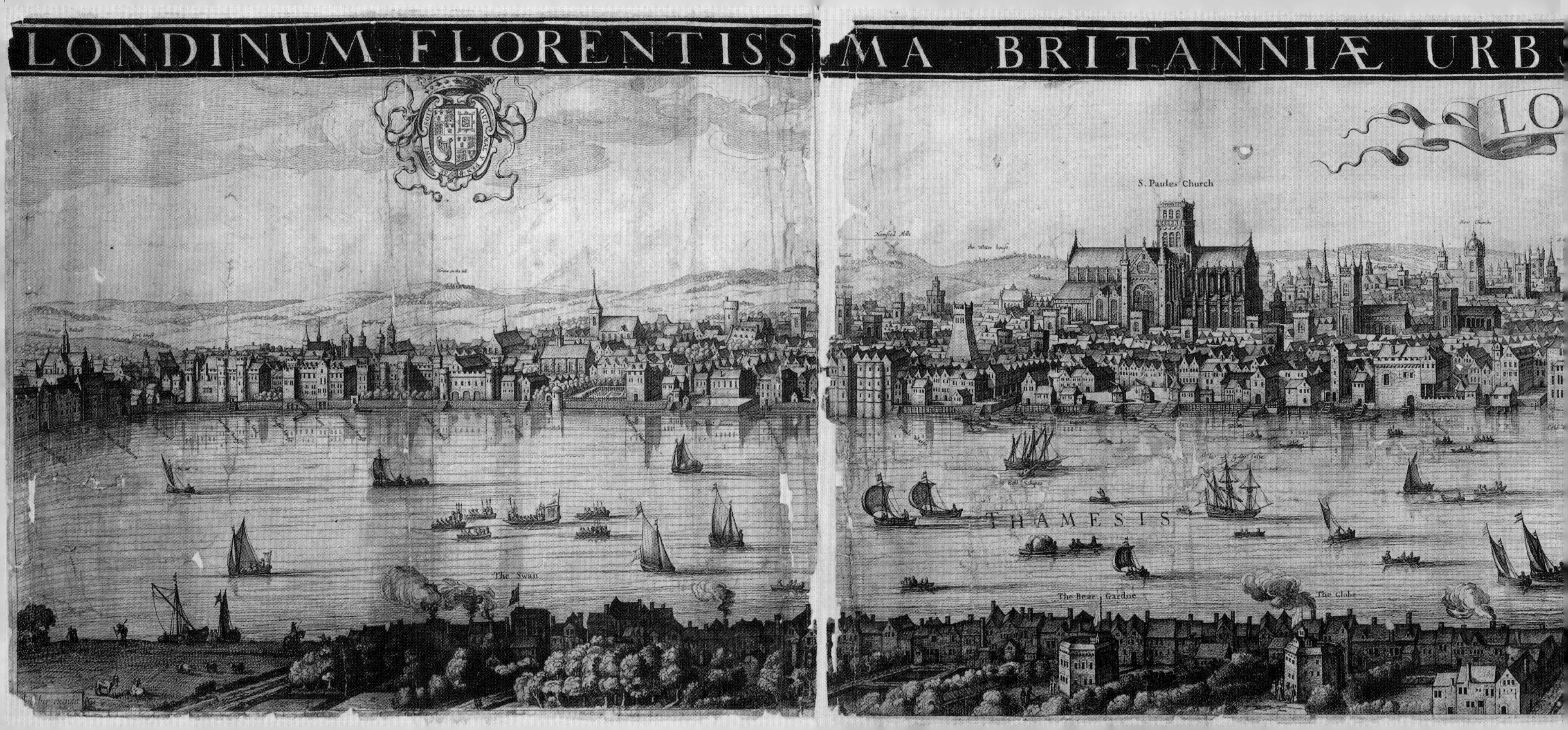
LONDINUM FLORENTISS
MA BRITANNIÆ URB
LO
S. Paules Church
THAMESIS
The Swan
The Bear Gardne
The Globe

EMPORIUMQUE TOTO ORBE CELEBERRIMUM.
ON
S. Laurens Poultney
S. Dunston the east
The Tower
THE BRIDGE
FLVIUS.
South
Winchester howse
Warke.
S. Mary Overis
S. Olafe

Only two existing images are considered authentic likenesses of William Shakespeare—the memorial bust at Stratford and the engraving by Martin Droeshout for the First Folio (page 156). Unfortunately, neither is very satisfying. Given the human desire to put a face with a name, a wealth of other images has been linked to Shakespeare over the years, and many were collected by the Folgers. The representative sampling that follows begins with this striking early seventeenth-century work. First recorded in 1847 in the possession of a schoolmaster from Ashbourne, Derbyshire, the painting is commonly known as the Ashbourne portrait.

Without a doubt, the portrait does not depict William Shakespeare, although Emily Folger probably thought it did when she purchased it in March 1931. It is also clear that the original was touched up, probably in the 1800s, to capitalize on its supposed resemblance to Shakespeare. The forehead was raised, the coat of arms obliterated, and the year of composition changed from 1612 to 1611—the year when William Shakespeare was forty-seven, which is given as the subject's age.

Most researchers believe that details uncovered in the painting's 1979 restoration, including part of a family motto and crest, identify the painting's subject as Sir Hugh Hamersley, later the Lord Mayor of London, who was indeed forty-seven in 1612. Although Hamersley's coat of arms was not assigned until 1614, it would have been unremarkable for him to have had it added later. Some of those who argue that Shakespeare's works were actually composed by Edward de Vere, the seventeenth earl of Oxford, however, contend the Ashbourne portrait originally depicted Oxford instead.

The question of whether it was Shakespeare who wrote the works attributed to him, often called the authorship controversy, existed well before the Folger was founded, although in the early 1900s the leading alternative was still Sir Francis Bacon (page 177). The Folger itself takes no position on the question; as a library open to scholars, it supports freedom of inquiry on any topic. Its holdings include extensive materials from the nineteenth century onward dealing with such proposed authors as Oxford; Bacon; William Stanley, sixth earl of Derby; the literary patron Edward Dyer; the playwright Christopher Marlowe; and many others.

Ashbourne portrait / 1612

ÆTATIS SVÆ. 47
A°: 1611

Painted on an oval mahogany panel, this large portrait of Shakespeare was presented to the Folger in 1975 by Mary Hyde, past president of the Shakespeare Association of America, who had written an article on the work ten years earlier in Shakespeare Quarterly. Discovered by a London dealer in 1962, the antique piece was almost certainly a commercial signboard, as is evidenced by two horizontal braces, a pair of closed iron loops at the back, and a pattern of nail holes that suggests it was once reinforced by metal edging. As Hyde pointed out in her article, the figure's scale—one and a half times life size—would also make it inappropriate for display inside a house.

The image itself is clearly based on the popular "Chandos portrait" of Shakespeare (the painting is named after a onetime owner, the third duke of Chandos, and is now in the National Gallery in London). Although never definitively linked to the Bard, the Chandos image is an informal and effective portrait that has inspired more copies than any other except the Droeshout engraving from the First Folio.

At first, the signboard was assumed to be the one that hung over the publishing house of Jacob Tonson, which produced Nicholas Rowe's 1709 edition of Shakespeare's works, the first collection of the plays with a named editor. Two points at least seemed to bear this out: Rowe's work includes two images of Shakespeare based on the Chandos portrait, and Tonson subsequently named his place of business the Shakespeare's Head. But there are many other possibilities. By the late 1600s to the early 1700s, when the signboard was probably created, Shakespeare had become a common motif for the signs outside English inns, taverns, and even other publishing houses.

The Shakespeare signboard is among numerous images of the Bard that enliven the meeting rooms and other working spaces at the Folger. Countless other pictures of Shakespeare may be found in sculptures, engravings, drawings, porcelains, and even comic books and films within the library's vast collection of Shakespeareana.

Shakespeare signboard / late 1600s to early 1700s

This stunning 1928 binding encloses a copy of James Boaden's An Inquiry into the Authenticity of Various Pictures and Prints of Shakespeare, *published in 1824. Boaden's work was one of the first serious attempts to study the numerous but often contradictory pictures of Shakespeare that were then emerging, and the Folger collection includes several more conventionally bound copies. This one, however, was among the very few books that Henry Folger purchased strictly for its cover, an exquisite example of a "Cosway binding," a type of binding named in honor of the earlier British miniaturist Richard Cosway (1742–1821) but invented in the early 1900s by J. H. Stonehouse, managing director of the Sotheran & Co. design firm. In a Cosway binding, miniature paintings on ivory are embedded like jewels in a leather background—in this case, goatskin gold-tooled with Tudor roses representing Elizabeth I, and by extension the Elizabethan age. The design by Stonehouse, executed by the London firm of Riviere & Son, is the perfect visual summary of the problem that Boaden presents. (A different, but equally remarkable, Riviere & Son binding may be seen on page 179.)*

At upper left, the painted miniature represents the Edward Marshall engraving of Shakespeare, a crude adaptation of Droeshout's First Folio engraving that reverses that portrait, squares off the ruff, and prettifies the hair. At upper right is the so-called Janssen portrait, a picture of uncertain origin that is now held at the Folger; it was once—probably incorrectly—attributed to the seventeenth-century painter Cornelius Janssen. The Droeshout engraving takes pride of place at the center of the binding, while the equally popular, but unauthenticated, Chandos portrait appears at lower left. Finally, at lower right, is a curiosity—the memorial bust at Stratford as it appeared for more than six decades after 1793, when the classical enthusiasms of the day led Shakespeare's first great biographer, Edmond Malone, to persuade the vicar of Stratford to paint it white. In 1861, the bust underwent restoration based on colored remnants of the original.

This binding was one of the outstanding pieces at the Folger's 1992 bookbindings exhibition; its portraits are the work of Miss C. B. Currie, who produced hundreds of miniatures for use in bookbindings before her death in 1940. Currie was among a number of woman miniaturists who flourished in the nineteenth and early twentieth centuries.

An Inquiry into the Authenticity of Various Pictures and Prints of Shakespeare / 1824

A romantic rendering of Shakespeare at the moment of inspiration, this 1757 terra-cotta sculpture by Louis François Roubiliac shows how ideas about artists, and Shakespeare in particular, had changed since the more straightforward Shakespearean images of the past. Although Roubiliac worked from one of those—the Chandos portrait—his sculpture is as much an effort to capture the playwright's creative process as his physical appearance.

Standing about twenty-two inches high on a sixteen-inch base, the sculpture was one of several studies Roubiliac made for a marble statue commissioned by the actor David Garrick for the Shakespeare Temple on the grounds of Garrick's Hampton villa. Although the features are meant to be Shakespeare's, Garrick himself may have served as a model and struck the dramatic pose shown here. In this early version, the playwright, leaning on a lectern with pen in hand, pushes an upthrust finger into his face as his eyes turn skyward for inspiration. Perhaps at Garrick's request, Roubiliac made the finished sculpture a more tranquil work in which the eyes are less animated and the left hand has moved so that it supports the Bard's chin rather than distorting his face.

Henry and Emily Folger's interest in sculpture found its best-known expression in the nine bas-reliefs by John Gregory that stretch across the library's facade and in the Brenda Putnam sculpture of Puck for the west side of the building. The Folgers also endowed the institution with a wealth of busts, statues, and other sculptures—most, like this one, on Shakespearean themes. One striking example, the bronze semirepresentational 1918 work Lady Macbeth *by the avant-garde sculptor Alice Morgan Wright, was itself given to the Folgers by Emily's older sister, Mary Augusta Jordan. A Vassar graduate and a professor of English at Smith College for more than forty years, Jordan had paid for Emily's education at Vassar and probably helped shape her interest in English literature.*

Louis François Roubiliac, sculpture of Shakespeare / 1757

The Folger Shakespeare Library may be best known in some circles for its collection of First Folios, but Henry and Emily Folger also sought out the quartos—small editions of the individual plays that began appearing during the late 1500s and early 1600s, some of which vary significantly from the text that appears in the Folio. Scholars have explained the text variations in several ways: they may reflect differences introduced by scribes or compositors, they may show different ways of cutting or adapting the plays for performance or for readers, or they may reflect Shakespeare's own revisions. Some early texts may also have been reconstructed by actors from memory or by spectators from shorthand notes. Inexpensive, unbound, and not always sold in great numbers, some of the quarto editions no longer survive.

For centuries, this was thought to be the case with the 1594 quarto of the early play Titus Andronicus. One can only imagine the Folgers' reaction to the news in 1904 that an immaculate copy had been discovered in the home of a Swedish postal clerk. As if to symbolize the luck of the find, the piece was found wrapped in a pair of eighteenth-century lottery tickets, which remain with it to this day (one may be seen at far right). Purchasing the quarto marked a new level of financial commitment for Henry Folger, who later wrote of himself at the time as "an enthusiast, whose means did not match his interest," adding, "It took three hours of tramping over city streets to clarify a bewildered mind sufficiently to cable the answer, Two Thousand Pounds," his ultimately winning bid.

The unique Titus—which, along with a 1594 version of 2 Henry VI, is the earliest extant printed Shakespeare play—thus holds a special place in Folger history. But the library owns more than 200 other quartos of Shakespeare's poems and plays. Those printed in 1598 or in later years often prominently display the name of William Shakespeare, presumably as a selling point. At the time of the printing of the Titus quarto, however, the printer followed the custom of displaying the name of the acting company rather than the author.

William Shakespeare, *Titus Andronicus* / 1594

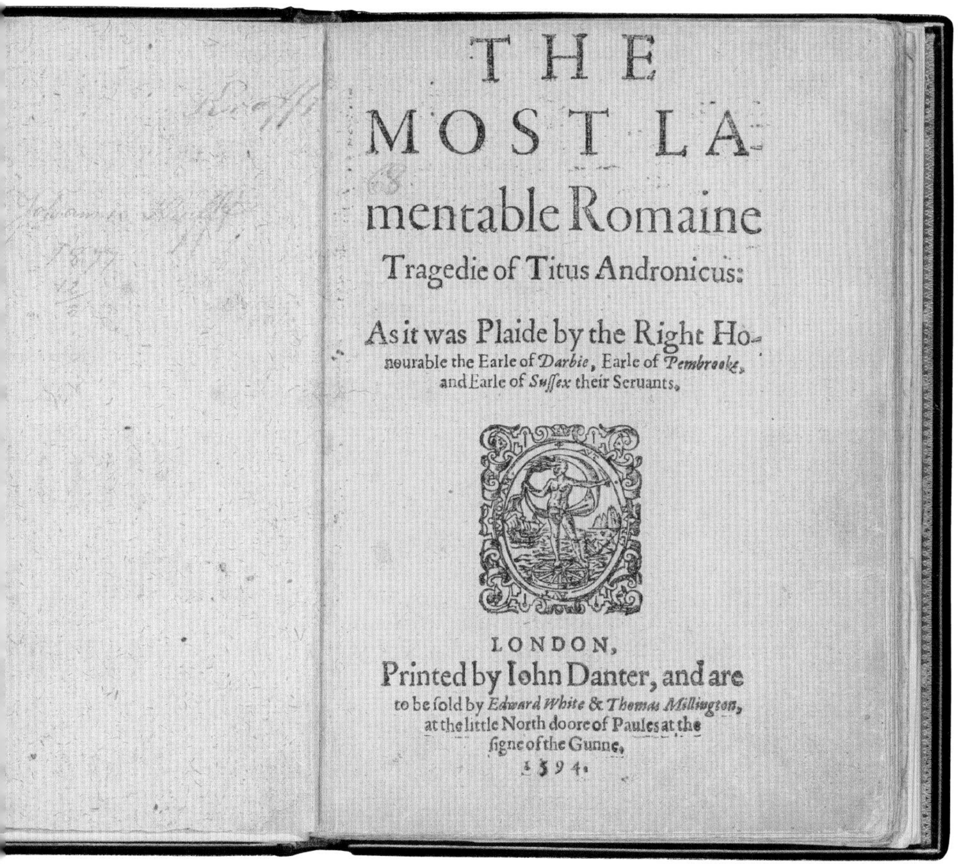

THE

MOST LA-

mentable Romaine

Tragedie of Titus Andronicus:

As it was Plaide by the Right Ho-
nourable the Earle of *Darbie*, Earle of *Pembrooke*,
and Earle of *Sussex* their Seruants.

LONDON,

Printed by Iohn Danter, and are
to be sold by *Edward White & Thomas Millington*,
at the little North doore of Paules at the
signe of the Gunne,
1594.

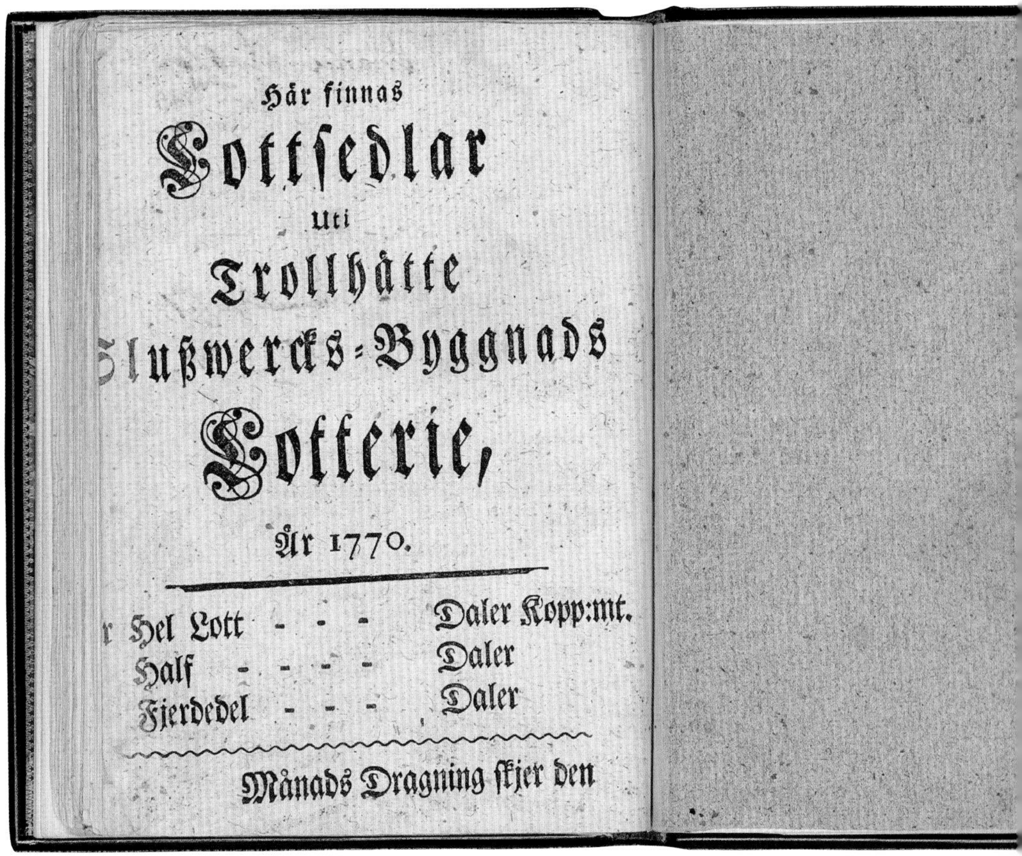

Här finnas

Lottsedlar

uti

Trollhätte

Slußwercks-Byggnads

Lotterie,

År 1770.

Hel Lott - - - Daler Kopp:mt.
Half - - - - Daler
Fjerdedel - - - Daler

Månads Dragning skjer den

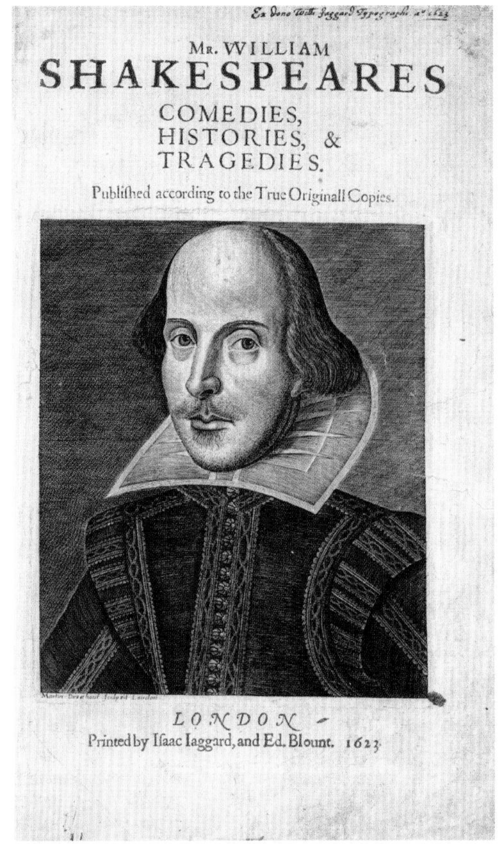

Ex dono Willi Jaggard Typographi a° 1623

MR. WILLIAM
SHAKESPEARES
COMEDIES,
HISTORIES, &
TRAGEDIES.
Publiſhed according to the True Originall Copies.

LONDON
Printed by Iſaac Iaggard, and Ed. Blount. 1623.

Seven years after the death of William Shakespeare, two of his fellow actors, John Heminge and Henry Condell, published this large, folio-sized volume of his collected works. The First Folio, as it was later called, contained thirty-six of Shakespeare's plays, eighteen of which had never before been printed and would otherwise have been lost. Among the plays that appeared for the first time in the Folio are Macbeth, The Tempest, *and* As You Like It.

The title page of the First Folio includes a portrait of Shakespeare engraved by Martin Droeshout that is one of only two authentic likenesses of the author. (The other is a memorial bust at Stratford's Holy Trinity Church; a replica appears in the Old Reading Room at the Folger.) Of approximately 750 printed copies of the First Folio, only about 240 can be accounted for today. Of these, the Folger collection includes 79, all acquired by Henry Folger.

The First Folio of which he was proudest was the so-called Vincent copy shown here, inscribed by its first owner, Augustine Vincent, with a note that he had received it from the printer, William Jaggard. A London bookseller first found the Vincent Folio in 1891 in a dusty stack of books piled in the coach house of one Coningsby C. Sibthorp of Canwick Hall in Lincolnshire. Learning of the find several years later, Folger offered to buy it. Sibthorp suggested a price of £5,000—more than $20,000 in 1899. Folger replied with a counteroffer of £4,000, only to discover that the Englishman was not about to bargain. Four years later, Folger did manage to acquire the volume, but not without paying Sibthorp over twice what he had originally offered.

Two other important copies of the First Folio that came into Folger's possession were one previously owned by the Baroness Burdett-Coutts that contains a canceled page from Troilus and Cressida, *and another from the earl of Roden that has the Droeshout portrait of Shakespeare in its rare original state. (As the book was coming off the press, both the text and the engraving were subject to minute corrections; the portrait soon developed a more natural shadow below the left ear, as in the Vincent copy.) Other First Folios in the collection offer insight into the foibles of their owners. One copy, for example, is inscribed by Elizabeth Okell as "her Book 1729" and contains two pages of children's drawings, probably dating from about the same period.*

William Shakespeare, "Vincent" First Folio / 1623

The second edition of Shakespeare's works, or the Second Folio, was printed in 1632 in the shop of Thomas Cotes, who took over the Jaggard print shop after the death of Isaac Jaggard, William's son, in 1627. It contains the same plays as the First Folio does, but with some textual emendations and corrections. Added to the preliminary poems in praise of the author is John Milton's "An Epitaph on Shakespeare," thought to be Milton's first published poem. An excerpt from Milton's verses appears in the Folger's west vestibule, over the corridor entrance.

There are some fifty-seven copies of the Second Folio at the Folger, including one signed by the British actor David Garrick and another that once belonged to Elizabeth of Bohemia, daughter of James I. Still another example is the copy shown here from the English college in Valladolid, Spain, which bears the certificate of Guillermo Sánchez, a censor for the Holy Office, or Inquisition. Charged with the detection and punishment of heretics and those guilty of any offense against Catholic orthodoxy, the Holy Office also routinely expurgated books by cutting out pages or blotting out offensive passages with printer's ink. Words, phrases, and whole sections, such as this closing scene from the play Henry VIII, *fell victim to the pen of the Inquisition.*

Extolling the infant princess Elizabeth (later to become Elizabeth I), Cranmer's praises in the play echo biblical passages and employ images generally used to describe the Virgin Mary. The similarity is hardly surprising, since Elizabeth I was often called the Virgin Queen by virtue of her unmarried state. But to Sánchez, the words were unacceptable. The expurgated lines read in part:

She must, the saints must have her; yet a virgin
A most unsported lily shall she pass
To th' ground and all the world shall mourn her.

William Shakespeare, Second Folio / 1632

[redacted]
In her dayes, Every Man shall eate in safety,
Vnder his owne Vine what he plants; and sing
The merry Songs of Peace to all his Neighbours.
[redacted]
And by those claime their greatnesse, not by Blood.
Nor shall this peace sleepe with her: But as when
The Bird of Wonder dyes, the Mayden Phœnix,
[redacted]
Shall then be his, and like a Vine grow to him;
Where ever the bright Sunne of Heaven shall shine,
His Honor, and the greatnesse of his name,
Shall be, and make new Nations. He shall flourish,
And like a Mountaine Cedar, reach his branches,
To all the Plaines about him: Our Childrens Children
Shall see this, and blesse Heaven.

Kin. Thou speakest wonders.

Cran. She shall be [redacted]
An aged Princesse; many dayes shall see her,
[redacted]
Would I had knowne no more: But she must dye,
[redacted]

Kin. [redacted]
I thanke ye all. To you my good Lord Maior,
And you good Brethren, I am much beholding:
I have receiv'd much Honour by your presence,
And ye shall find me thankfull. Leade the way Lords,
Ye must all see the Queene, and she must thanke ye,
She will be sicke els. This day, no man thinke
'Has businesse at his house; for all shall stay:
This little-One shall make it Holy-day. *Exeunt.*

THE EPILOGVE.

'Tis ten to one, this Play can never please
All that are heere: Some come to take their ease,
And sleepe an Act or two; but those we feare
W'have frighted with our Trumpets: so 'tis cleare,
They'l say 'tis naught. Others to heare the City
Abus'd extreamly, and to cry that's witty,
Which we have not done neither; that I feare
All the expected good w'are like to heare,
For this Play at this time, is onely in
The mercifull construction of good women,
For such a one we shew'd 'em: If they smile,
And say twill doe; I know within a while,
All the best men are ours; for 'tis ill hap,
If they hold, when their Ladies bid 'em clap.

FINIS.

The Prologue.

In Troy there lyes the Scene: from Iles of Greece
The Princes Orgillous, their high blood chaf'd,
Have to the Port of Athens sent their shippes
Fraught with the ministers and instruments
Of cruell Warre: Sixty and nine that wore
Their Crownets Regall, from th'Athenian Bay
Put forth toward Phrygia, and their vow is made
To ransacke Troy, within whose strong Immures
The ravish'd Helen, Menelaus Queene,
With wanton Paris sleepes, and that's the Quarrell.
To Tenedos they come,
And the deepe-drawing Barkes doe there disgorge
Their Warlike frautage: now on Dardan Plaines
The fresh and yet unbruised Greekes doe pitch
Their brave Pavillions. Priams six-gated City,
Dardan and Timbria, Helias, Chetas, Troien,
And Antenonidus with massy Staples
And corresponsive and fulfilling Bolts
Stirre up the Sonnes of Troy.
Now Expectation tickling skittish spirits,
On one and other side, Troian and Greeke,
Sets all on hazard. And hither am I come,
A Prologue arm'd, but not in confidence
Of Authors pen, or Actors voyce; but suited
In like conditions, as our Argument;
To tell you (faire Beholders) that our Play
Leapes ore the vaunt and firstlings of those broyles,
Beginning in the middle: starting thence away,
To what may be digested in a Play:
Like, or find fault, doe as your pleasures are,
Now good, or bad, 'tis but the chance of Warre.

The fourth of the eighteenth-century editions of Shakespeare's works, Sir Thomas Hanmer's 1744 edition in six volumes, is remembered today not for its editorial choices but for its Shakespearean illustrations, some of the most effective and original to that date. For each play, Hanmer commissioned a drawing by the artist Francis Hayman that was then engraved by Hubert Gravelot. These matched images from Measure for Measure *are from a unique copy of the Hanmer edition held at the Folger, in which the original watercolor drawings have been inserted near the corresponding engravings. The handwritten contract between Hayman and Hanmer, which was reproduced in* Shakespeare Quarterly *in 1953, is bound into the first volume of the set.*

Although Hayman did not base his drawings on actual stage productions, he set them in a theatrical space. In the climactic confrontation shown here, the tyrannical Angelo, left in charge of Vienna by its duke, faces the returned duke, who has just removed his disguise as a friar. Angelo's victims, including the lovely Isabella, look on.

Less sunny than As You Like It *and the other traditionally popular Shakespearean comedies,* Measure for Measure *interests modern students because of its gender issues and ambiguous moments—most notably, the duke's final speech, a proposal of marriage to Isabella, which goes unanswered as the curtain falls. Such unresolved plot elements, because they are open to different interpretations, help keep Shakespeare's works alive for each generation. In 1995–96, members of a yearlong NEH-sponsored Folger Institute performance institute constructed and distributed an online edition of the play in which movie clips, explanations of terms, and facsimiles of pages from the First Folio all illuminate the script. Two years later, high-school teachers at the Folger's Teaching Shakespeare Institute tackled the play, too, coming up with lesson plans—also posted online—meant to make the piece more accessible to secondary-school students. One exercise, "Unspoken Answers and Unscripted Scenes," asks students to invent and act a scene in which Isabella replies to the duke, basing their work on words and events elsewhere in the play, and acting out some of Shakespeare's other scenes to match their invented reply.*

Francis Hayman, scene from *Measure for Measure* / ca. 1740–41
Hubert François Gravelot, scene from *Measure for Measure*, after Hayman / ca. 1740–41

F. Hayman Inv. H. Gravelot Sculps.

"Of all the people associated with the magic name of Shakespeare," the bookseller A. S. W. Rosenbach once wrote, "Mr. Folger liked David Garrick best." The leading actor-manager of the 1700s, Garrick revolutionized English theatre with a lively, naturalistic acting style that held audiences spellbound. In three decades at the Drury Lane Theatre, Garrick offered an abundance of Shakespeare's plays, relieved of the stilted acting and wholesale reworking of the past. While he strove for a "purer" Shakespeare, Garrick nevertheless had no qualms about reworking the plays himself—adding the death scene of Romeo and Juliet illustrated here, for example, while also restoring much of Shakespeare's original text.

A natural self-publicist who encouraged the production of hundreds of portraits of himself, Garrick played a key part in the cult of bardolatry that continues today. Words he wrote for a 1759 pantomime are carved in the Folger's Exhibition Hall: "Thrice happy the nation that Shakespeare has charm'd. / More happy the bosoms his genius has warm'd! / Ye children of nature, of fashion and whim, / He painted you all, all join to praise him." In 1769, he helped organize the Shakespeare Jubilee in Stratford, an event that culminated in yet another Garrick poem on the Bard.

The Folger's collection of Garrick-related materials, perhaps the largest in the world, ranges from promptbooks, playbills, and correspondence to portraits, porcelains, and even a set of Garrick's silverware. Some pieces explore the same subject in different ways, as do the mezzotint, playbill, and painted copper roundel shown here, all of which document Garrick's performances of Romeo and Juliet *with George Anne Bellamy between 1750 and 1753; the roundel is among several Garrick pieces donated in the 1990s as part of the Babette Craven collection of theatrical memorabilia. Others are unique, like the wooden model of the Shakespeare Temple at Garrick's Hampton estate. Dating from about 1830, long after Garrick's day, it may have been a coronation gift for William IV, whose arms are stamped on the miniature Shakespeare editions stored inside (to make room, a model of the Roubiliac statue was displaced to the roof). Many of the Folger's Garrick holdings, however, have been uncataloged or difficult to pull together across collections. To solve that problem, the Folger embarked in the year 2000 on its first multimedia cataloging initiative—*Raising the Curtain: David Garrick at the Folger, *a project aimed at making the Folger's Garrick materials in all media more accessible to scholars worldwide.*

Mezzotint and playbill, David Garrick in *Romeo and Juliet* / ca. 1753 and 1751
David Garrick in *Romeo and Juliet* / 1765
Model of David Garrick's Shakespeare Temple / ca. 1830

THEATRE ROYAL in Drury-Lane,
To-morrow, being Thursday the 31st of JANUARY,
ROMEO and JULIET.
The Part of ROMEO to be perform'd
By Mr. GARRICK,
Capulet by Mr. BERRY,
Tibalt by Mr. BLAKES,
Fryar Lawrence by Mr. BURTON,
The Part of Mercutio by Mr. WOODWARD,
Lady Capulet by Mrs. BENNET,
Nurse by Mrs. JAMES,
And the Part of JULIET to be perform'd
By Miss BELLAMY.
The Funeral PROCESSION
To the MONUMENT of the CAPULETS.
Mr. Beard, Mr. Reinhold, Mrs. Clive, Miss Norris, &c.
QUEEN MAB.
Harlequin, Mr. WOODWARD,
The Other CHARACTERS by
Mr. LIVIEZ,
Mr. BLAKES,
Mr. COSTOLLO,
Mr. LAYFIELD,
The Little SWISS,
Mrs. TOOGOOD,
Master VERNON,
Mad. MARIET, and Others.
Mr. GARRICK and Mrs. BELLAMY in the Characters of ROMEO and JULIET

ART Flat,

A respected and commercially successful portrait painter, the eighteenth-century British artist George Romney longed to make a name for himself in the more highly regarded field of history painting, a genre that encompasses literary scenes as well as actual past events. In between the portrait sittings that paid his bills, Romney produced vast numbers of sketches for his planned paintings, only some of which were ever created. The Folger possesses the second-largest collection of these Romney drawings in America and the third-largest in the world, many of which are on Shakespearean subjects. Romney's drawings offer a glimpse of his private world and his astonishing talents as a draftsman.

Together with a small number of the artist's paintings, 116 of the drawings were exhibited at the Folger in the winter of 1998–99 in 'Designs from Fancy': George Romney's Shakespearean Drawings. *As with many Folger exhibitions, it was curated by a specialist in the field, Trinity College art historian Yvonne Romney Dixon, who had also cataloged the Folger's collection of Romney drawings several years earlier. Dixon—a descendant of the artist—noted that the works on display traced an evolution in Romney's drawings from highly controlled classical studies to free-flowing lines. The example shown here, a study of King Lear, dates from about 1773, toward the beginning of that change, with classical, academic shading that carefully indicates the shape of the face, recalling ancient Roman sculpture. Throughout his life, Romney returned again and again to Lear, who had been the subject of Romney's first history painting in 1762 and would be the subject of his last attempt at a picture in 1798.*

George Romney, drawing of the head of Lear / ca. 1773–75

Born in the colony of Pennsylvania in 1738, the American artist Benjamin West was so well received during a stay in England in the 1760s that he moved there permanently, becoming a founding member of the Royal Academy and Historical Painter to King George III. In 1792, he succeeded Sir Joshua Reynolds as president of the academy. (West's American pupils, who included Gilbert Stuart and John Singleton Copley, ensured his continuing influence across the Atlantic.)

Known for such history paintings as Penn's Treaty with the Indians, *West was also attracted to Shakespeare's plays, and in the course of his career painted scenes from* Romeo and Juliet, Hamlet, Macbeth, *and* King Lear. *As with Romney, the scenes are drawn directly from Shakespeare's text, rather than depicted as stage productions.*

King Lear was a popular subject during this period, and the play seems to have had considerable appeal for West, who painted Lear in the Storm *in 1788 as well as several depictions of the scene shown here, usually called King Lear and Cordelia. This version, from 1793, is his fourth and last. With either Kent or a physician steadying the battered Lear, Cordelia tenderly greets her father as he awakes from the sleep that has cured his madness—albeit too late to ward off the tragic deaths of both.*

Benjamin West, King Lear and Cordelia / 1793

Henry Fuseli's dreamlike 1793 painting, Macbeth Consulting the Vision of the Armed Head, *is perhaps the finest artwork collected by Henry and Emily Folger. Many also consider it the Swiss-born artist's greatest achievement, with a subject well suited to his favored themes of nightmare, fantasy, and terror. The painting depicts Macbeth's second encounter with the witches, in which they conjure up a series of apparitions beginning with a disembodied head—bearing a grotesque resemblance to Macbeth in Fuseli's conception. As the head delivers its warning to "beware Macduff," the murderer-king recoils at an unbalanced angle that adds to the picture's sense of unreality. In 1993, the work served as an apt cover image for the first complete catalog of the Folger's paintings, researched and written by art historian William Pressley; it was also displayed that year in* As Imagination Bodies Forth, *the first Folger paintings exhibition in the institution's history.*

Like many other paintings produced in England in the late 1700s, Fuseli's work was originally commissioned for a "Shakespeare Gallery"—an exhibition that charged an entry fee and sold engravings of the works displayed. Invented by Alderman John Boydell in 1789, the idea was widely imitated; this painting appeared in a Dublin-based Shakespeare Gallery that later moved to London. In 1997, the Folger agreed to lend this work and two other Fuselis to a European exhibition on the artist. During preliminary cleaning, the neatly lettered words "MACBETH ACT 4 SCENE 1 Hy FUSELI" were discovered on the frame above the painting, just as spectators at the Shakespeare Gallery would have seen them two centuries before.

One of the four Shakespeare plays most often taught in the United States (the others are Hamlet, Romeo and Juliet, *and* Julius Caesar*),* Macbeth *is a favorite choice for elementary-school groups performing scenes for the Folger's annual Children's Shakespeare Festival. Children, it seems, are drawn to the work's uncanny blend of murder and the supernatural—the same elements that inspired Fuseli.*

Henry Fuseli, Macbeth Consulting the Vision of the Armed Head / 1793

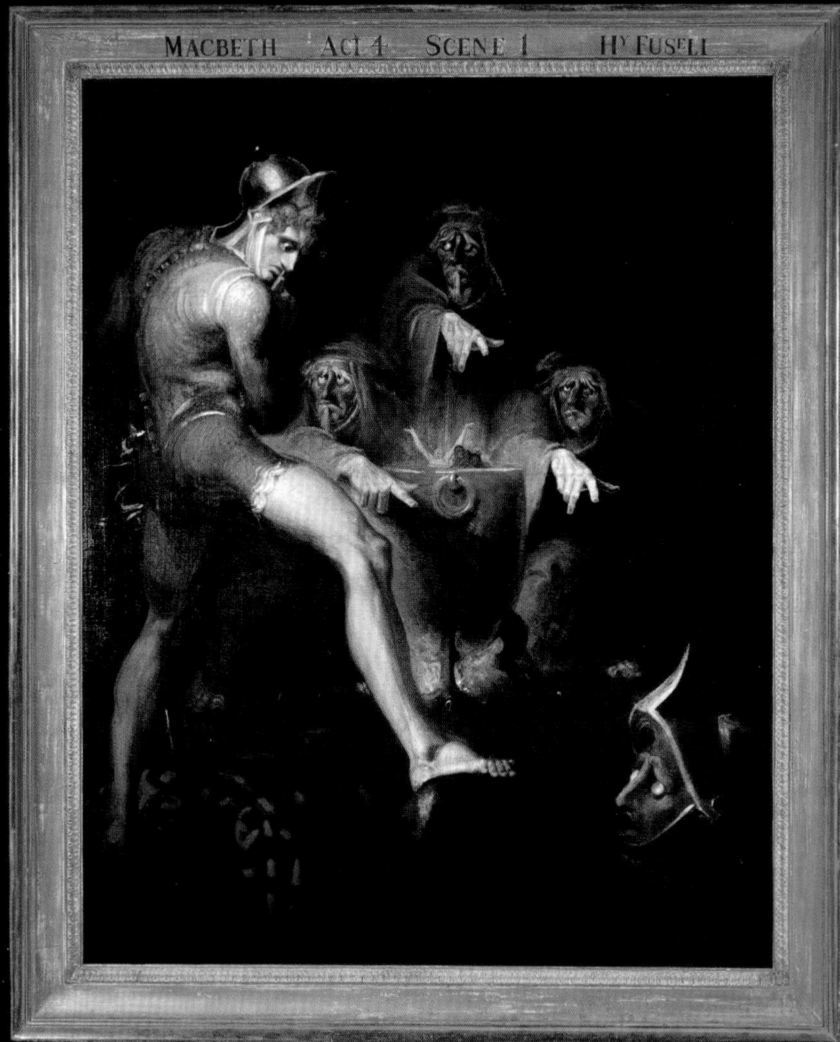
MACBETH Act 4 SCENE 1 H Fuseli

Hermione
The Winter's Tale

Hermione
The Winter's Tale

A poet, dramatist, novelist, critic, musician, actress, and dramatic reader, Fanny Kemble was, by all accounts (including her own), a person of unusual talent. She remains best known as an actress, a profession upon which she embarked in 1829 in the role of Juliet at Covent Garden. "I ran straight across the stage, stunned with the tremendous shout that greeted me," Kemble wrote years later of her first entrance. By the balcony scene, "for aught I knew, I was Juliet; the passion I was uttering sending hot blushes over my neck and shoulders while the poetry sounded like music to me as I spoke it."

Audiences took this newest star of the Kemble family to their hearts, and images of Fanny Kemble in her debut as Juliet circulated widely. In 1832, at the age of twenty-two, Kemble left for New York, where the popular young actress sparked a craze for "Fanny Kemble caps." Then she married Pierce Butler of Philadelphia. Unhappy from the start, the marriage fractured completely after he inherited a Georgia plantation and a large contingent of slaves—an abhorrent situation for Fanny, who held abolitionist views. The couple separated several times and divorced in 1849.

Kemble took up acting once again, although she never regained her earlier success, and later turned to touring with staged readings of Shakespeare instead. Among the Folger's holdings related to Kemble is this set of twenty-five costume designs on transparent mica, representing her Shakespearean roles. Each has a blank oval in lieu of a face, suggesting that an image of Kemble might have been slipped behind a given costume as it was examined; the picture of her face shown in the second photograph is a modern copy supplied by the Folger and used in a display for its 1985 exhibition The Kemble Family. *One of England's great theatrical dynasties, the family also included Fanny Kemble's uncle John Phillip Kemble, her aunt Sarah Siddons, and numerous other actors and performers, many of whom, like her, performed on both the British and the American stage.*

Fanny Kemble costume for Hermione / undated

Theatre is a fleeting art, and even with modern filming techniques a stage performance can never be fully captured. The problem of reconstruction is even greater in the case of productions put on before movies or even photography was invented. Among the best evidence for details of staging, effects, costumes, and other aspects of a performance are promptbooks, the marked copies of plays prepared for professional productions. Promptbooks also provide information about cuts and adaptations of the text—often quite extensive in the case of Shakespeare's plays. The Folger collection includes more than 1,800 promptbooks, about half of them for Shakespearean productions, including some used by David Garrick, Edwin Booth, members of the Kemble family, John Barrymore, and Paul Robeson (page 184). Invaluable for students of theatre and social history, the books were the focus of a comprehensive conservation and cataloging effort begun in 1992 with funding from the NEH.

This example, compiled by prompter T. W. Edmonds for Charles Kean's 1859 production of Hamlet *at the Princess's Theatre in London, was a souvenir promptbook available for sale; it was one of a very few copies to which watercolors of the sets were added, as well as handwritten notes recording cues and the blocking, or positions, of actors. Kean and his actress wife, Ellen Tree, were for many years the managers and leading players of the Princess's Theatre, and they were well known for spectacular productions and a devotion to authenticity. In place of the generic stage costumes of the day, often nothing more than contemporary clothing, Kean substituted costumes based on meticulous, perhaps even excessive, research. Before presenting* King John, *for example, he visited Worcester Cathedral and measured the monarch's skeleton to determine his height. Similarly, his elaborate stage sets, such as the one shown here for the castle of Elsinore, reflected the best contemporary knowledge of the sites portrayed.*

Charles Kean, souvenir promptbook for 1859 *Hamlet* / undated straight: Come, give us a taste of your quality;[58] come, a passionate speech.

1st Play. (L.H.) What speech, my lord?

Ham. I heard thee speak me a speech once,—but it was never acted; or, if it was, not above once; for the play, I remember, pleased not the million; 'twas caviare to the general:[59] but it was an excellent play, well digested in the scenes, set down with as much modesty as cunning.[60] One speech in it I chiefly loved: 'twas Æneas' tale to Dido; and thereabout of it especially, where he speaks of Priam's slaughter: If it live in your memory, begin at this line; let me see, let me see;—

The rugged Pyrrhus, like the Hyrcanian beast,—'tis not so: it begins with Pyrrhus:

The rugged Pyrrhus,—he, whose sable arms,
Black as his purpose, did the night resemble,
Old grandsire Priam seeks.

Pol. (R.) 'Fore Heaven, my lord, well spoken, with good accent and good discretion.

Ham. (C.) So proceed you.

1st. *Play.* (L.) *Anon he finds him*
Striking too short at Greeks; his antique sword,
Rebellious to his arm, lies where it falls,
Repugnant to command: Unequal match'd,
Pyrrhus at Priam drives; in rage strikes wide;
But with the whiff and wind of his fell sword[61]
The unnerved father falls.

[58] —*quality;*] Qualifications, faculty.

[59] —*caviare to the general;*] Caviare is the spawn of fish pickled, salted, and dried. It is imported from Russia, and was considered in the time of Shakespeare a new and fashionable luxury, not obtained or relished by the vulgar, and therefore used by him to signify anything above their comprehension—general is here used for the people.

[60] —*as much modesty as cunning.*] As much propriety and decorum as skill.

[61] *Falls with the whiff and wind of his fell sword*] Our author employs the same image in almost the same phrase:

"The Grecians *fall*
"*Even in the fan and wind of your fair sword.*"
Tr. & Cress. V. 3. Tr.

all retire up except the 1st Actor

Guil.

Ros.

Actors.

Ham.

1st Act.

Pol.

Among the more striking pieces of theatre history held at the Folger is this faded but still-regal coat worn by Edwin Booth when he played Richard III. The son of the well-known tragedian Junius Brutus Booth, Edwin took New York by storm in 1857 and remained a dramatic force until his retirement in 1891. Several of his costumes are housed at the Folger, which has about three dozen complete or partial costumes in its collection, most of them from nineteenth-century Shakespearean productions.

During the 1864–65 season, Booth secured his place at the top of America's theatrical world by playing Hamlet one hundred nights in a row at the Winter Garden, a remarkable feat at a time when most plays were performed for only one or two weeks. Less than a month later, he and the nation were stunned by the news that his younger brother John Wilkes Booth, also an actor, had assassinated Abraham Lincoln. Briefly, Edwin Booth went into seclusion. But he returned in time to new triumphs, establishing Booth's Theatre in New York (a theatrical success, though a financial disaster) and founding the Players Club in the same city.

In keeping with his era's interest in historical accuracy, Edwin Booth derived many of his costumes from the reference works of James Robinson Planché. Planché was almost certainly the source for this garment, which incorporates the royal coat of arms of Richard's day—British lions quartered with French fleurs-de-lis—and has a padded shoulder to indicate Richard's identity as a hunchback. As shown in this hand-colored engraving from 1872, one of twelve showing Booth in various costumes, the actor wore it over stage armor in the final scenes at Bosworth Field.

In 2001, the Folger's holdings related to Booth and many other nineteenth-century performers gained new strength with the addition of a wide array of materials associated with the American theatre critic William Winter, donated by his great-grandson, Robert Young. The Winter collection is of particular value because of the critic's close ties to many leading performers of his time; he and Booth, for example, collaborated on fifteen published promptbooks. Among the materials in the collection are journals, letters, scrapbooks, works of art, and personal mementos, including a picture signed "Wm Winter, with the kindest regard of Edwin Booth."

Coat worn by Edwin Booth as Richard III / undated
Edwin Booth as Richard III / 1872

HAMLET

British caricaturist, author, and bon vivant Sir Max Beerbohm irreverently summarized the "Baconian" theory of Shakespeare authorship in this 1904 color lithograph, which shows Shakespeare underhandedly receiving a copy of Hamlet *from Sir Francis Bacon. In 1994, Beerbohm's work was among a wealth of often entertaining images in the Folger's* Roasting the Swan of Avon *exhibition, which brought together many less-than-reverential materials on the Bard. The show included critics of Shakespeare's plays (among them, George Bernard Shaw), examples of censorship of his works by bodies ranging from the Spanish Inquisition to American textbook publishers, and materials related to the authorship controversy, including the theory that Sir Francis Bacon wrote the plays.*

That idea had its roots in the writing of an American woman, Delia Bacon, who believed herself to be descended from the Elizabethan philosopher. In her 1857 work on the subject, Delia Bacon actually proposed that Francis Bacon was one of several eminent figures who wrote the plays; later Baconians credited him alone, and some have tried to prove it by locating cryptographs within Shakespeare's texts. In its day, the Baconian theory had a considerable vogue, convincing no less a figure than Mark Twain of its merits.

To illustrate this idea, the 1994 exhibition could draw on a wealth of Folger materials. As A. S. W. Rosenbach wrote in his 1931 recollections of Henry Folger, "Although not a believer in the Baconian theory, Mr. Folger formed an almost complete library on this subject, including many manuscripts and autograph letters." Those holdings were further enhanced in December 1968 with a gift from three members of the Bacon family of 300 letters and other papers from 1821 to 1859 relating to Delia Bacon. In advocating her theories, Bacon sought the support of literary and other important figures of her day, most of whom were unconvinced of her ideas but personally sympathetic to her. The correspondence in this collection includes letters from Ralph Waldo Emerson, Nathaniel Hawthorne, Thomas Carlyle, James Buchanan, and Harriet Beecher Stowe.

Max Beerbohm, *William Shakespeare, His Method of Work* / 1904

Alberto Sangorski was a master craftsman in the esteemed London book-binding firm of Riviere & Son. On December 23, 1926, the Times Literary Supplement *reported, "He has just completed . . . a richly illuminated manuscript of Shakespeare's* Songs and Sonnets, *[which] has been in hand for five years, and every detail, designing, engrossing, illumination, painting and binding has been done by Mr. Sangorski."*

The result is one of the most beautifully designed and handcrafted books of the twentieth century. No expense was spared in the choice of materials. Passages from the works of Shakespeare are written in an exquisite calligraphic hand on the finest vellum, with 23-karat gold leaf in the illuminations. Each page is interleaved with moiré silk (in the photographs shown on pages 180–181, the silk has been rolled up so that the facing pages may be seen). The front cover of the binding has sapphires in the corners and incorporates Shakespeare's coat of arms in 18-karat gold, embellished with a ruby and black and blue enamels. Henry Folger bought the book soon after it was finished. Together with a sixtieth-anniversary binding created by conservator Frank Mowery in the 1990s, the Sangorski book is one of only two jeweled bindings in the Folger Shakespeare Library.

Songs and Sonnets by William Shakespeare / 1926

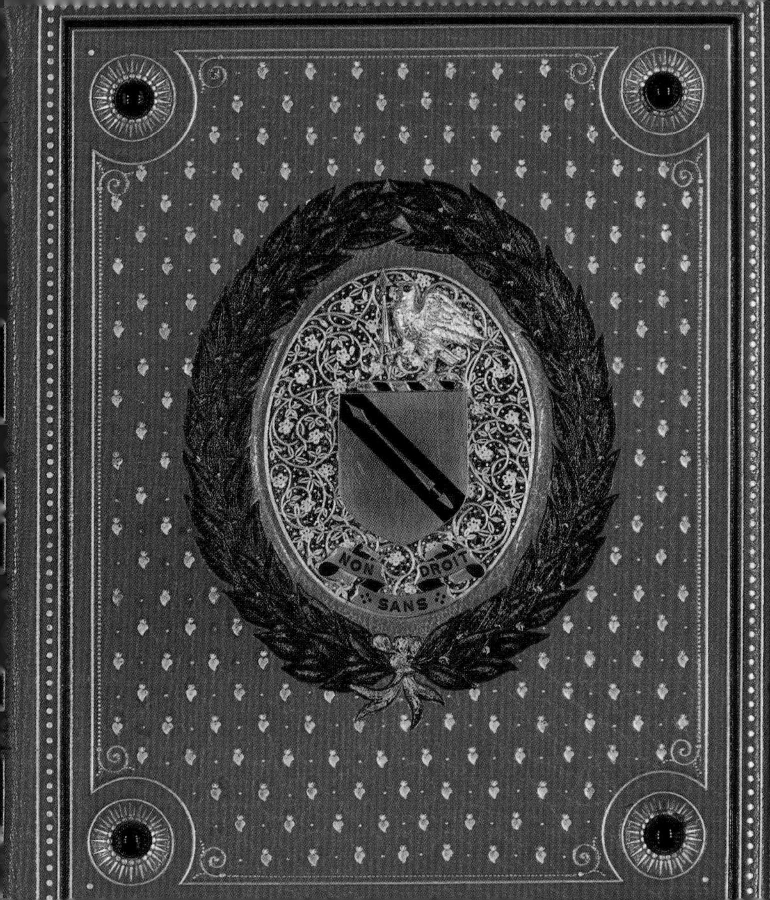
NON SANS DROIT

SONGS
AND
SONNETS
BY
WILLIAM
SHAKESPEARE

The Sea Dirge

FULL fathom five thy
father lies;
Of his bones are coral
made:
Those are pearls that
were his eyes:
Nothing of him that
doth fade,
But doth suffer a sea-change
Into something rich and
strange.
Sea-nymphs hourly ring
his knell:
Ding-dong.
hark! now I hear them,—
ding-dong, bell.

Tempest Act I. Scene II.

Ophelia's Songs—

How— should I your true love
know
From one another
By his cockle hat and staff
And his sandal shoon.

He is dead and gone, lady—
He is dead and gone;
At his head a grass-green turf,
At his heels a stone.

White his shroud as the mountain snow,—
Larded with sweet flowers;
Which bewept to the grave did go—
With true-love showers.

. . . . .

And will he not come again?
And will he not come again?
No, no, he is dead;
Go to thy death-bed,
He never will come again.
His beard was as white as snow
All flaxen was his poll
He is gone, he is gone,
And we cast away moan:
God ha' mercy on his soul!

Hamlet Act. IV. Scene V.

The American film industry's earliest attempts at Shakespeare were very much in the classic theatrical tradition, as can be seen in this sketch by Dan Sayre Groesbeck for one of the 1,200 costumes in MGM's 1936 film of Romeo and Juliet. *Pictured in the role of Juliet's nurse is Edna May Oliver. An experienced character actress who had previously played such stalwart figures as Aunt Betsey Trotwood in* David Copperfield *and Aunt March in* Little Women, *Oliver was so effective as the Nurse that some reviewers felt she stole the picture.*

Like Oliver, Groesbeck was a film-industry veteran. From his first job for Cecil B. DeMille in 1923, he produced thousands of drawings and sketches to suggest the look of costumes, sets, and other details for historical films, although he rarely received a direct credit. This sketch, donated to the Folger in 1969 by Colonel Charles E. Hammond, is among several Folger holdings relating to the film, including two gifts from MGM in 1936: a specially produced, noninflammable copy of the film in steel containers, and a volume of one hundred still photographs. While the Folger has included filmed works in its collection since the 1930s, it was not until 1975 that a grant from the Rockefeller Foundation established a permanent film archive for the library.

MGM's Romeo and Juliet *owed its existence to the talented but always frail producer Irving Thalberg, who cast his wife, Norma Shearer, and British actor Leslie Howard as the star-crossed lovers. Its cost of more than $2 million proved impossible to recoup at the box office, however. Slow-paced and overly reverential—William Strunk Jr. of Cornell was retained to "protect" Shakespeare's text—the film became Thalberg's only commercial failure. Just three weeks after its release, Thalberg died of pneumonia at thirty-seven, a real-life tragedy that some have attributed in part to his overexertion in producing and promoting the movie. The film subsequently received four Oscar nominations, including Best Picture, Best Actress, Best Art Direction, and Best Supporting Actor, for Basil Rathbone as Tybalt.*

Dan Sayre Groesbeck, Edna May Oliver as the Nurse in 1936 MGM film *Romeo and Juliet* / undated

A football All-American at Rutgers and a 1923 graduate of Columbia Law School, Paul Robeson soon left the legal profession to pursue an acting career. But as a black actor in the segregated United States, he was frustrated by the limited opportunities available. Like Ira Aldridge, a nineteenth-century African-American actor whom he greatly admired, Robeson sought success on the London stage. (Aldridge himself is represented at the Folger by holdings that include playbills, engravings, and a short manuscript poem.) In London Robeson played the title role in Eugene O'Neill's Emperor Jones *in 1925 and stood out in the 1928 musical* Show Boat. *In 1930, he played Othello to Peggy Ashcroft's Desdemona, a mixed-race casting unthinkable in the United States at that time for the classic play. The promptbook shown here documents that production, an unsuccessful venture that closed in about six weeks.*

As American racial attitudes began to change, Robeson appeared at home as Othello, first in 1942 in Cambridge, Massachusetts, and then in 1943 at the Schubert Theatre in New York. The New York Othello *had the longest run to that time of any Shakespeare production on Broadway, with more than 280 performances. It also took a more contemporary approach than the London production, which had used heavy, period costumes. Instead, costume designer Robert Edmond Jones devised looser garments that literally as well as figuratively added flexibility to the role. In this sketch by Jones, swatches of four fabrics show how Robeson's costume looked.*

Othello *has often been an avenue through which to explore racial perceptions, and in 1971 it was the impetus for a popular Folger Booklet,* The Elizabethan Image of Africa *by the African scholar Eldred D. Jones, which incorporated many images from the Folger collection. Still other pictures from the collection were used in the 1990s in lesson plans developed as part of the Folger's Teaching Shakespeare Institutes. In 1996, a faculty member at one institute, American University professor Caleen Sinnette Jennings, was inspired by the group's study of* Othello *and other plays to write* Casting Othello, *a one-act drama exploring issues of race relations within a small theatre company. A combination of that work and Jennings's earlier* Playing Juliet *was produced by the Folger Theatre and the Source Theatre Company in 1998, earning a nomination for a Helen Hayes Award for best new play.*

Paul Robeson, promptbook for *Othello* (London) / 1930
Robert Edmond Jones, costume for Paul Robeson as Othello (New York) / 1943

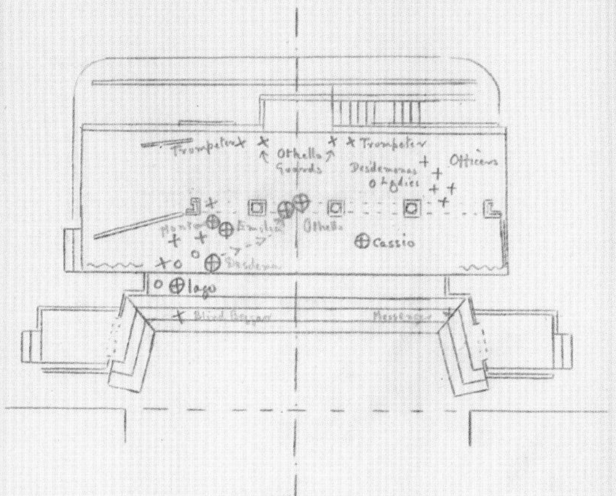

Positions for Othello's Entrance

CUE LIGHTS UP (2:58) 2-4 to full

~~not learn of him, Emilia, though he be thy husband.~~ How say you, Cassio? is he not a most profane and liberal counsellor?

Cas. He speaks home, madam: you may relish him more in the soldier than in the scholar.

TRUMPETS. off L. Othello & Officers off stage left start singing "Bou-la-de-re" as trumpets & drums finish. They continue singing until they reach their positions on stage

~~*Iago.* [*Aside*] He takes her by the palm: ay, well said, whisper: with as little a web as this will I ensnare as great a fly as Cassio. Ay, smile upon her, do; I will gyve thee in thine own courtship. You say true; 'tis so, indeed: if such tricks as these strip you out of your lieutenantry, it had been better you had not kissed your three fingers so oft, which now again you are most apt to play the sir in. Very good; well kissed! an excellent courtesy! 'tis so, indeed. Yet again your fingers to your lips? would they were clyster-pipes for your sake!~~—[*Trumpet within.*] The Moor! I know his trumpet.

Cas. 'Tis truly so.

Des. Let's meet him and receive him.

Cas. Lo, where he comes!

Trumpeters, Othello Guards, messenger, 2 officers, Othello

Enter Othello and Attendants.

MON. OTHELLO!

Oth. O my fair warrior!

Des. My dear Othello!

Des. x to Oth. C.

Oth. It gives me wonder great as my content
To see you here before me. O my soul's joy!
If after every tempest come such calms,
May the winds blow till they have waken'd death!
~~And let the labouring bark climb hills of seas~~
~~Olympus-high, and duck again as low~~
~~As hell's from heaven!~~ If it were now to die,
'Twere now to be most happy; for I fear,
My soul hath her content so absolute
That not another comfort like to this
Succeeds in unknown fate.

Des. The heavens forbid
But that our loves and comforts should increase,
Even as our days do grow!

Oth. Amen to that, sweet powers!
I cannot speak enough of this content;
It stops me here; it is too much of joy:
And this, and this, the greatest discords be [*Kissing her.*
That e'er our hearts shall make!

WARN SWITCHBOARD
WARN TRAILERS

Iago. ~~[*Aside*] O, you are well tuned now!~~
~~But I'll set down the pegs that make this music,~~
~~As honest as I am.~~

Oth. Come, let us to the castle. — All CHEER
News, friends; our wars are done, the Turks are drown'd.
How does my old acquaintance of this isle? — SHAKE HANDS WITH MON.
Honey, you shall be well desired in Cyprus;
I have found great love amongst them. O my sweet,
I prattle out of fashion, and I dote
In mine own comforts. I prithee, good Iago, — Iago x to Othello. HANDSHAKE
Go to the bay, and disembark my coffers:
~~Bring thou the master to the citadel;~~
~~He is a good one, and his worthiness~~
~~Does challenge much respect.~~ Come, Desdemona,
Once more well met at Cyprus. — MUSIC CUE.

[*Exeunt all but Iago and Roderigo.* and BEGGAR.

ROD x to Iago.

Iago. HIST Do thou meet me presently at the harbour. — Iago throws Beggar off R. 1
Come hither. If thou be'st valiant—as, they — ROD down to Iago
say, base men being in love have then a nobility in their natures more than is native to them—list me. The lieutenant to-night watches on the court of guard. First, I must tell thee this: Desdemona is directly in love with him.

EXIT: OTHELLO GUARDS, OTHELLO & DES, Emil & Cassio, 2 attendant ladies, Montano and Lieut, Montano Officers, messenger, Trumpeters, Cassio officers, Cyprus Ladies and Lieuts off R. 2

Rod. With him! why, 'tis not possible.

Iago. Lay thy finger thus, and let thy soul be instructed. Mark me with what violence she first loved the Moor, but for bragging and telling her

WHEN ROD CLEAR
CLOSE TRAILERS
FLYS DROP BACKING
CUE SWITCHBOARD.
LIGHTS Behind to out.
½ amber in FLOATS.
WORKING LIGHT

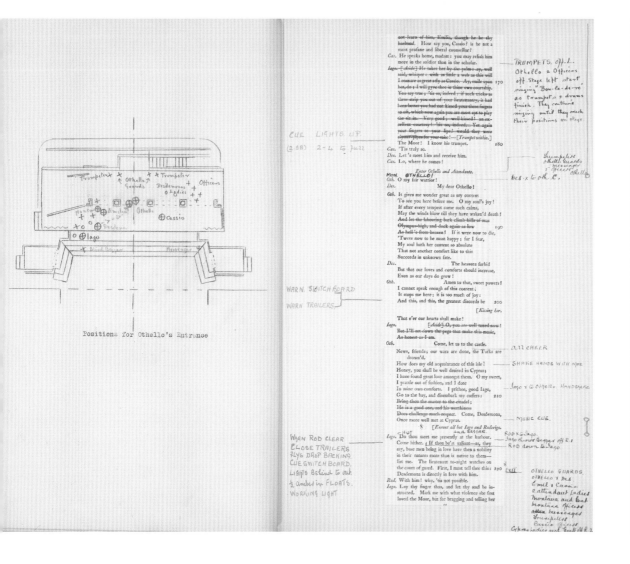

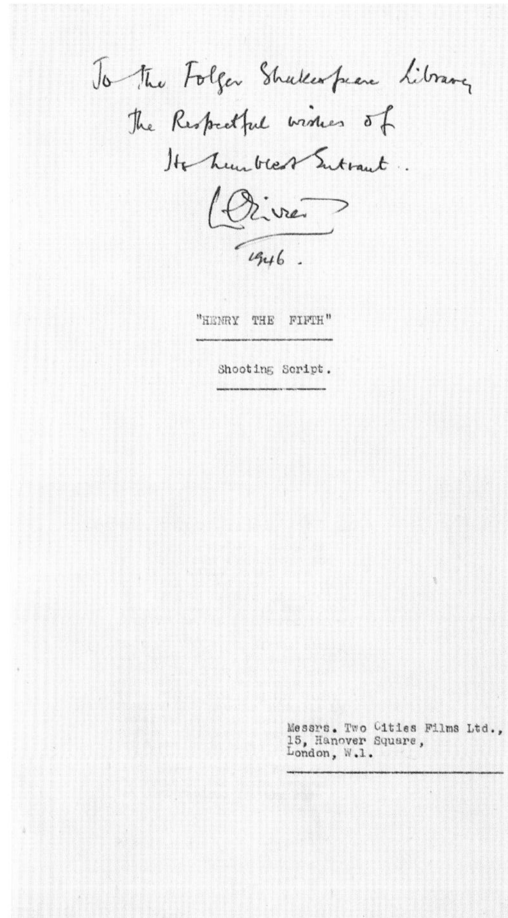

To the Folger Shakespeare Library
The Respectful wishes of
Its humblest Servant.
L Olivier
1946.

"HENRY THE FIFTH"

Shooting Script.

Messrs. Two Cities Films Ltd.,
15, Hanover Square,
London, W.1.

The world was still at war when, at the request of the British government, Laurence Olivier directed, produced, and played the leading role in a film of Shakespeare's Henry V. *The resulting movie was not only a remarkable treatment of Shakespeare's work but also a brilliant piece of wartime propaganda, presenting as it did a hopelessly outnumbered band of Britons prevailing over a Continental foe—and all through the words of the Englishman who has been called history's greatest playwright. Few at the time of filming could have missed the relevance of Henry's cry before the siege of Harfleur of "Once more unto the breach, dear friends," although the war was on the way to its European conclusion by the time the movie was released in late 1944.*

Filmed in brilliant Technicolor, Henry V *was a remarkably successful attempt to solve the problem that had defeated so many others—putting the archaic language and staged situations of an Elizabethan play into the modern medium of film. In a directorial sleight of hand, Olivier set the first portion of the play inside the Globe Theatre—the "wooden O" of the prologue—so that when the camera at last moved outward to the greater world audiences felt liberated, and the inherent "staginess" of the work was obscured. He audaciously cut Shakespeare's original text by almost half, and in some scenes incorporated surrealistic painted backdrops based on period illustrations. Elaborate costumes like the one worn by Olivier in this hand-colored publicity photograph added still more to the cost of production, which ultimately exceeded that of any previous British film. The result has been called "one of the canonical works of the Shakespearean cinema."*

Like many men and women of the stage, Olivier knew and appreciated the Folger Shakespeare Library, where he attended a memorable tea with readers and staff members one day in 1961. Years before, he gave the Folger the shooting script of Henry V, *shown here with a gracefully phrased inscription in his own hand, and the post-production script of his subsequent film* Hamlet. *The institution continues to document Shakespearean productions on film and the stage in its growing collection, which includes films, television shows, and other Shakespearean materials from earlier times right up to the present day.*

Laurence Olivier, publicity photograph for *Henry V* / 1945
Laurence Olivier, shooting script for *Henry V* / 1944

The modern Folger is a busy place. Hundreds of researchers a year come to study in its reading rooms and take part in a diverse array of conferences, seminars, and other programs. At the same time, the Folger conducts numerous programs to make the subjects represented by its collections more accessible to the larger public, young and old alike. Countless visitors annually explore the Folger's remarkable architecture, its Elizabethan Garden, the displays in its great Exhibition Hall and Shakespeare Gallery, and its shop full of books, prints, and other items on Renaissance and Shakespearean themes. Every year, tens of thousands enjoy plays, early music concerts, readings, lectures, and other programs in its Elizabethan Theatre. More than 12,000 students and 750 teachers a year get the chance to perform Shakespeare themselves, whether onstage at the Folger, in its nationwide workshops, or in Folger-inspired classroom exercises. Other members of the public contact the Folger every year with specific questions related to Shakespeare or its collections. Folger recordings and publications at both the scholarly and the popular level reach across the nation and around the world, as do the institution's offerings online.

To support these and other activities, the Folger relies on a combination of its endowment funds and aid from the National Endowment for the Humanities, philanthropic foundations, corporations, and individual donors, including, among others, the Friends of the Folger and those who attend the Spring Gala. Some of this support has put certain Folger efforts on a more permanent footing through the creation of restricted endowment funds, such as, for example, funds dedicated to exhibitions and conservation. More than twenty of the permanent funds go toward yet another important priority: the acquisition of both rare materials and modern works, the lifeblood of any research library. Aided by these funds, the Folger continues to purchase broadly in books, manuscripts, and art. Folger staff members stay in close touch with the world's rare book dealers, including a number of the same firms engaged by Henry Folger, and the library is represented at the world's great auction houses whenever appropriate material is on the block. Some of the results are displayed annually at the Folger's popular Acquisitions Night benefit.

Fallen trees form a multilevel Forest of Arden set for a Folger Theatre production of As You Like It. *Poised above the exiled Duke (in vest) and his companions, a desperate Orlando demands food.*

Every year, the Folger also receives generous donations in kind, from single rare items to entire collections—some of which have taken a lifetime to assemble. Important gift collections in recent years have included such specialized materials as early printed herbals, decorative papers, Renaissance books about public celebrations, and nineteenth-century theatrical memorabilia. In what social scientists sometimes call a "virtuous circle"—the happy opposite of a vicious circle—these and other additions to the Folger collection often lead in turn to new projects and initiatives, including exhibitions, catalogs, lectures, public programs, and academic inquiries, as the Folger's inventive staff continues to imagine satisfying ways for scholars and the public alike to learn from and enjoy its remarkable collection.

READERS, FELLOWS, AND OTHER SCHOLARS

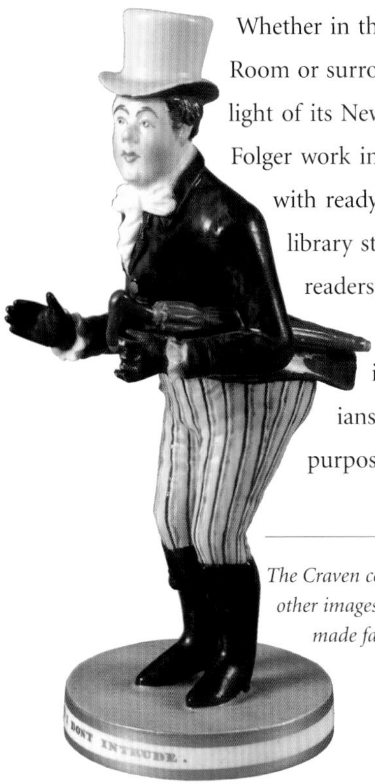

Whether in the Elizabethan ambience of the Folger's Old Reading Room or surrounded by Shakespearean paintings in the cool white light of its New Reading Room, visiting scholars, or readers, at the Folger work in a quiet setting conducive to concentrated thought, with ready access to the collection and help at hand from the library staff, many of them scholars in their own right. Most readers, who must apply to conduct research at the library, have doctorates or are doctoral candidates; others include writers, private collectors, curators and librarians, and theatre artists. Some visit only once for a special purpose—to study a unique manuscript, for example, or a set of nineteenth-century playbills. Others work more steadily in the collection, returning at the same time every year or every other year, or even relocating permanently to be near the Folger for more frequent research. A few have been honored with the designation of Folger scholar in residence.

The Craven collection, donated in the 1990s, includes many figurines and other images of the busybody Paul Pry (left), an umbrella-toting character made famous in the 1800s by British comic actor John Liston.

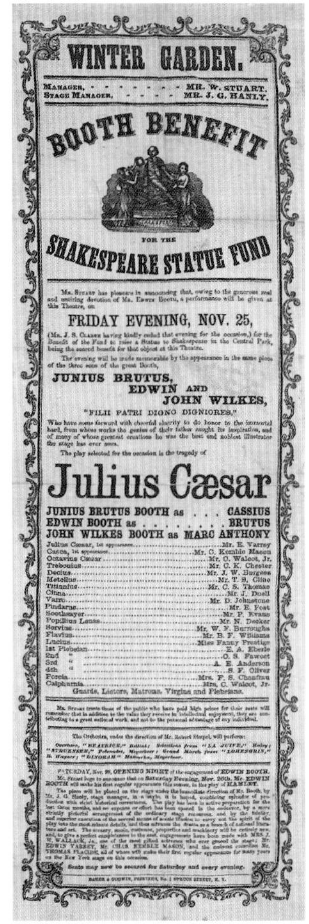

While such solitary study is central to intellectual life, the Folger also prides itself on fostering scholarly discourse, both through academic programs and through less formal encounters. "Many of my most important academic contacts and continuing academic relationships have originated and been sustained at the Folger," one reader commented at the start of the twenty-first century, going on to call the institution "an intellectual center that promotes and supports in every sense the best academic work." The Folger's most storied locale for such exchanges is its daily afternoon tea, an informal gathering of staff and scholars that promotes discussion and can lead to new approaches toward research problems, teaching, and analysis. Many conversations begun there later find more polished expression in scholarly publications, including the Folger's own *Shakespeare Quarterly* *(page 194)*. Over the years, readers' varied interests have also suggested topics for Folger exhibitions and other programs.

Above, a member of the reading room staff consults a book on the balcony of the Old Reading Room. Among the great variety of materials available for study at the Folger are a quarter of a million playbills; the remarkable example shown at left is for a benefit starring the brothers Edwin, Junius Brutus Jr., and John Wilkes Booth in November 1864, five months before John Wilkes assassinated Abraham Lincoln at Ford's Theatre.

New ideas, publications, college classroom materials, and reinvigorated teaching also regularly arise from the lively annual array of programs offered by the Folger Institute. A partnership between the Folger and a consortium of more than three dozen universities, the institute has long benefited from the support of the NEH and the Andrew W. Mellon Foundation, among other donors. Institute programs come in many forms, among them intensive workshops, semester-length seminars, blockbuster conferences attended by more than 350 scholars, and, in the summer, four-week institutes for college teachers. Most concentrate on some aspect of the early modern period, such as the history of the book, the nature of scientific inquiry, or the Reformation. Participants run the gamut from advanced graduate students to tenured university faculty and are encouraged, while at the Folger, to pursue their own research interests within the topic at hand. The Folger Institute also includes specialized centers for Shakespeare studies and the history of British political thought.

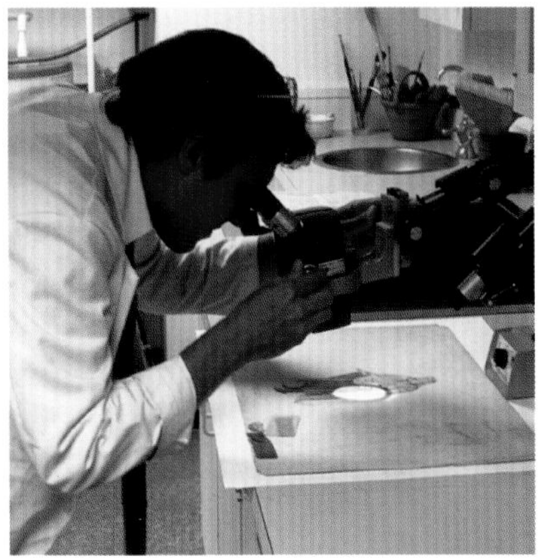

Research methods fall within the institute's purview as well, including the work of paleography—the art of reading Renaissance handwriting, in which letters were formed very differently than they are today. Although paleography is an essential tool for early modernists at and above the graduate level, it is no longer widely taught in the United States. The Folger's popular paleography courses are attended by students from around the country and the world.

In many ways, the plum of academic work at the Folger is the fellowships program, which supports the research of individual scholars with the assistance of the NEH, the Andrew W. Mellon Foundation, and the American Council of Learned Societies. Every year, the Folger sponsors several dozen short-term and long-term research fellowships, ranging in length from several weeks to nine months. The long-term fellowships are particularly prized, as they provide a special opportunity for focused study to busy academics who normally must divide their efforts among committee work, teaching, and research. For long-term fellows, as for other visiting scholars, the Folger's combination of collegial interchange and productive study offers a rare oasis amid the many demands of modern academic life.

CONSERVING RARE HOLDINGS

Although many Folger activities are highly visible to the public, some crucial parts of its work occur largely behind the scenes, most notably the treatment and conservation of rare materials by the Folger's skilled conservators. The challenge faced by the Folger conservation department is hard to overstate. By some estimates, 4 to 5 million pairs of hands have picked up, opened, and examined Folger resources under light bright enough to read by since the library opened in 1932. Folger treasures have been seen by millions of visitors in more than 250 exhibitions in the United States and abroad. The total effect is seismic, placing the physical properties of each part of the collection under stress as its content is absorbed. Every type of holding, from printed works to art, costumes, furniture, musical instruments, photographs, and film and sound recordings, presents its own conservation problems, as do materials from every century.

Folger head of conservation Frank Mowery examines a drawing from the collection with a stereomicroscope, an optical device for stereoscopic, or three-dimensional, viewing of fine detail.

While the text blocks of early printed books may be structurally sound even after 500 years, insects, moisture, and frequent handling have often severely damaged individual leaves. Early bindings deteriorate; clasps are lost, hinges crack, and boards become detached. Iron gall ink and some colored pigments eat through the finest paper. Ironically, however, certain more recent materials can be far more problematic. Paper from the nineteenth century, when wood pulp generally replaced rag paper, has a high content of lignin, a chemical component of wood, which causes the paper to rapidly turn yellow and brittle when exposed to air.

In coping with these and other forms of damage, Folger conservators emphasize modern techniques that stabilize materials to halt further deterioration, and in some cases restore materials to an earlier state—a task that may involve reversing the well-meaning but sometimes harmful efforts of previous conservators. Department members also protect fragile books and other items by constructing custom housings; produce new bindings to replace disintegrating old ones; and prepare books, manuscripts, artworks, and other materials so they may be safely photographed, exhibited, and studied. The Folger conservation department attracts visitors and students from around the world, many of whom come to learn its approach to advanced techniques such as leaf casting and paper splitting.

Leaf casting refers to the use of a fine slurry to fill small pits or holes in pages, or leaves, of old paper, a repair that strengthens the entire leaf. Folger chief conservator Frank Mowery was among the first in the world to computerize paper measurements that ensure the right amount of slurry is prepared to match the paper's original thickness precisely. In paper splitting, a technique that strengthens embrittled paper, conservators literally split apart one face of the paper from the other, place a vanishingly thin sheet of Japanese paper in between, and then reunite the pieces. Although safe when

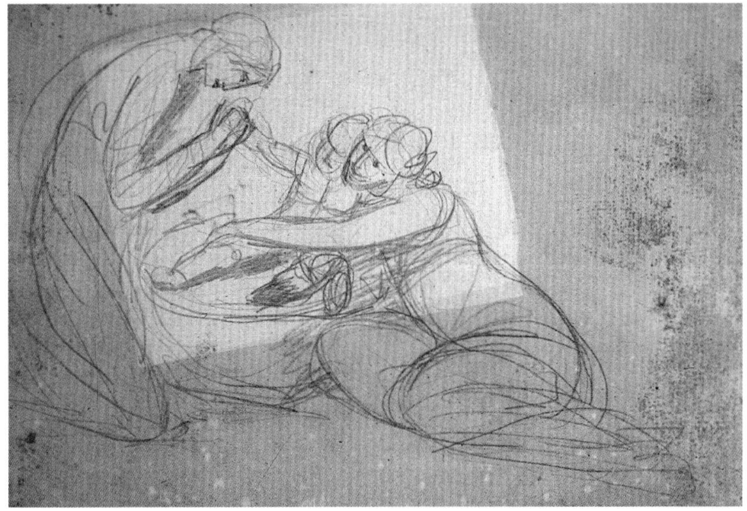

Dating from the late 1700s, George Romney's drawing The Infant Shakespeare Nursed by Comedy and Tragedy *became grossly discolored over the years. Folger conservators restored the drawing to its original color through carefully administered exposure to tungsten lights.*

performed by skilled hands, the process has struck at least one observer as "heart-stopping to watch."

Many aspects of the Folger's work outside the conservation laboratory are also devoted to protecting the library's rare books and other materials from further damage. Temperature and humidity are monitored daily in the Folger reading rooms, and security and fire-prevention systems throughout the library are periodically upgraded. Within the reading rooms, readers consult rare works as gently as possible. Rare books, for example, are supported by foam cradles while in use so that they never lie flat, a position that can weaken bindings. To hold a book open, readers use soft, weighted cords or handmade weighted cloth tubes called book snakes. Light in the reading rooms is kept at a moderate level, with supplementary reading lamps, so that only books actively in use are illuminated fully. Through such measures, combined with the conservators' thoughtful care, the Folger seeks to protect the centuries-old materials in its keeping for many years to come.

A WORLD OF PUBLICATIONS

Since its inception, the Folger has produced a great variety of publications. Folger exhibitions have yielded many engagingly illustrated catalogs that incorporate original essays, transcriptions of rare documents, and other scholarly contributions; several Folger catalogs have won national awards from the American Institute of Graphic Artists. The Cambridge University Press has a special Folger Institute imprint for works resulting from Folger conferences and institutes. The Folger's education department collaborated in the 1990s with several teachers from its Teaching Shakespeare Institutes to produce a seminal curriculum series, *Shakespeare Set Free,* that inspired teachers throughout the country to involve their students in Shakespeare's text through acting and other classroom exercises. And still other Folger works in print abound.

The Folger's flagship publications, however, are both associated with Shakespeare: the popular New Folger Library Shakespeare edition of the plays, and the scholarly journal *Shakespeare Quarterly.* Since the 1950s, the Folger has been known to high-school and college students as well as general readers for its affordable editions of Shakespeare's plays, published primarily in paperback, which place the text of each play or poem cleanly on the right-hand page with explanatory notes and illustrations on the left. Launched in 1992, the New Folger Library Shakespeare edition incorporates that successful format, but with a complete reediting of Shakespeare's text, based on early printed sources, by Barbara Mowat, director of Folger academic programs, and Paul Werstine, professor of English at King's College and the Graduate School of the University of Western Ontario.

In response to classroom research conducted before publication, the New Folger Library Shakespeare includes introductory essays on such topics as Shakespeare's use of language. In the body of each play, newly written notes explain historical or mythical references as well as archaic words, and illustrations selected particularly for this edition

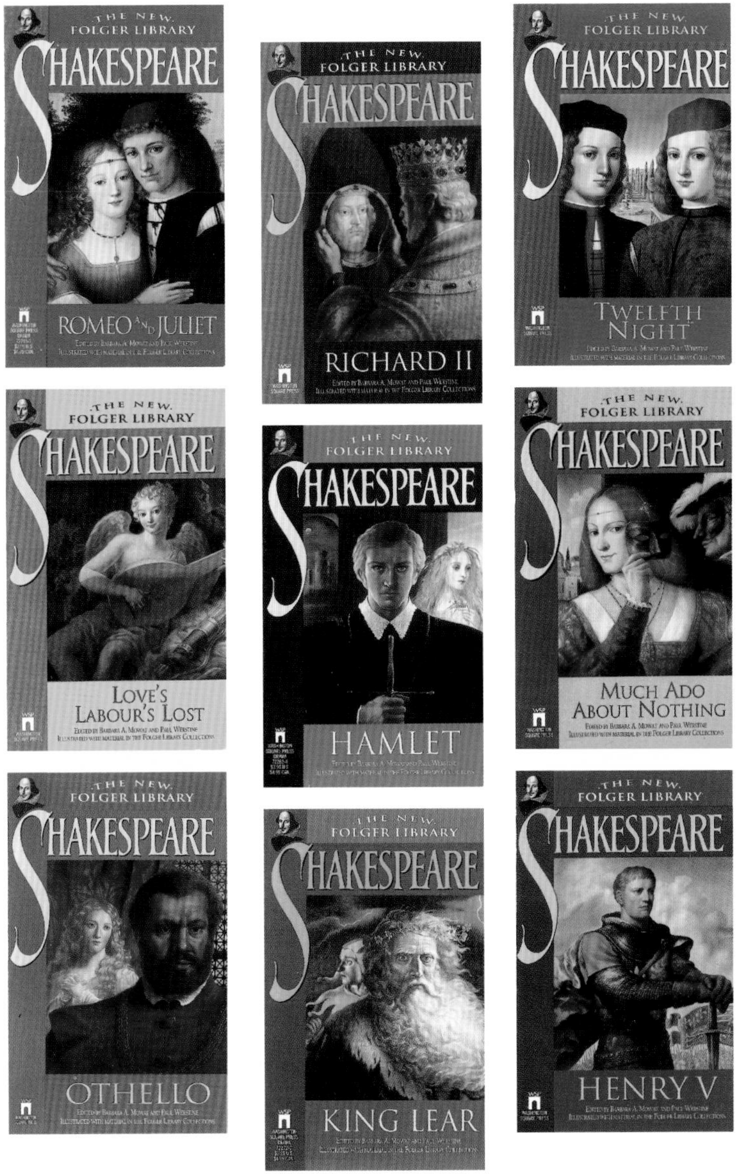

from the Folger collection shed light on bygone customs, popular beliefs, myths, historical figures and events, and other topics. A modern essay by an influential scholar follows each play, as does a locator for familiar lines. Together, these and other aids encourage students and others to follow John Heminge and Henry Condell's urging in the First Folio, carved on the Folger's north facade: "His wit can no more lie hid, then it could be lost. Reade him, therefore; and againe, and againe."

That advice surely also rings true for the readers of *Shakespeare Quarterly,* the preeminent Shakespeare journal in the world. Furthering research at the highest level, the journal serves a professional audience of Shakespeare scholars and enthusiasts. Begun in 1936 as the *Bulletin* of the Shakespeare Association of America, it was retitled *Shakespeare Quarterly* in 1950 and came to the Folger in 1972. Since 1998, George Washington University has contributed to the cost of publication.

Today *Shakespeare Quarterly* publishes scholarly articles and notes on a wide variety of topics within the field of Shakespeare studies. Articles range from postmodern criticism to biography, bibliographic and textual scholarship, and theatrical and art history, often bringing to light new information on Shakespeare and his age. *SQ,* as it is affectionately known, also reviews books in the field of Shakespeare studies, assesses important contemporary productions in its "Shakespeare Performed" section, and publishes an annual *World Shakespeare Bibliography.* As with a variety of Folger-related materials, many current and archival issues of *Shakespeare Quarterly* are available online. With the addition of the Internet, the Folger publishing tradition gains a new dimension while continuing to share images and ideas through books and other materials in print.

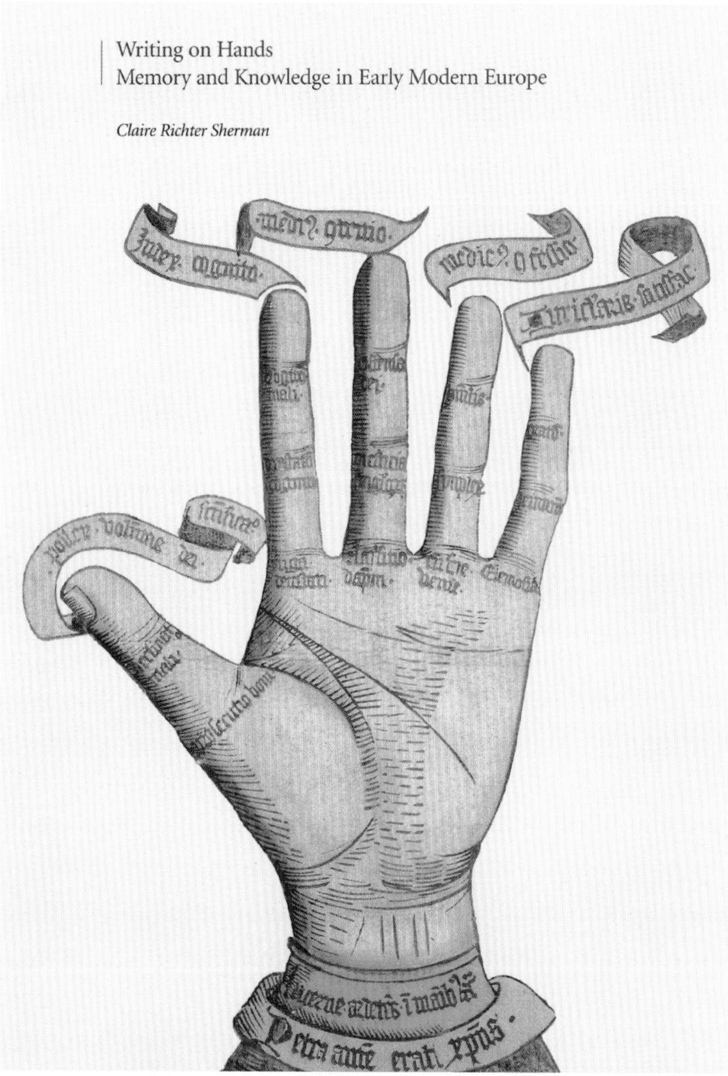

Writing on Hands
Memory and Knowledge in Early Modern Europe
Claire Richter Sherman

A pair of catalogs complement the themes of two exhibitions: above, for an exhibition jointly sponsored with Dickinson College, early modern ideas and images of the hand; opposite, at upper right, the recurring motif of Lady Fortune in Shakespeare's time.

DISPLAYS TO ELUCIDATE, ENTERTAIN, AND INFORM

Just inside the doors of the library building is the oak-paneled Exhibition Hall, designed to recall a long gallery like that in an Elizabethan house. During the Folger's early years, most of the hall was devoted to a standing exhibition on Shakespeare and Elizabethan England. Today, a multimedia computer installation and video display in the adjoining Shakespeare Gallery serve that purpose, providing not only sound and moving pictures but also images of far more Folger holdings than the former semipermanent display could accommodate. In the Exhibition Hall itself, the Folger now presents two or three major exhibitions a year. Most are drawn from its collections, making the Folger's treasures accessible to visitors and bringing Shakespeare's world to life.

Exhibitions at the Folger have ranged from topics as ambitious in scope as "time" to particular aspects of the collection, important historical or literary anniversaries, and topics of current scholarly interest, many of them suggested by Folger readers, who may also serve as guest curators. In the exhibition *The First Folio of Shakespeare,* twenty-four copies of the most famous book at the Folger were on display; no other library in the world could have mounted this exhibition from its own collections. Curated by Peter W. M. Blayney, a distinguished scholar in residence at the Folger and an authority on the First Folio, the exhibition showed how this remarkable book came to be printed in 1623, how it was put together, and what its fortunes have been down to the present day. A very different, but equally intriguing, look at matters Shakespearean was supplied by the exhibition *Shakespeare's Unruly Women,* which examined how the Victorian era and its actresses coped with Shakespeare's spiritedly independent female characters. Paintings, photographs, costumes, and stage properties traced the public's changing views of Shakespearean figures such as Cleopatra, depicted in images

that varied from a tightly corseted portrayal of the 1840s to a more wanton fin de siècle colored engraving.

Several exhibitions have examined how Shakespeare and his contemporaries lived, beginning with *Elizabethan Households,* which used texts, illustrations, and artifacts to explore the goods and rooms of a typical Elizabethan house and the people who made up the household. A subsequent outing entitled *The Housewife's Rich Cabinet* surveyed a wealth of domestic "how-to" ideas from the early modern age. Among the materials on view were a Renaissance-style mousetrap newly constructed according to directions from Leonard Mascall's 1590 *Booke of engines* and a cap embroidered after a pattern in Thomas Trevelyon's 1608 commonplace book. The use of artifacts in conjunction with rare books and manuscripts is a hallmark of Folger exhibitions, offering visitors yet another way to visualize the past.

For the Columbus quincentenary, the NEH funded a particularly ambitious exhibition, *New World of Wonders: European Images of the Americas, 1492–1700.* Featuring not only maps and travel accounts but also drawings, artifacts, natural histories, costume books, and images of plays, masques, and pageants, the exhibition examined the many ways in which Europeans formed their images of the New World and was supplemented by lectures, workshops, and other programs. As one reviewer commented in praising this display, "The truly important voyages we make are the intellectual ones." Visually diverse and always stimulating, exhibitions at the Folger take their visitors on just such intellectual travels to myriad lands.

TEACHERS, STUDENTS, AND THE PUBLIC AT LARGE

Four words sum up the Folger's educational philosophy: Shakespeare is for everyone. Educational programs at the Folger are designed to encourage an interest in and excitement about Shakespeare's work in teachers, students from elementary to high school, and members of the public. In recent years, some programs have brought the study of other poets and writers into the classroom as well.

The Folger regularly offers Teaching Shakespeare Institutes, NEH-funded summer sessions in which secondary-school teachers from around the country work intensively to develop active ways to engage students in reading and performing Shakespeare. A mixture of scholarly lectures, curriculum sessions, acting exercises, and focused discussions, each institute concentrates on four of Shakespeare's plays, including at least one that is rarely taught. Many of the results are posted on the Folger Web site, extending the program's reach beyond the national level to provide teachers worldwide with up-to-date curriculum resources, including digitized images of some of the Folger's primary sources.

Other Folger programs work directly with students, among them Bill's Buddies, an educational outreach troupe whose shows encourage students to act, speak, and experiment with Shakespeare's language; and

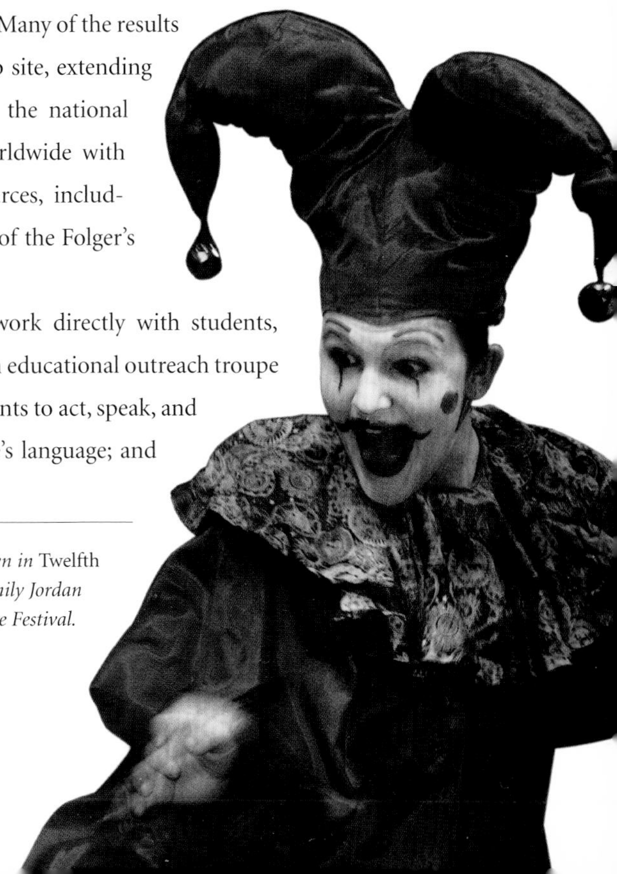

An animated teenage Feste, the clown in Twelfth Night, *takes the stage during the Emily Jordan Folger Secondary School Shakespeare Festival.*

Above, students offer a classically costumed look at Shakespeare in the secondary-school festival. At lower right, this third-grade student's portrait of Shakespeare was one of many posters adorning a fence in 1999 during renovations for the Haskell Center for Education and Public Programs.

Shakespeare Steps Out, a multidisciplinary arts-based program for Washington, DC, public schools in disadvantaged neighborhoods. Launched in the late 1990s, Shakespeare Steps Out brings Shakespeare to elementary-school teachers and to students in the third through sixth grades through classroom visits that draw on dance, art, and drama to explore Shakespeare's life, culture, language, and plays; professional-development workshops encourage teachers to expand the program's lessons beyond Shakespeare to other subjects as well. After several sessions, the program concludes by transporting students to the Folger for a tour and a performance workshop on the stage of the Elizabethan Theatre.

Although teaching Shakespeare at the elementary-school level is somewhat unusual in the United States, the young students involved in Shakespeare Steps Out in some ways demonstrate a more direct appreciation for Shakespeare's texts than older students do. In one memorable session at Washington's Davis Elementary School, for example, a fifth grader shared his favorite passage from *Macbeth,* "Will all great Neptune's ocean wash this blood / Clean from my hand? No, this my hand will rather / The multitudinous seas incarnadine, / Making the green one red." His classmates liked the passage too, tirelessly repeating the beguiling phrase "multitudinous seas incarnadine." Children, it seems, often understand Shakespeare's language through the sounds, wordplay, rhythm, and images without anxiously pondering the meaning of each word as a high-school student or an adult might do.

Students of all ages perform at the Emily Jordan Folger Children's Shakespeare Festival and the Emily Jordan Folger Secondary School Shakespeare Festival, two rites of spring at the Folger that have grown to involve more than a thousand participants a year from some seventy public and private schools. On each festival day, school groups present scenes from the plays, often with highly inventive costumes and staging, for each other and their parents and friends. The Folger offers a two-month director-in-residence program to help some schools prepare for the event, as well as special workshops.

Reaching out to a still-wider audience are the Folger's docents, who may be said to embrace the full sense of the original Latin verb *docere,* "to teach." These stalwart and extremely well-informed volunteers are often the first point of contact for casual visitors, tour groups, or schoolchildren visiting the Folger. Among many other activities, they conduct walk-in tours of the institution and the Elizabethan Garden and assist at the annual Shakespeare's Birthday Open House and performance festivals. On the days of the elementary-school festivals in particular, as miniature Lady Macbeths and small, cloaked Prosperos fill the grounds, the carved relief of "child masquers" over the door to the Elizabethan Theatre seems to resonate with new meaning. Whether through the festivals or other Folger programs, a generation of youngsters newly attuned to the possibilities of Shakespeare and his language is both the goal and the delight of educational programs at the Folger.

THE FOLGER ONSTAGE

In a sense, the Folger's plays, concerts, readings, and lectures bring its outreach programs full circle to the setting where Shakespeare's works began—almost literally so, given the evocative setting of the Elizabethan Theatre. Through original Folger Theatre productions as well as fine touring presentations, the Folger is known for innovative productions that forge strong connections with modern audiences, adding to the lively continuing legacy of Shakespearean stagecraft. While Shakespeare is central to its mission, the Folger has also produced a variety of other works, among them dramas by Shakespeare's contemporaries, and has staged the premieres of new plays, including several related to or inspired by Shakespeare and other Renaissance playwrights. Furthering the Folger's outreach to schools, a small group of high-school fellows spends twelve weeks each year in seminars with noted

Actors from the Bill's Buddies educational outreach troupe—including, from left to right, Cam Magee, John Worley, and Chuck Young—coach a young participant in a Shakespeare's birthday performance.

scholars and theatre professionals and attends several productions at both the Folger and the Shakespeare Theatre, which cosponsors the program. Most Folger Theatre productions are also performed for school groups in matinees during the week, with associated workshops.

Among many Folger Theatre highlights over the years have been an award-winning production of *Romeo and Juliet;* a *Hamlet* in which four actors—three of them women—simultaneously portrayed the title character; and an *As You Like It* in which the Folger's permanent onstage columns were joined by a host of similar structures, which were abruptly lowered in midplay to become fallen tree trunks in the Forest of Arden *(page 188).*

If the Folger Theatre concentrates primarily on Shakespeare, the resident Folger Consort evokes the institution's broader focus on the early modern age. In fact, the Consort's repertoire extends even further, ranging from medieval works to the baroque—and in some instances, to the twentieth century: in 1998, the group commissioned and performed a new musical setting of verses and lines from *The Tempest* for Elizabethan-era instruments by the modern composer James Primosch. The performance of Primosch's music is preserved on one of more than a dozen recordings on the Consort's Bard Records label. Working with a variety of guest vocalists and other instrumentalists, the Consort has performed in Washington's National Cathedral; in New York's Abraham Goodman House, Frick Gallery, and Carnegie Recital Hall; and in other venues as well as in live and recorded broadcasts on National Public Radio and public television. In addition to its

Bathed in eerie green light, Lady Macbeth (Lucy Newman-Williams) sinks into madness during a Folger Theatre production of Macbeth *set in the Louisiana of the late 1950s and early 1960s. Innovative lighting and an original soundtrack gave the production a distinctly film noir feeling, dubbed by one reviewer "film vert."*

*Scenes from Folger Theatre productions either inspired by Shakespeare or presenting Shakespeare's own work include—clockwise from upper left—*Playing Juliet / Casting Othello, *a backstage drama coproduced with the Source Theatre Company; a modern-dress* Tempest *that incorporated this dance scene between Prospero and a vampish Ariel; and* Shakespeare's R & J, *an adaptation of* Romeo and Juliet *in which the work is performed by four Catholic schoolboys. Here, Juliet, played by Student #2 (Christopher Borg), laments Tybalt's death at Romeo's hands. All three productions were nominated for Helen Hayes Awards, with* The Tempest *winning for lighting and sound design.*

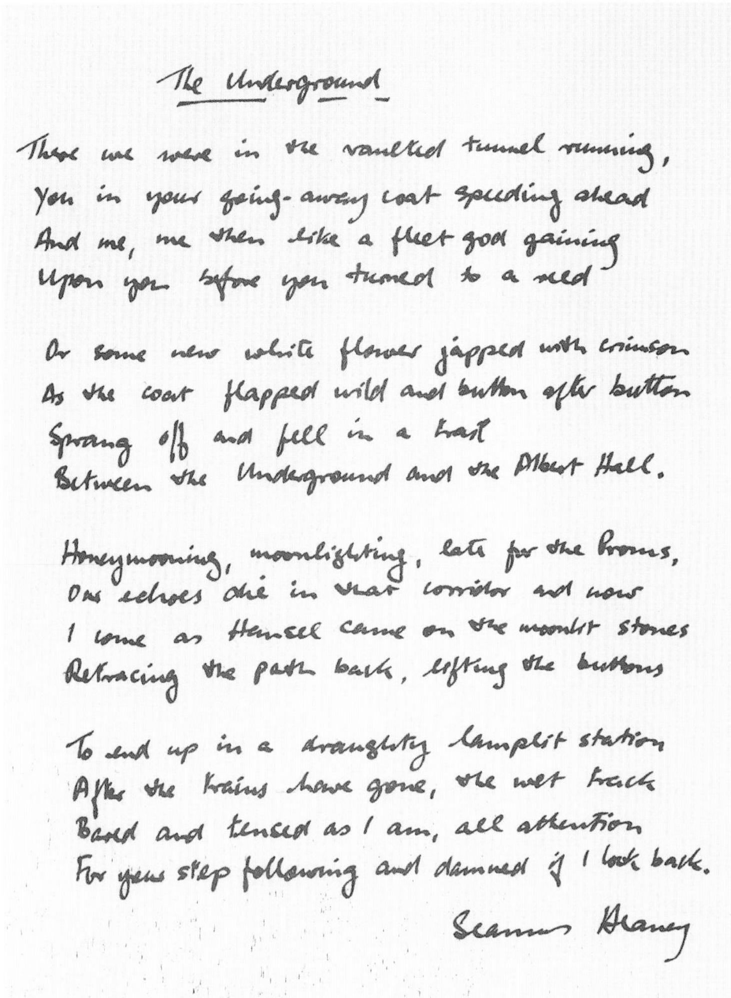
The Underground

There we were in the vaulted tunnel running,
You in your going-away coat speeding ahead
And me, me then like a fleet god gaining
Upon you before you turned to a reed

Or some new white flower japped with crimson
As the coat flapped wild and button after button
Sprang off and fell in a trail
Between the Underground and the Albert Hall.

Honeymooning, moonlighting, late for the Proms,
Our echoes die in that corridor and now
I come as Hansel came on the moonlit stones
Retracing the path back, lifting the buttons

To end up in a draughty lamplit station
After the trains have gone, the wet track
Bared and tensed as I am, all attention
For your step following and damned if I look back.

Seamus Heaney

Greek myth, fairy tale, and the London Underground interweave in this poem hand-copied for the Folger by its author—and later Nobel recipient—Seamus Heaney, who inaugurated the Folger Poetry Board Reading series. Audience members receive their own copies of such manuscripts at Folger Poetry readings, adding another dimension to the literary experience.

regular concerts at the Folger, the Consort has staged a full-dress production of Henry Purcell's English opera *Dido and Aeneas* and a rare modern re-creation of John Milton's masque *Comus,* the latter in conjunction with a Folger Institute conference on the piece.

And the list of revels does not end there, for the Folger has long played host to lectures and readings. In 1998, Harold Bloom combined the two forms, interspersing his speech with scenes by three actors with whom he shared the stage. Among a multitude of other distinguished speakers have been such figures as director Peter Brook, Nobel Prize winners Seamus Heaney and Octavio Paz, and a diverse array of prominent and often cutting-edge playwrights, actors, writers, scholars, and observers of the modern scene.

The PEN/Faulkner Foundation, which makes its home at the Folger, presents the PEN/Faulkner Award for Fiction every year at the library and also sponsors an annual series of readings there, among other activities. In the world of poetry, the Folger itself sponsors the O. B. Hardison Jr. Poetry Prize, named after the former director, which honors poets who are also gifted teachers. The Folger Poetry Series continues to hold a broad range of modern poetry readings that have included several American poets laureate, among them Rita Dove, Robert Pinsky, and Stanley Kunitz, as well as a great diversity of other poetic voices.

Contemporary poetry readings and lectures were first proposed as part of the library's mission as early as 1932. Then as now, supporters and friendly observers of the Folger perceived it as an institution that embraces the modern era as well as the past and finds new and powerful connections between the two. The extraordinary and ever-changing programs through which it does so—from literary readings to activities as diverse as scholarly conferences and children's performance festivals—if not quite infinite, surely constitute variety of a high order indeed.

Folger Consort cofounders Christopher Kendall and Robert Eisenstein relax with reproductions of period stringed instruments in hand. Two of the early music ensemble's many recordings, which include guest vocalists and instrumentalists, appear above.

PROLOGUE: THE YEARS BEFORE 1932

1879 Amherst College senior Henry Clay Folger attends a lecture by Ralph Waldo Emerson on "superlative or mental temperance." Inspired, Folger reads several of Emerson's other works, including an 1864 speech on Shakespeare that shapes Folger's life as a devotee of the Bard and collector of Shakespeareana.

1885 Henry Folger and Emily Jordan marry.

1896 Emily Folger earns a master's degree from Vassar College. Her thesis title is "The True Text of Shakespeare."

1914 Henry Folger is awarded an honorary doctorate by Amherst College in recognition of the Folgers' growing Shakespeare collection.

1919–27 Through an agent, Henry Folger assembles a parcel of land in the 200 block of East Capitol Street, SE, for a library to house the collection acquired by the Folgers over several decades.

1928 Henry Folger retires from his position as chairman of the board, Standard Oil of New York.

1929 Paul Philippe Cret of Philadelphia selected as architect; Cret subsequently recommends New York sculptor John Gregory to create bas-reliefs for the library's facade.

Construction of the library begins.

1930 June 11, 1930. Henry Folger dies at age 73.

Henry Folger's will reported in the *New York Times,* including his plan for the library. The will designates the trustees of Amherst College as the library's administrators.

1931 After Henry Folger's estate proves much smaller than expected because of the 1929 stock market crash, Emily Folger provides more than $3 million in securities and other gifts; she supplies additional funds a year later.

William A. Slade, formerly of the Library of Congress, named as director; shares leadership responsibilities with Joseph Quincy Adams of Cornell University, who becomes the director of research.

First books arrive at the library from warehouse storage.

DECADE I: 1932–41

1932 April 23, 1932. Folger Shakespeare Library dedicated on the traditional date of Shakespeare's birthday. President Herbert Hoover attends; Emily Folger presents the key to the building to the Amherst trustees; Joseph Quincy Adams delivers the first annual Shakespeare's birthday lecture, "Shakespeare and American Culture."

Emily Folger awarded honorary doctorate by Amherst College.

1933 Reading Room made regularly open to accredited scholars.

1934 The Folger observes the 370th anniversary of Shakespeare's birthday with a musical program broadcast to a nationwide radio audience.

William Slade returns to the Library of Congress; Joseph Quincy Adams becomes acting director, assuming full administrative responsibility.

1935 Trustees establish two annual fellowships available to "young scholars of unusual promise in the field of Elizabethan research."

Library initiates first card catalog of its books under the direction of chief bibliographer, E. E. Willoughby.

1936 February 21, 1936. Emily Folger dies at age 78.

Joseph Quincy Adams becomes first regularly appointed director.

A facsimile of the Folger's unique first quarto of *Titus Andronicus* (1594) is the library's first scholarly publication. Between 1936 and 1941, a total of six facsimile volumes are published, including copies of *The Passionate Pilgrim* (1599) and *The Ghost of Lucrece* (1600).

To foster social and scholarly dialogue, the Folger begins serving afternoon tea to staff and visiting researchers. At first, tea is in the Founders' Room; later, it moves to a separate tea room.

1938 The Folger buys the collection of the late Sir Robert Leicester Harmsworth, comprising more than 8,000 rare books printed in England between 1475 and 1640. Together with later acquisitions of Continental material, the Harmsworth purchase expands the Folger's focus beyond Shakespeare studies to include virtually all aspects of the early modern world.

In the first of several purchases from the manuscript collection at England's Loseley Park, the Folger acquires the official records of Sir Thomas Cawarden, Master of the Revels for Henry VIII, Edward VI, Lady Jane Grey, Mary I, and the young Elizabeth I.

1939 To celebrate the 500th anniversary of the invention of printing in the West, some of the collection's earliest books are placed on display.

DECADE II: 1942–51

1942 In early January, 30,000 rare items sent secretly by train to underground storage at Amherst College to avoid wartime dangers.

1944 Items safely returned from Amherst to the Folger in November by special express train.

1946 Joseph Quincy Adams dies; James McManaway serves as acting director.

1947 Elizabeth Pope becomes the first woman fellow at the Folger, taking as her subject the religious background of Shakespeare's plays.

1948 Louis B. Wright, formerly of the Huntington Library, appointed director.

First conference of the Folger Research Group, a monthly event for scholars interested in Renaissance studies.

1949 In the first theatrical performance at the Elizabethan Theatre, the Amherst Masquers present *Julius Caesar.* Plays are not regularly staged at the theatre until 1970.

1950 First publication of *Shakespeare Quarterly* by the Shakespeare Association of America. Long-standing ties between the *Quarterly* and the Folger staff culminate in the periodical's transfer to the Folger in 1972.

DECADE III: 1952–61

1954 Trustees of Amherst College pass a resolution emphasizing the Folger's traditional policy "granting permission to any qualified scholar to use the rare materials in its possession."

1958 Publication of Dorothy E. Mason's *Music in Elizabethan England,* the first of the Folger Booklets on Tudor and Stuart Civilization, a series designed to provide concise information on the social and intellectual history of the Tudor and Stuart periods. The booklet series continues until 1971.

1959 First large-scale renovation of the building begins, adding office space, new underground storage, and a terrace.

1960 University and high-school teachers meet at a Folger conference to discuss new methods of teaching Shakespeare.

General Reader's Shakespeare paperback editions debut, starting with *Richard III, King Lear, As You Like It,* and *Henry V.* Edited by director Louis B. Wright and Virginia LaMar, these accessible annotated editions of the plays and sonnets use materials from the Folger's collection to put Shakespeare's works in context. The series continues through 1969.

DECADE IV: 1962–71

1964 The Folger marks the 400th anniversary of Shakespeare's birth with three major exhibitions, several small traveling exhibitions and loans, lectures on Shakespeare's life and work, an Elizabethan dinner, and a reception at the White House hosted by President and Mrs. Lyndon Johnson.

1968 Louis B. Wright retires. Philip A. Knachel becomes acting director.

1969 O. B. Hardison Jr., professor of English at the University of North Carolina, appointed director.

1970 Formation of the Folger Institute, a joint venture of the Folger and a university consortium to promote Renaissance and eighteenth-century studies through seminars and symposia. The consortium begins with two institutions, American and George Washington Universities, soon joined by the University of Maryland. By the institute's thirtieth anniversary, the consortium has thirty-eight members.

The Folger launches its series of modern poetry readings, starting with poet and Shakespearean scholar Paul Ramsey.

Elizabethan Theatre brought into compliance with District of Columbia fire-safety laws governing public theatres that charge admission. The Folger Theatre Group forms; its first production, *Dionysus Wants You!,* is a rock-musical adaptation of *The Bacchae.*

First volunteer docents complete a four-session training course. The docent program, begun as a way to provide tours and lectures for visitors, later expands to include helping with the annual Shakespeare's Birthday Open House and education programs, as well as other projects.

1971 Friends of the Folger formed to encourage individual giving as a supplement to the endowment.

First Folger Institute seminars held. Topics include Renaissance musicology, intellectual history, and the world of Erasmus.

Folger Theatre Group performs its first play by Shakespeare, *Twelfth Night.*

DECADE V: 1972–81

1972 The Folger celebrates its fortieth anniversary with two exhibitions on its own history and a conference, "The Widening Circle," on the interplay between religion and politics in sixteenth-century Europe.

Folger Shakespeare Library building enrolled in the National Register of Historic Places.

Publication of *Shakespeare Quarterly* transferred from the Shakespeare Association of America to the Folger.

Andrew W. Mellon Foundation provides the Folger with a separate, half-million-dollar endowment fund for general operating support.

Folger–British Academy Exchange Program begins, annually sending two American researchers to the United Kingdom and two British researchers to the Folger Shakespeare Library.

Start of the DC Schools Project, a cooperative endeavor between the Folger and the Washington, DC, public school system to develop methods and materials for teaching Shakespeare to inner-city students.

1973 Earliest recorded purchase of one of Shakespeare's works discovered by curator of manuscripts Laetitia Yeandle in the recently acquired diaries of Richard Stonley, an Elizabethan official; according to one entry, Stonley bought *Venus and Adonis* in 1593. In a separate literary development, researchers locate the long-lost Restoration comedy *The Country Gentleman* in the Folger's manuscript collection.

Items added to the Folger's collection during the past year are highlighted at the first of several Acquisitions Benefits.

1974 The Folger hosts an international Petrarch congress. Among the highlights is an academic procession from the Folger to the US Capitol to celebrate the 633rd anniversary of the poet's coronation as poet laureate on the Capitoline Hill in Rome.

Charlton Heston performs several readings from Shakespeare at the second Acquisitions Benefit.

Library acquires a copy of the rare first edition of *Areopagitica; A Speech of Mr. John Milton For the Liberty of Unlicenc'd Printing* . . . (1644).

1975 Lunchtime Midday Muse program begins, accommodating a growing number of poets and musical groups eager to appear at the Folger.

Friends of the Folger form the Collectors Club to encourage members with a special interest in rare books to contribute to the library's collection.

Shakespeare Film Archive established with a grant from the Rockefeller Foundation. The archive later adds materials related more generally to the library's collection.

1976 International Shakespeare Congress hosted by the Folger on the bicentennial theme "Shakespeare in America"; during the conference, Jorge Luis Borges delivers annual Shakespeare's birthday lecture, "The Riddle of Shakespeare." Bicentennial exhibition, *Shakespeare on the American Stage.*

First restricted acquisitions endowment fund established by Mrs. H. Dunscombe Colt.

1977 Folger Consort, the Folger's resident early modern music ensemble, opens its first season with the program "England: Chapel and Chamber Music, 1400–1600."

In a major acquisition, the Folger purchases the Stickelberger collection of some 850 early Reformation books and pamphlets.

The Folger assumes responsibility for publication and distribution of books bearing its imprint, Folger Books; previously, most of the library's books were produced and marketed under copublishing arrangements.

1978 Separate conservation fund established.

1979 The Folger hosts its first annual Shakespeare's Birthday Open House. On the preceding day, National Public Radio broadcasts a live concert by the Folger Consort; on the day of the open house, classical-music radio station WGMS hosts *Shakespeare Fair on the Air,* a fund-raiser benefiting the Folger Theatre Group and Consort.

Reading Room closes for renovation and expansion. During this period, the Folger arranges the first large-scale traveling exhibition of objects from its collection, *Shakespeare: The Globe and the World,* with an illustrated catalog of the same name by S. Schoenbaum. The show travels to seven cities in twenty-six months.

1980 Folger Consort releases its first recording, *Shakespeare's Music,* on the Delos label.

Emily Jordan Folger Children's Shakespeare Festival established, starting an annual tradition that continues today. This first three-day festival includes scenes from Shakespeare performed by some 250 fourth, fifth, and sixth graders from eleven area schools.

1981 The Folger starts a new fellowship program for high-school students in which sixteen students participate in small group discussions with eminent scholars and experience the Folger's atmosphere and resources.

Reading Room reopens. Festivities include an open house and a speech by the archbishop of Canterbury at the April annual meeting of the Friends.

Dedication of the Patterson Conservation Laboratory and the Charles A. Dana Wing, a case-lined room outside the entrance to the vaults where rare and outstanding objects from the collection can be displayed.

The Folger's first Secondary School Shakespeare Festival, an outgrowth of the successful children's festival, takes place at Madeira School in McLean, Virginia.

DECADE VI: 1982–91

1982 Marking its fiftieth year, the Folger celebrates with a two-day observance of Shakespeare's birthday that includes the annual open house, a lecture by S. Schoenbaum, and a performance of Ian McKellen's *Acting Shakespeare.* At a White House reception, President and Mrs. Ronald Reagan are made members of the Order of the Folger Shakespeare Library and presented with specially designed medals.

Dedication of the Theodora Sedgwick Bond–William Ross Bond Memorial Reading Room; once opened for use, the room adds much-needed space for visiting readers. The project later receives an award from the American Institute of Architects.

Bill's Buddies, an educational outreach acting troupe, makes its debut.

1983 Two years after its founding, the PEN/Faulkner Foundation makes its home at the Folger. PEN/Faulkner presents the largest peer-juried award for fiction in the United States and jointly sponsors a fiction-reading series with the Folger.

In October, O. B. Hardison resigns as director, effective December 31; Philip Knachel serves as acting director through June 1984.

1984 First annual Founders' Day Dinner benefit, known in later years as the Spring Gala.

Werner Gundersheimer, professor of history and director of the Center for Italian Studies at the University of Pennsylvania, appointed director; takes office in July.

The Folger announces plans for a senior fellowship program to include a dozen full-year positions filled by internationally distinguished scholars and educators.

National Endowment for the Humanities (NEH) provides a grant to establish the Folger Institute's Center for the History of British Political Thought.

The Folger Institute hosts an NEH-funded summer seminar, cosponsored by the Newberry Library, on the archival sciences.

NEH funds the first Teaching Shakespeare Institute, a monthlong summer program at the Folger for high-school teachers from across the country. The institutes continue to be held to the present day.

During the rebinding of two sixteenth-century medical books, conservator Frank Mowery finds the earliest-known example of writing from the British Isles, a manuscript fragment predating AD 800; the fragment is later sold at auction and the proceeds used to establish an acquisitions endowment.

1985 The Folger announces the establishment of two new endowments to support long-term fellows; subsequently, an NEH grant is awarded to support additional long-term fellowships.

Folger Theatre Group is discontinued and reincorporates, with the library's support, as a new not-for-profit organization, The Shakespeare Theatre at the Folger. The Shakespeare Theatre performs at the Folger for the next six years.

Docents complete *Shakespeare: A Guide for Young Readers,* an annotated bibliography of materials pertaining to Shakespeare and his times that are written or abridged for children.

1986 For the first time since 1932, the Folger's Exhibition Hall is refurbished, adding state-of-the-art exhibition cases, solar-veil window treatments, and other improvements.

The Folger collaborates with the US Department of Education on the Folger Shakespeare Education and Festival Project, bringing the Folger method of teaching Shakespeare to educators nationally through in-service workshops.

Emily Dickinson: Letter to the World, a conference and exhibition, becomes the first Folger exhibition consisting primarily of borrowed materials, including the poet's famous white dress.

Folger Institute's Center for Shakespeare Studies, underwritten by NEH, founded.

1987 Dedication of the Patterson Loft, study carrels on the balcony of the Old Reading Room.

1988 Folger Consort presents Hildegard von Bingen's *Ordo Virtutum* at the Washington National Cathedral, establishing a tradition of Consort performances in this national landmark.

1989 Elizabethan Garden opens. Located on the east side of the original library building, the garden incorporates herbs and other plants mentioned in Shakespeare's works or commonly used in his day.

1990 In an ambitious project, the Royal Shakespeare Company and the Folger jointly sponsor a program that takes twenty-five American and fifteen British secondary-school teachers to Stratford-upon-Avon and Washington, DC, to attend workshops on teaching Shakespeare.

1991 Poet Seamus Heaney presents the first annual Folger Poetry Board Reading, reciting or reading works by his favorite authors as well as his own poems.

Queen Elizabeth II becomes the first reigning British monarch to visit the Folger Shakespeare Library.

First annual O. B. Hardison Jr. Poetry Prize awarded to poet Brendan Galvin. Named for the Folger's late director, the Hardison prize recognizes both poetry and teaching excellence.

Actress Lynn Redgrave creates and presents for the Folger an evening of Shakespeare inspired by her love of Shakespeare and her father, Sir Michael Redgrave. She later develops the one-woman show into the full-length play *Shakespeare for My Father,* a Tony Award nominee.

DECADE VII: 1992–2001

1992 The Folger celebrates its diamond jubilee year with a presentation at the White House hosted by President and Mrs. George Bush.

Launch of The Jubilee Campaign, "To Turn a Page Anew," with a goal of more than $20 million to be raised over three years.

New Folger Library Shakespeare paperback series, edited by Barbara A. Mowat and Paul Werstine in light of contemporary trends in Shakespearean criticism, begins publication with *The Taming of the Shrew, Macbeth, Julius Caesar, The Merchant of Venice, Hamlet,* and *Romeo and Juliet.*

New World of Wonders exhibition, underwritten by an NEH grant, commemorates the 500th anniversary of Columbus's arrival in America.

1993 In the largest philanthropic award to the Folger to date, a multiyear $2.5 million grant from the Lila Wallace–Reader's Digest Fund supports expanded outreach programs; renovation of public facilities, including improved disabled access; and creation of the Shakespeare Gallery, an interactive exhibition area for visitors.

Publication of *Shakespeare Set Free: Teaching Romeo and Juliet, Macbeth, and A Midsummer Night's Dream,* a teaching guide begun at the 1988 and 1989 Teaching Shakespeare Institute summer sessions; two other books in the series follow.

Organized to encourage the study of Shakespeare, the Capitol Hill Shakespeare Partnership joins the Folger with two nearby schools: Stuart Hobson Middle School, of the DC public school system, and Capitol Hill Day School, a private school.

1994 Library begins retrospective conversion of card catalog in preparation for an integrated library system, including an online catalog.

Electrical fire in Elizabethan Theatre destroys original sky canopy and causes other damage.

Donation from Mary P. Massey of her collection of more than 300 rare, early herbals.

1995 First direct Folger access to the Internet.

Festive Renaissance exhibition celebrates more than two decades of donations by Mrs. H. Dunscombe Colt of early modern festival books commemorating royal births, pageants, tournaments, funerals, and other occasions.

1996 In-house debut of the library's online catalog, Hamnet, named after Shakespeare's only son, who died in 1596 at the age of eleven.

The Folger launches its first Web site.

Arrival of the first installment of the late Babette Craven's collection of theatrical memorabilia, a major donation of the 1990s that includes paintings, manuscripts, porcelain figures, and other records of theatre history.

1997 At a White House gathering, First Lady Hillary Clinton celebrates the Folger's sixty-fifth anniversary.

Funding from NEH and the Mellon Foundation makes possible the most ambitious cataloging project in the history of the library, a multiyear effort to create online records for tens of thousands of early English books.

In a new theatre initiative, the Folger Theatre presents *Romeo and Juliet.* The production wins three Helen Hayes Awards.

Shakespeare Steps Out, a program to introduce Shakespeare to elementary-school children, begins in four DC public schools.

1998 Among other rarities, the Folger acquires one of seven extant copies of the first edition of Edmund Spenser's *The Shepheardes Calender* (1579); the earliest Shakespeare play on film, an 1899 silent movie of *King John;* and, in a bequest from the late Francis T. P. Plimpton, the 1579 "sieve" portrait of Elizabeth I.

Teaching Shakespeare Web site launched, sharing ideas and updated lesson plans for teaching Shakespeare.

Taking as its theme "the bistros, booksellers, and Bohemians of Paris," the Spring Gala successfully breaks with Washington, DC, convention by presenting a roving black-tie affair with faux bistros and no formal dinner seating.

1999 Director Werner Gundersheimer announces $7.5 million campaign to support the growth of public programs endowments and the renovation of a building at 301 East Capitol Street to become the new education and public programs center.

Tea room, board room, and kitchen undergo renovation.

Launch of the *Seven Ages of Man* multimedia interactive exhibition within the Shakespeare Gallery space. The exhibition includes more than 250 images of key objects from the Folger collection; Sir Derek Jacobi records the monologue of the same name, which greets visitors as they activate the display.

2000 Hamnet catalog becomes available to the public through the Folger Web site.

Wyatt R. and Susan N. Haskell Center for Education and Public Programs opens at 301 East Capitol Street. The same year, the Folger's educational programs win the Washington, DC, Mayor's Art Award.

With partial funding from SOS! (Save Outdoor Sculpture), restoration work begins on *Puck,* the outdoor marble sculpture by Brenda Putnam commissioned for the opening of the library in 1932.

The Folger collaborates with the Massachusetts Institute of Technology and other institutions to create the Shakespeare Electronic Archive; this effort includes a Hamlet on the Ramparts Web site complete with film clips from historic productions, facsimile pages, sketches, and paintings.

2001 After four years of work, 50,000 additional records of English books printed between 1475 and 1700 are added to the Hamnet catalog. In a separate development, selected digital facsimile pages from several items in the Folger's collection become available online as well.

Folger Consort and the Folger Institute collaborate in the production of John Milton's masque *Comus,* an effort resulting in a scholarly conference and multiple performances in the Elizabethan Theatre.

2002 Werner Gundersheimer retires as director of the Folger Shakespeare Library.

DIRECTORS OF THE LIBRARY

1932–34	William A. Slade (Librarian / Director)
1936–46	Joseph Quincy Adams
1948–68	Louis B. Wright
1969–83	O. B. Hardison Jr.
1984–2002	Werner Gundersheimer

CHAIRMEN OF THE FOLGER SHAKESPEARE LIBRARY COMMITTEE OF THE AMHERST COLLEGE BOARD OF TRUSTEES

1930–31	Dwight Morrow
1931–33	Calvin Coolidge
1933–45	Harlan Fiske Stone
1945–46	William Long Thorpe
1946–47	Richard Harrington Gregory
1947–64	Eustace Seligman
1964–67	Alfred Friendly
1967–72	Francis T. P. Plimpton
1972–79	W. Willard Wirtz
1979–81	Mrs. John Farr Simmons
1981–85	Mrs. Caspar Weinberger
1985–88	Charles R. Longsworth
1988–91	B. Francis Saul II
1991–94	Kenneth H. Bacon
1994–97	Louis B. Thalheimer
1997–	Karen Hastie Williams

All photographs by Julie Ainsworth, unless otherwise noted. Credits below provide source information for books, manuscripts, artworks, and other artifacts where appropriate, including Folger call numbers.

Front and back cover:
Claudius Ptolemaeus. *Geographie opus novissima.* Strassburg, Johann Schott, 1513. Folger call number G87 P8 L3 1513 Cage. Photograph by Horace Groves.

Frontispiece:
Photograph by Nathan Benn.

10 First two photographs by Antonio Alcalá.
Remaining photographs copyright 2001 Lloyd Wolf. All rights reserved.

12 Ticket. Folger Archives, Folger Shakespeare Library.

13 J. L. Covell, portrait photographs. Gallery Studio, Amherst, Massachusetts. Lifshey Studio, Brooklyn, New York.

14 William Shakespeare. *The handy-volume Shakspeare.* New York, George Routledge and Sons, undated. Folger call number PR2754 13a3b-2 Sh. Col.

15 Pach Bros., New York.

16 CC Soda bottle. Washington, DC, distributed by Coca-Cola Bottling Company, ca. 1930–32. Folger call number Ac. 249621.

17 Photograph and leaf. Folger Archives, Folger Shakespeare Library.

18 Harris and Ewing, Washington, DC.

19 B. F. Stevens and R. Brown Ltd., Library, Literary, & Fine Art Agents. Telegram to Folger Shakespeare Library. August 11, 1938. Folger acquisitions files.

20 Postcard. Folger Archives, Folger Shakespeare Library. The gift of Julie Ainsworth.

23 Photograph by Folger Shakespeare Library.

25 *Shakespeare: The Globe and the World* was made possible by the National Endowment for the Humanities, the Corporation for Public Broadcasting, the Metropolitan Life Insurance Company, and Exxon Corporation. Photograph by Folger Shakespeare Library.

26 Nicholas Hilliard. Lettice Knollys, countess of Leicester. Watercolor on vellum, ca. 1590–95. Folger call number FPm9. The gift of Dorothy Rouse-Bottom.

27 Concept and design by Adworks.

28 Photograph by Ken Cobb.

29 Poster created for PEN/Faulkner by William Dunlap incorporating a photograph by Ed Meek. Calligraphy by Rose Folsom.

33 Frank O. Salisbury. Henry Clay Folger. Oil on canvas, 1927. Folger call number FPb57.

33 Frank O. Salisbury. Emily Jordan Folger. Oil on canvas, 1927. Folger call number FPb58.

33 Flemish allegorical tapestry. Early 1500s. Folger call number Tapestry 7. The gift of Mary Weinmann, in memory of her grandmother, Ethel Sperry Crocker.

34 Theodora Sedgwick Bond–William Ross Bond Memorial Reading Room. Hartman-Cox Architects, Washington, DC, Warren Cox, architect.

37 Armillary sphere / sundial. The gift of current and former Folger docents. Elizabethan Garden design by J. Carl Webster of Garden Arts, Baltimore. Photograph by Antonio Alcalá.

38 Brenda Putnam. *Puck.* Marble, dedicated 1932. Folger call number FSa1. Photograph by Adams Studio Custom Photography, Washinton, DC.

39 Photograph by Anice Hoachlander, Hoachlander Davis Photography.

41 George Gower. The Plimpton "sieve" portrait of Queen Elizabeth I. Oil on panel, 1579. The bequest of Francis T. P. Plimpton. Folger call number ART 246171.

46 Thomas à Kempis. *Opera.* Nuremberg, Kaspar Hochfeder, [November 29,] 1494. [And] Saint Albertus Magnus. *Compendium theologice veritatis.* [Strassburg, Johann Prüss], 1489. Folger call number INC T320.

48 Juan Luis Vives. *De concordia & discordia in humano genere . . . libri quattuor.* Antwerp, Michiel Hillen, 1529. Folger call number PA8588 A13 1529 Cage.

48 *A defence of priestes mariages.* [London, by John Kingston for Richard Jugge, 1567?]. Folger call number STC 17518.

49 Angelo Petricca. *De nobilitate eiusque origine.* Rome, Ignazio de Lazari, 1659. Folger call number Ac. 180084.

49 Esther Inglis. *Argumenta psalmorum Davidis.* Manuscript, 1608. Folger call number V.a.94. The gift of Lessing J. Rosenwald. Photograph by Nathan Benn.

51 *The Castle of Perseverance.* Manuscript ca. 1400–25. Folger call number V.a.354.

52 Geoffrey Chaucer. [*Canterbury Tales.* Westminster, printed by William Caxton, 1477.] Folger call number STC 5082. Photograph by Horace Groves.

55 Euclid. *Preclarissimus liber elementorum Euclidis perspicacissimi.* Venice, Erhard Ratdolt, 1482. Folger call number INC E86.

56 [The Bible. German.] *Disz durchleuchtigist werck der gantzen heyligen geschrifft, genant dy bibel.* [Nuremberg,] Anton Koberger, [February 17, 1483]. Folger call number INC B566. The gift of Mrs. H. Dunscombe Colt.

58 [Catholic Church. Hours.] *Incipiunt hore beate marie virginis secu[n]dum usum sarum.* Paris, [Philippe Pigouchet, 1498]. Folger call number STC 15889.

61 Marcus Tullius Cicero. *Commentū familiare in Ciceronis officia.* [Lyons], 1502. Folger call number PA6295 A3 1502 Cage. Purchased with the assistance of Arthur A. Houghton Jr.

63 [Catholic Church. Hours.] *Enchiridion preclare ecclesie Sarisburiensis.* Paris, Germain Hardouyn, [1533?]. Folger call number STC 15982.

65 *The. holie. Bible.* [London, Richard Jugge, 1568]. Folger call number STC 2099 copy 3.

66 George Gower. The Plimpton "sieve" portrait of Queen Elizabeth I. Oil on panel, 1579. The bequest of Francis T. P. Plimpton. Folger call number ART 246171.

69 Robert Dudley, earl of Leicester. Letter to Elizabeth I. [August 3, 1588]. Folger call number MS Add 1006. The gift of Dorothy Rouse-Bottom.

71 Elizabeth I. Letter to Henry IV of France. ca. 1595. Folger call number V.b.131.

72 James I. Royal warrant for the release of Sir Walter Raleigh. January 30, 1617. Folger call number L.b.358. Photograph by Horace Groves.

75 Claudius Ptolemaeus. *Geographie opus novissima.* Strassburg, Johann Schott, 1513. Folger call number G87 P8 L3 1513 Cage. Photograph by Horace Groves.

76 Martin Luther. *Eyn Sermon von dem unrechten Mammon.* Wittenberg, [Johann Rhau-Grunenberg], 1522. Folger call number Ac. 218-463q.

78 Edmund Spenser. *The Shepheardes Calender.* London, Hugh Singleton, 1579. Folger call number STC 23089. Purchased with the assistance of James O. Edwards, The Andrew W. Mellon Foundation, The Trustees Fellowship and Acquisitions Fund, and Friends of Eric Weinmann.

81 Abraham Ortelius. *Theatrum orbis terrarum.* Antwerp, Officina Plantiniana, 1595. Folger call number G1015 O6 1595 Cage.

82 John Donne. Letter to Sir George More, March 1601/1602. Folger call number L.b.532.

85 Edward Topsell. *The Historie of Foure-Footed Beastes.* London, William Jaggard, 1607. Folger call number STC 24123 copy 2. Photograph by Horace Groves.

86 Esther Inglis. *Octonaries upon the vanitie and inconstancie of the world.* Manuscript, December 23, 1607. Folger call number V.a.92. The gift of Lessing J. Rosenwald. Photographs by Horace Groves.

89 Thomas Trevelyon. Pictorial commonplace book. Manuscript, 1608. Folger call number V.b.232. The gift of Lessing J. Rosenwald.

91 Johann Remmelin. *Catoptrum Microcosmicum.* Frankfurt am Main, Heirs of Anton Humm, 1660. Folger call number Ac. 209024.

97 Leonhart Fuchs. *De historia stirpium.* Basel, Michael Isengrin, 1542. Folger call number Massey 46f. The gift of Mary P. Massey.

98 Henry Barrett. *A breife booke unto private captaynes.* Manuscript, 1562. Folger call number V.a.455.

101 John Foxe. *Actes and monumentes.* London, John Daye, 1570. Folger call number STC 11223.

102 Lucas Janszoon Waghenaer. *The mariners mirrour.* [London, John Charlewood, 1588?]. Folger call number STC 24931. Photograph by Horace Groves.

105 Niccolò Tartaglia. *Three bookes of colloquies concerning the arte of shooting in great and small peeces of artillerie . . . now translated into English by Cyprian Lucar.* London, [Thomas Dawson] for John Harrison [the elder], 1588. Folger call number STC 23689 copy 3.

106 Christopher Saxton. [*Atlas of the counties of England and Wales*]. [London, 1590?]. Folger call number STC 21805.5. Photograph by Horace Groves.

109 Thomas Hariot. *A briefe and true report of the new found land of Virginia.* Frankfurt am Main, Johann Wechel for Theodor de Bry, [1590]. Folger call number STC 12786.

111 Elizabeth I. *Orders, . . . by her Majestie, and her privie Counsell, to be executed . . . in such Townes, Villages, and other places, as are, or may be hereafter infected with the plague, for the stay of further increase of the same.* London, deputies of Christopher Barker, 1592. Folger call number STC 9199.

111 [London. Plague Bill.] *From the 24 Auguste to the 31, 1609.* Bill of mortality, London, 1609. Folger call number STC 16743.8.

112 Vincentio Saviolo. *Vincentio Saviolo his practise.* London, [Thomas Scarlet for] John Wolfe, 1595. Folger call number STC 21788 copy 1.

115 John Dowland. *The First Booke of Songes or Ayres of fowre partes with Tableture for the Lute.* [London], Peter Short, 1597. Folger call number STC 7091.

117 Lute. Workshop of Michielle Harton, ca. 1598, Padua.

119 Hugh Alley. *Caveatt for the Citty of London.* Manuscript, 1598. Folger call number V.a.318.

120 Sarah Longe. *Mrs. Sarah Longe her Receipt Booke.* Manuscript, ca. 1610. Folger call number V.a.425.

123 Thomas Coryate. *Coryats Crudities.* [London,] W[illiam] S[tansby], [1611]. Folger call number STC 5808 copy 1.

124 Costumes and scenes from the time of James I. Watercolor, early 1600s. Folger call number ART Vol. c91, nos. 1b, 1c, 8b. Photographs by Horace Groves.

126 *The Wonders of this windie winter.* London, G. Eld for John Wright, [1613]. Folger call number STC 25949.

126 Henry Goodcole. *Natures Cruell Step-Dames: or Matchlesse Monsters of the Female Sex.* London, for Francis Coules, 1637. Folger call number STC 12012.

126 *A Brief Narrative of A Strange and Wonderful Old Woman that hath A Pair of Horns Growing upon her Head.* London, Thomas Johnson, 167[8]. Folger call number B4610.2 Bd. w. STC 20863.5.

126 Samuel Wiseman. *A Short and Serious Narrative of Londons Fatal Fire.* London, for Peter Dring, 1667. Folger call number S3551.

129 Jean Puget de la Serre. *Histoire de l'entrée de la reyne mere du roy trés-Chrestien, dans la Grande-Bretaigne.* London, Jean Raworth for George Thomason and Octauian Pullen, 1639. Folger call number STC 20488.

133 Wenceslaus Hollar. *Unus Americanus ex Virginia. Aetat: 23.* Etching, 1645. Folger call number ART Box H737.5 no. 29. Purchased as the gift of Barbara Fahs Charles.

133 Wenceslaus Hollar. Portrait of a young African man. Etching, [1645?]. Folger call number ART 236023. The Elizabeth Niemyer Acquisitions Fund.

133 Wenceslaus Hollar. Portrait of a young African woman. Etching, 1645. Folger call number ART Vol. b35, no. 46.

135 Sir Isaac Newton. *Philosophiae naturalis Principia Mathematica.* London, The Royal Society, 1687. Folger call number Ac. 207976.

139 Final Concord. 1602. Folger call number Z.c.36 (110–111).

140 Blackfriars Gate-House Conveyance, March 10, 1613. Folger call number Z.c.22 (45).

142 Claes Jansz. Visscher. *Londinum florentissima Britanniae urbs.* Engraving, ca. 1625. Folger call number GA 795 L6 V5 1625 Cage.

147 The Ashbourne portrait of Shakespeare / Sir Hugh Hamersley. Oil on canvas, 1612. Folger call number FPs1.

149 Shakespeare signboard. Oil on mahogany panel, late 1600s to early 1700s. Folger call number FPs9. The gift of Mary Hyde. Photograph by Horace Groves.

150 James Boaden. *An Inquiry into the Authenticity of Various Pictures and Prints of Shakespeare.* London, R. Triphook, 1824. Folger call number ART Vol. f111 copy 2.

152 Louis François Roubiliac. Sculpture of Shakespeare. Study for statue for David Garrick's Shakespeare Temple. Terra-cotta, 1757. Folger call number FSs1.

155 William Shakespeare. *The Most Lamentable Romaine Tragedie of Titus Andronicus.* London, by John Danter for Edward White and Thomas Millington, 1594. Folger call number STC 22328.

156 William Shakespeare. *Mr. William Shakespeares Comedies, Histories, & Tragedies.* London, Isaac Jaggard and Ed. Blount, 1623. Folger call number STC 22273, Fo. 1, no. 1.

159 William Shakespeare. *Mr. William Shakespeares Comedies, Histories, & Tragedies.* London, Thos. Cotes, 1632. Folger call number STC 22274, Fo. 2, no. 7.

161 Francis Hayman. Act 5, scene 4 from *Measure for Measure*. Drawing for Sir Thomas Hanmer's 1744 edition of *The Works of William Shakespeare*, ca. 1740–41. Folger call number PR2752 1744 copy 2 vol. 1 Sh. Col.

161 Hubert François Gravelot. Act 5, scene 4 from *Measure for Measure*. Engraving after the drawing by Francis Hayman for Sir Thomas Hanmer's edition of *The Works of William Shakespeare*, ca. 1740–41. Folger call number PR2752 1744 copy 2 vol. 1 Sh. Col.

163 Robert Laurie. *Mr. Garrick and Mrs. Bellamy in the Characters of Romeo and Juliet*. Mezzotint after the painting by Benjamin Wilson, ca. 1753. [And] Playbill. Drury Lane production of *Romeo and Juliet*, January 31, 1750/1751. Interleaved in Thomas Davies, *Memoirs of the Life of David Garrick*. London, 1780. Folger call number W.b.473 no. 358 and following no. 358.

163 David Garrick as Romeo in *Romeo and Juliet*, after original painting by Benjamin Wilson engraved by Ravenet. Enamel plaque, [1765]. Folger call number ART 241283. Babette Craven Collection of Theatrical Memorabilia.

163 Model of David Garrick's Shakespeare Temple and Roubiliac statue at Hampton. Mixed material, ca. 1830. Contains thirty-eight-volume miniature edition *Shakspeare, from the text of Johnson, Steevens, & Reed*. London, W. Pickering, 1823–25. Folger call number PR2752 1823–1825a, copy 5 Sh. Col.

164 George Romney. Drawing of the head of Lear. Black chalk, ca. 1773–75. Folger call number ART Flat b5 no. 5.

167 Benjamin West. King Lear and Cordelia. Oil on canvas, 1793. Folger call number FPa82.

169 Henry Fuseli. Macbeth Consulting the Vision of the Armed Head. Oil on canvas, [1793]. Folger call number FPa27.

170 Small notebook containing twenty-five half-length oval paintings of Fanny Kemble as Beatrice, Juliet, Portia, Hermione, and others. Watercolor on mica. Folger call number ART Vol. c88.

173 Charles Kean. Souvenir promptbook for *Hamlet, Prince of Denmark*, by William Shakespeare. Marked and corrected by T. W. Edmonds, Prompter. Performed at the Princess's Theatre, January 10, 1859. London, John K. Chapman and Co. Folger call number PROMPT Ham. 20.

175 Blue and red velvet coat ornamented with fleurs-de-lis and lions in gold thread, side pocket attached. Worn by Edwin Booth as Richard in *Richard III*. Folger call number 12-4-08-6 Boo., Costume Collection.

175 W. J. Linton after W. J. Hennessy. *Richard III*. Hand-colored wood engraving, 1872. Folger call number ART File B725.4 no. 82.

176 Max Beerbohm. *William Shakespeare, His Method of Work*. Color lithograph from *The Poet's Corner*, London, William Heinemann, 1904. Folger call number ART Vol. f3.

179 William Shakespeare. *Songs and Sonnets by William Shakespeare*. [London], manuscript and binding by Alberto Sangorski, 1926. Folger call number W.b.260.

182 Dan Sayre Groesbeck. Costume design for Edna May Oliver as Nurse in *Romeo and Juliet*. Watercolor. Executed for 1936 MGM film. Folger call number ART Box G874 no. 1. The gift of Colonel Charles E. Hammond.

185 Paul Robeson. Promptbook for *Othello* by William Shakespeare. Produced and directed by Maurice Browne, with Paul Robeson as Othello. Performed at the Savoy Theatre, London, May 19, 1930. Folger call number PROMPT Oth. Fo. 2. The gift of Maurice Browne.

185 Robert Edmond Jones. Costume design for Paul Robeson in *Othello.* Ink and gouache over pencil indications, fabric swatches attached. Executed for 1943 production of *Othello* staged in New York at the Shubert Theatre. Folger call number ART Box J79 no. 1. The gift of James O. Belden in memory of Evelyn Berry Belden.

186 Laurence Olivier in *Henry V.* Publicity photograph, 1945. Folger call number ART File O49.3 H1 no. 1 PHOTO. The gift of United Artists. Courtesy of Carlton International.

186 Laurence Olivier. Shooting script for *Henry V* by William Shakespeare, produced and directed by Laurence Olivier. London, Two Cities Films, [1944]. Folger call number PROMPT Hen. V Fo. 1. The gift of Laurence Olivier and United Artists.

188 Photograph by Ken Cobb. Directed by Aaron Posner. Set design by Tony Cisek.

190 Figure of Paul Pry. Derby porcelain, ca. 1826–30. Folger call number ART 241132. Babette Craven Collection of Theatrical Memorabilia.

190 Winter Garden, New York. *Booth Benefit for the Shakespeare Statue Fund. Julius Caesar.* Playbill, November 25, 1864. Folger call number Bill box U4 W781864–65, no. 2a.

193 George Romney. *The Infant Shakespeare Nursed by Comedy and Tragedy.* Graphite drawing, ca. 1783–91. Folger call number ART Box R766, no. 6. Photographs by Frank Mowery.

197 Photograph by Gayle Krughoff.

200 Photograph by Claire Newman-Williams. Directed by Joe Banno. Lighting by Dan Covey. Original music and sound design by Scott Burgess.

201 Photographs by Ken Cobb. *Playing Juliet / Casting Othello* by Caleen Sinnette Jennings. Directed by Lisa Rose Middleton. *The Tempest* directed by Joe Banno. Lighting design by Dan Covey. Original music and sound design by Scott Burgess. *Shakespeare's R & J* adapted and directed by Joe Calarco.

203 Photograph by Ken Cobb.

The Folger wishes to thank Joe Banno, Mark Cinnamon, MD, Robert Eisenstein, Donna Hamilton, Pamela O. Long, Cam Magee, Jean Miller, Peggy O'Brien, Francie Owens, Gail Kern Paster, Penelope Rahming, Paul Statt, and Alden Vaughan.

Design by Studio A, Alexandria, Virginia
Antonio Alcalá, Mary Dunnington, Helen McNiell

Printed by Balding + Mansell

Typeset in Minion and Minion Expert

Printed on Scheufelen Job Parilux Silk